EFFECTIVE LEGAL RESEARCH

4th edition

JOHN KNOWLES
Law Librarian,
Queen's University Belfast

1st edition co-authored by
PHILIP A. THOMAS
Professor of Socio Legal Studies,
Cardiff Law School,
University of Wales, Cardiff

SWEET & MAXWELL

THOMSON REUTERS

Published in 2016 by Thomson Reuters (Professional) UK Limited, trading as
Sweet & Maxwell, Friars House, 160 Blackfriars Road, London, SE1 8EZ
(Registered in England & Wales, Company No. 1679046. Registered office and
address for service: 2nd Floor, 1 Mark Square, Leonard Street, London, EC2A 4EG).

For further information on our products and services, visit:
http://www.sweetandmaxwell.co.uk

Typeset by Servis Filmsetting Ltd, Stockport, Cheshire
Printed in Great Britain by CPI Group (UK) Ltd, Croydon, CR0 4YY.

*No natural forests were destroyed to make this product;
only farmed timber was used and re-planted.*

A CIP catalogue record for this book is available from the British Library

ISBN 978-0-414-05191-1

Contents

Acknowledgments

The author and publishers would like to thank those organisations who have allowed their copyrighted materials to be reproduced as examples throughout this book. Grateful acknowledgment is made to the following:

British and Irish Legal Information Institute (*http://www.bailii.org*)
HeinOnline (*http://www.heinonline.org*)
Incorporated Council of Law Reporting (*http://www.iclr.co.uk*)
LexisNexis (*http://www.lexisnexis.co.uk*)
Oxford Journal of Legal Studies, 2011, Vol.31, issue 3, p.437, by permission of Oxford University Press
TSO (*http://www.tsoshop.co.uk*)
Westlaw UK (*http://www.westlaw.co.uk*)

Preface

A new law student is faced with a potentially bewildering variety of sources of law. A recent case mentioned in a lecture might be found in a database of law reports, a printed report, or a website providing access to recent court judgments. There might be journal articles or newspaper reports that discuss the case. The text of an Act can be found in a number of different ways, using both online sources and editions of statutes found in a law library. It can be difficult to know where to start. This book aims to help you make effective use of the law resources to which you have access. Finding and using primary sources of law is now largely a matter of learning how to best make use of online databases and websites. However, coverage of traditional print sources has been retained in this book and their use explained, in order that you can make the best possible use of both print and online sources.

In a sense, this book is a labour-saving device. Use it as a reference throughout your time as a student, or indeed thereafter, should you decide to go into legal practice. Though some of the more detailed coverage is most likely to be of use if you are embarking on a legal research module (or a post-graduate qualification), it is not intended to be a textbook associated with a particular course. It is a reference aid to be consulted whenever you have a problem. Consequently, you might use the book selectively, referring to those sections that are useful at a particular point in your studies, or when recommended to look up a case, statute or issue by a member of the teaching staff.

The book concentrates on the law in England and Wales. Detailed coverage is also given of European human rights law and the law of the European Union. A brief appendix covers sources of law for Scotland, Northern Ireland and Wales, along with sources of international law.

Effective Legal Research owes much to the contribution made by Philip A. Thomas, as co-author, not only of the first edition of *Effective Legal Research*, but also of the four editions of *Dane & Thomas: How to Use a Law Library*. The coverage of print resources is based, in large part, on the coverage of print materials in *How to Use a Law Library*.

Chapter 5 (Journals) has been largely re-written for this edition to take into account changes in academic publishing, including open access. Coverage of online sources has also been extensively revised and changes in UK official publishing incorporated. Citation follows OSCOLA (Oxford University Standard for the Citation of Legal Authorities) throughout. However, abbreviations for printed sources are punctuated according to the publisher's citation style. OSCOLA uses light punctuation for print sources. All website addresses are given as accessed December 2015.

1
Making the most of a law library

INTRODUCTION

A law library might seem the most traditional of libraries. A university law library contains many shelves of heavy bound volumes of statutes and law reports, along with a wide variety of academic journals and textbooks. Sometimes the law library will be housed in a separate building; more often it will form one area within a larger library. 1.1

Imposing as these print collections can be, however, they constitute only one part of what a law library offers. The library is also a gateway to online collections of legal materials. The extent of the online collections of case law and journal articles is likely to greatly surpass that of the library print collections. There will also be library access to e-books, complementing the range of print books available on the library shelves. To learn how to research the law efficiently and effectively is to learn how to make use of both the online and the print collections of a law library.

THE LIBRARY CATALOGUE

The online library catalogue is your guide to the extent of the print and online materials available to you. It will also be supplemented by library web pages which usually provide access to online services. Online catalogues are easy to use and computers providing catalogue access will be available throughout the library building. You should also be able to connect to the catalogue online from wherever you are using your own computer, smart phone, or other mobile device. Find the library catalogue and web pages as soon as you can and familiarise yourself with the way they work. If you are not already well acquainted with the law library, make use of library induction talks and seek out guides provided for you, both in print and on the library website. Remember that librarians are there to support you and so do not be afraid to ask for help, especially at the start of your course. 1.2

BOOKS

The books held in a university library are usually the best starting point for legal research. Making good use of them can save a great deal of wasted effort. 1.3

You will find three different kinds of book on the library shelves. Textbooks designed for undergraduates explain the fundamentals of law in a particular area. These are complemented by research texts (sometimes called monographs) which offer detailed descriptions of the law and usually a more advanced level of discussion. These often assume the knowledge set out in undergraduate textbooks. Practitioner texts and looseleaf updating services, in contrast, aim to provide a detailed, authoritative, statement of the law in a particular area. They are designed first and foremost for the legal profession. All three types of book can be useful to legal research. Check dates of publication, to ensure that you are using the most recent edition.

Books of all kinds are usually grouped on the shelves according to their subject. The subject dealt with in each book is indicated by numbers, or letters and numbers, which are usually printed on the spine of the book. These symbols indicate the exact subject matter of each volume. They are known as the classification number or classmark and bring together, in one area of the library, all books dealing with the same subject, such as torts, criminal law and constitutional law.

There may be a number of separate sequences in the library. Large books (folios and quartos) and very thin books (pamphlets) may be kept in a separate part of the library. As a result, the size of the book may be important in helping you to find it on the shelves. There will normally be some indication on the catalogue entry for a book, if a book is shelved separately.

E-books

1.4 It is no longer the case that you are restricted to print volumes when searching for books that might be of value to your research. Significant numbers of books are now available online from most university libraries. These e-books are purchased by your library in much the same way as print volumes and can usually be accessed through the library catalogue. Instead of providing a library location for a book, the catalogue displays a link to an online version of the book's printed text. In many cases complete collections of e-books can be searched from a single dedicated search page. Examples include the ebrary collection of e-books and MyiLibrary. Check library web pages to confirm their availability. Access restrictions will be similar to those for subscription database services (see para.2.8).

It is not usually possible to download the full text of library e-books. Unlike e-books held on hand-held book readers, these books are designed to be read online from a networked computer. In almost all cases a relatively limited amount of text can be downloaded and retained, but if substantial downloads are permitted, there will be time limits placed on your access to the text. Printing is usually restricted to relatively brief sections of the book. In most cases it is also possible to set bookmarks and add your own notes to a library e-book. You will need to create a personal account on the e-book website to do this, but once you have done so, e-books can be searched and annotated in much the same way as an e-book held on an e-book reader.

You will not, unfortunately, find many online versions of key student textbooks in the library catalogue. These are usually only available for personal download to e-book readers. Publishers do however release e-book versions of research texts to libraries. These are often released a little while after the publication of the initial hardback print version. Many legal practitioner texts are also available in current updated versions from the Lexis Library (para.2.3) and Westlaw UK (para.2.4). These include titles such as *Rayden & Jackson on Divorce and Family Matters* from

> **TIPS** • *When using library catalogue searching, combine title keywords with the author surname if known.*

the Lexis Library and *Archbold: Criminal Pleading, Evidence and Practice* from Westlaw UK. Using these books online means that you no longer have to check edition dates, or look for supplementary volumes to the main print editions to be sure that the statement of the law you are reading is completely up to date. If the print version of the text you are reading comes in a looseleaf format, it means you no longer have to check that the latest versions of the pages you are using have been filed into the binder volume.

Searching the library catalogue

Library catalogues allow you to search for books using the author's name, or the title of the book. It is usually easier and quicker to search by title (ignoring words such as "The" or "A" in the title), or alternatively by a combination of author surname and title. If you do not have the exact title, search for words occurring anywhere in the title. In most cases, the initial search page of the library catalogue contains only a single search box. If this is so, enter author surnames and title words in a single search phrase. Further search options can usually be found under an "advanced search" link. Search results can also be filtered to display books from particular locations or collections, or to display only details of e-books, for example, rather than all books in the library collection. 1.5

If the library has the book you want, the catalogue entry will give you its full details (e.g. its publisher, the date of publication and the length of the book in pages) and either the location of the book on the shelves, or a link to the full text of an e-book.

One potential cause of confusion is the tendency of law books, which have run to a number of editions, to be known by the name of the original author, even though that author may no longer be involved in the writing of the book. This is something you will need to take account of when using the catalogue. *Winfield and Jolowicz on Tort*, for example, is in its nineteenth edition and Winfield has not been involved with the work for many years, but his name is still associated with the book. You will usually find an author entry under Winfield, but there will also be entries for Edwin Peel and James Goudkamp who are the authors of the current edition. If you are using a title search you need to search for "Winfield and Jolowicz on Tort", not "Tort", which was the original title of the book.

Many law books have been written jointly by two or more authors. You may be referred for example to Craig and de Burca (*EU Law*) or Clayton and Tomlinson (*The Law of Human Rights*). There will be an entry in the catalogue for both authors, and title searches could combine the name of either author with "EU Law" or "Law of Human Rights".

Author searches should be used with care. Even if you are sure of the author of the book, a number of different authors may share the same name. The form of name you have might also not match that used in the catalogue. Suppose you have a reference to a book written by John Jackson. The library catalogue might use any of the following variations of the name (among others):

- Jackson, J.A., John Archer, 1929–;
- Jackson, J.D, John Dugland, 1955–;
- Jackson, J.E., John Ellwood;
- Jackson, John, 1887–1958; and
- Jackson, John E.

If you are using an author index, it is necessary to work down the list of authors to find the right author. Standard catalogue searches will display results for all author names containing "John" and "Jackson". In this case, the second author listed is a writer on legal subjects.

Sometimes a book does not have an individual as the author. It is published by an organisation or society and the organisation is, in effect, the author. In this case, you will find an entry in the catalogue under the name of the body, e.g. Law Commission, Law Society, Legal Action Group, United Nations.

Finding and borrowing books

1.6 The classification number for a book appears prominently in the library catalogue entry. It is usually combined with letters and numbers based on the author's name, which enable you to trace the precise place the book should appear on the shelves. Remember to check also for any indication that the book you wish to find may be shelved in a separate sequence—(pamphlets, large-sized books etc.).

If the book is on loan to another reader, the library catalogue will give the current return date for the book. It is usually possible to request the book using the catalogue, in which case the book will be recalled from its present borrower.

A book may be mis-shelved or missing, or have been removed by library staff for some reason, e.g. re-binding. If you have any problems finding a book, ask a member of the library staff for help.

When you borrow a book from a library issue desk (or use a self-service issue machine), you will be given a return date for the book. Remember that you could be asked to return the book before that date if another reader has requested it. There will also be fines for late return. These fines can be significant if the book has been borrowed from a short-loan, reserve, or consultation collection.

LAW REPORTS AND JOURNALS

1.7 In the course of your legal studies you will often need to look at reports of cases which have been heard in courts in the UK, the EU and elsewhere. These reports are published in a number of publications called law reports. Amongst the best known series of law reports are the *All England Law Reports*, the *Weekly Law Reports* and the *Law Reports*. These are examined in more detail in Ch.3. There is a standard form of writing references to law reports, and this is explained in para.3.3.

The bound volumes of law reports found on library shelves are usually held in a separate sequence. These volumes are not for loan. In a well-established library, the collections of law reports will be extensive. A single series of these reports, the *Law Reports*, first published in 1864, occupies many metres of shelving in the law library. Although this is the most extensive series, there are many others. In addition to the shelves containing such bound volumes, the library will also have prominently located display shelves for recent, unbound issues of law reports.

Most law reports are also available online and access is provided almost exclusively by database services such as the Lexis Library and Westlaw UK. These are described in para.2.2. It is worth keeping in mind just how much information these services contain. The *Law Reports* are almost certainly available to you online and they form only one part of a single database within the Lexis Library and Westlaw UK.

You will find, in addition, that you are referred to articles and case notes in journals (or periodicals). Journals provide commentary on cases and advanced discussion of legal issues. They are published for the most part either weekly, monthly or quarterly (hence the name, periodical). A journal reference should give you the author and title of a journal article, the year, the volume number, an abbreviation for the title of the journal in which the article appeared and the page number of the first page of the article itself, e.g.:

Asha Kaushal "The Politics of Jurisdiction" (2015) 78 M.L.R. 759

Law database providers such as the Lexis Library and Westlaw UK provide access to the full text of journal articles as well as to law reports. However, not all UK journals are available online from these databases. Many other journals can be accessed directly from publishers' websites or through intermediary sites. If your library has a subscription for online access, the full text of articles will be available.

As is the case with law reports, the bound print volumes of printed journals are usually shelved in a separate sequence in the library. There is usually a display area for recent unbound issues similar to the display area for unbound law reports.

Abbreviations

The tradition adopted by lecturers and authors of referring to journals and law reports only by an abbreviated form of their full title can present a major difficulty for new students. Instead of writing the name of the journal or law report in full, they are invariably shortened to such cryptic abbreviations as: 1.8

- (2015) 78 M.L.R. 759;
- [2011] 3 W.L.R. 322

This may make it difficult for you to know whether you are looking for a law report or a journal article. To make things even more difficult, library catalogues use the full unabbreviated title of a journal or law report. As a result, abbreviations need to be de-coded before you can use them to check for online or print access. If you are in any doubt as to the nature of a reference, ask a member of the library staff for advice. Many of the references are also confusingly similar, e.g. L.R. can be the abbreviation for both "law report" and "law review". This can be frustrating if you are looking for print volumes in the library. The law reports are shelved together, but separately from the law reviews, which are journals. Consequently, if you are looking along the shelves of bound volumes for a publication, you could find yourself looking in the wrong sequence. A common mistake, for instance, is to assume that a reference to a report of a case in "Crim. L.R." means that you must search amongst the law reports for a series entitled the *Criminal Law Reports*. There is no such series (although there is a series called the *Criminal Appeal Reports*). The reference "Crim. L.R." is to the *Criminal Law Review*, which is a journal shelved with the other journals. It contains both articles and reports of cases.

The meaning of abbreviations can be checked both online and in print and key sources are noted in para.3.5.

Tracing journals and law reports

1.9 A title search using the library catalogue can usually establish what journals and law reports are available either online or in print. Sometimes a specific journal title search will be provided. A separate journal finder or A–Z list of journals is often also available. It is important to search using the full title of a journal or law report, not its abbreviation.

If you are looking for a journal, which includes the name of an organisation in its title, you may be unsure of the precise title to use. Is it the *American Bar Association Journal*, for example, or the *Journal of the American Bar Association?* In these cases it is usually possible to search for the journal by the name of the organisation that produces it. If the publication you wish to find has "Bulletin", "Transactions" or "Proceedings" at the start of its title, retain these words when you make your search or use a "keyword" search.

Most libraries are likely to have significantly more journal titles available online than they hold in print, as explained in para.5.2. However, it is important to remember that your access to journals will be limited to those for which the library has a subscription. This is just as true for journals and reports accessed online as it is for the journals and reports held in print on the library shelves.

If your search is successful, you will find a catalogue entry which displays a link to the appropriate online source, or the location of a print journal or report in the library. There are usually separate entries for the online and print versions of a journal or report. Catalogue entries for print journals or reports display library locations and classmarks, which work in much the same way as book locations and classmarks. Just as for books, look for any indication that a journal or report might be shelved apart from the main sequence, in an area for large-sized journals for example, or in library special collections. Be sure, in addition, to check the precise holdings the library has of a particular journal or report. Whether online or in print, it is not always the case that the library has a report or journal from its first volume or issue onwards. Cancellations and limitations on subscriptions may also mean that the current year is not available.

Some, but by no means all, of the journals available online from your library may also be found in the journals sections of the Lexis Library (para.2.3) and Westlaw UK (para.2.4), assuming these services are available. However, journals and reports available from Lexis and Westlaw should also be listed in the library catalogue. Browse options within the journals section of each database service, will establish which journals can be accessed online and the year of publication of the first available issue (para.5.3). Tracing law reports online using Lexis, Westlaw and other online sources is covered in Ch.3.

REFERENCE SOURCES

1.10 A number of reference sources are available for legal research, both online and in print. The key legal encyclopedia is *Halsbury's Laws of England* (para.7.3), accessed online from the Lexis Library.

Dictionaries

1.11 Lawyers have a language of their own, which is a mixture of Latin, French and English. There are several small single volume dictionaries of law, which may be useful for your research.

Some may be available in the library reference section. Examples include the *Dictionary of Law* from Oxford Reference (2015) and *Osborn's Concise Law Dictionary* (2013). The library shelves are also likely to contain more substantial multi-volume law dictionaries such as *Stroud's Judicial Dictionary of Words and Phrases*. The Index of Legal Terms available from the Westlaw UK home page (para.2.4) can be used to search entries drawn from *Stroud's Judicial Dictionary of Words and Phrases*, *Jowitt's Dictionary of English Law* and *Osborn's Concise Law Dictionary* online. Standard English dictionaries may also be useful. The multi-volume *Oxford English Dictionary* should be available, in most cases in both online and print versions.

Latin phrases and maxims may cause difficulties. Latin phrases appear in most legal dictionaries and a collection of legal maxims can be found in the various editions and reprints of H. Broom, *A Selection of Legal Maxims*. If you are carrying out research in legal history, you may need J.H. Baker, *Manual of Law French* (1990).

Tracing people and addresses

Solicitors and barristers can be easily traced from the online listing provided by the directory websites. The Waterlow website (at *http://www.waterlowlegal.com*) provides a means of finding contact details of solicitors and barristers using the site's Legal Search. The website also contains a careers and development section, which includes basic careers advice and information on continuing professional development. If you want to trace a solicitor by area of specialisation, this can be done by using the Law Society website (at *http://www.lawsociety.org.uk*) which provides a "Find a solicitor" search. The sections of the *Bar Directory* covering barristers' chambers by location and barristers in private practice can be searched online using the legal hub website from Sweet & Maxwell (at *http://www.legalhub.co.uk*). The Legal500 website (at *http://www.legal500.com*) is more selective, providing profiles of leading commercial firms. 1.12

Biographical details of prominent members of the legal profession can also be found in *Who's Who*. *Debrett's Correct Form* is also useful in this context, providing advice on the correct form of address when writing to, or addressing, members of the judiciary and other eminent people. Check the library catalogue for online subscription access to both *Who's Who* and *Debrett's*. The Legal Aid Agency administers the legal aid scheme in England and Wales. Contact details for its local offices can be found on the Legal Aid Agency section of the GOV.UK website (at *http://www.gov.uk*).

2
Using online sources of law

INTRODUCTION

2.1 The start of the century saw a dramatic shift in the scope and availability of information online. At the same time, the use of a web search engine such as Google to find useful information has become second nature for anyone with internet access. Beware, though, of assuming that a search engine is the only route to online information, especially when undertaking legal research. A great deal of relatively recent case law and legislation, along with important parliamentary and government publications, can be found using a web search engine. The response will also be gratifyingly quick and apparently comprehensive. However, restricting your search to Google will mean that a great deal of useful source material for research will be missed.

To make effective use of online sources of law also requires that you learn how to use the database services already noted in Ch.1. Services such as the Lexis Library and Westlaw UK are the only sources, for example, that can give you a complete, up-to-date statement of law in force for England and Wales. They, and other subscription services, also contain extensive archives of case law, which are not otherwise available online. Just as important, the full text of the vast majority of journal articles currently accessible online is only available from database services, or from other subscription websites. All of these information sources—cases, legislation in force and journal articles—are inaccessible in the absence of a subscription access route. Unless you have access to subscription sources made available by a library, they will be closed to you.

Searching subscription database services such as the Lexis Library and Westlaw UK using keywords and indexes also requires a different approach to that used in searching internet search engines. You will need to be more precise in the keywords and phrases you use, but there will be a corresponding gain in the precision of the results obtained. Database searching is described in more detail in para.2.11. The coverage of the database services themselves is noted from para.2.2 onwards.

It would be wrong, however, to suggest that subscription services provide the only important source of law online. The BAILII website, the legislation.gov.uk website and the EUR-Lex pages that form part of the EU's Europa website all provide free public access to primary sources and their use should not be ignored. Further information on these sites is provided in para.2.12.

Understanding the way both subscription and non-subscription law sites work will help you get the best from the online sources available to you. You will find them referred to a great deal in the following chapters. Throughout the book the use of an online resource for legal research is outlined first, followed by an outline of how to use the print alternative, if there is one. Remember, there remain advantages to the use of print sources in your legal research (para.2.17).

SUBSCRIPTION SERVICES

Your university library or law school is likely to have subscriptions to at least two of the services provided by the major commercial database providers. These are services that provide access to a package of case law, legislation, and often either index references to journal articles, or access to the full text of the articles themselves. Practitioner texts may also be included as online books. 2.2

These services are web-based and the home page of the service once found looks much like any other web page on the internet; so too will the search and results pages. One difference is that the web pages you see when you are using one of the online subscription services are part of a live interactive session in which you are sending questions and commands to a database and receiving information in response. There will be some form of logging on and exit procedure to start and finish your online session and you may also be "timed out" if you leave a page for a long period of time and then wish to restart. Because you are logged on to a remote service it is also not advisable to use the "forward" and "back" commands of your web browser, as this can mean that the pages you are using become out of step with the server at the other end of your search session. The logging on procedure will also ensure that you are a valid user of the system. Standard logging on and authentication procedures for UK universities are covered in para.2.8.

There are a number of advantages to using these services, beyond their search capabilities, which you might want to take into account. They offer Word-based or PDF file printing and saving options, for example, which are not always available on public websites. Documents can also be emailed to your email account. Another feature of these services is the integration of links to law reports and legislation into the text of the document you are reading. This means that if a particular section of an Act is referred to in a law report, it is possible to link directly to that section. More specialist features include the ability to save and re-run searches and receive the results as update emails, or the ability to view current awareness updates in particular subject areas.

For these reasons, it is worth spending time getting to know how subscription services work, even though the need for a logging in procedure can be off-putting. Later chapters of this book will highlight search strategies to use when finding law reports, legislation and journals using the Lexis Library (para.2.3) and Westlaw UK (para.2.4) in particular.

The database coverage of each of the major subscription services is outlined in the following sections. Understanding the different coverage of the database providers can help you decide where to start your legal research online. Though both the Lexis Library and Westlaw UK contain comparable legislation databases, for example, the specialist law reports and to a large extent the journals contained in their databases will be different. This is because the Lexis Library is linked to LexisNexis publishing, while Westlaw UK is linked to Sweet & Maxwell.

Other services, such as Lawtel (para.2.5) and Justis (para.2.6) are also able to offer additional services and content not available from either the Lexis Library or Westlaw UK.

The Lexis Library

2.3 The Lexis Library provides access to case law databases, which have been available to academic libraries and the legal profession since the mid-1980s, as part of the Lexis and LexisNexis Professional database services. In 2007 these case law databases were merged with online journal, specialist law report and legislation databases provided by LexisNexis Butterworths to create the content of the current Lexis Library.

UK universities usually subscribe to a core set of databases which form the content of the "Cases", "Legislation" and "Journals" sections of the service. The content of the "Commentary" and "Forms and Precedents" sections will depend on additional library subscriptions.

The "Cases" section of the service includes over 50 specialist law reports in full text, along with the full text of the *All England Law Reports*, the *Law Reports* (from 1864) and the *All England Law Reports Reprints*, covering 1558 to 1935. Transcripts of judgments made in "unreported cases" (see para.3.19) are available from the mid-1980s onwards. These transcripts are sometimes of particular value, as transcripts of judgments pre-dating 2000 are often difficult to obtain from other sources. The Lexis Library is also the only subscription source for Northern Ireland case law.

The "Legislation" section of the service provides the full text of Public General Acts in force in England and Wales, a full statutory instruments database for England and Wales, and the full text of Scottish Parliament Acts and statutory instruments.

EU cases and legislation can also be found in the "Cases" and "Legislation" sections of the Lexis Library, though these are currently somewhat confusingly found under shortcuts to "International Cases" and "International Legislation" respectively.

The "Journals" section of the service includes the full text of around 100 law journals and newsletters, many aimed at an academic audience, some at the legal practitioner. Most of the titles are only available online through the Lexis Library, though some—those published by Oxford University Press in particular—are available online from other sources.

Much of the supplementary content available from the Lexis Library can be found in the "Commentary" section of the service. The database sources available will depend on the additional subscriptions taken out by your university, but may well include *Halsbury's Laws of England* (para.7.3), the major legal encyclopedia for England and Wales. Specialist titles, which aim to give a comprehensive statement of law in a particular area, may also be found. These include *Harvey on Industrial Relations and Employment Law*, for example, and *Clarke Hall & Morrison on Children.* The *Encyclopaedia of Forms and Precedents* is also likely to be available in most universities as it is of particular value to students undertaking legal practice courses. It can be found in a "Forms and Precedents" section of the service.

The international content of the Lexis Library can be found by exploring the "Sources" section of the service. Sources are listed by country, or can be traced using keyword searches. Substantial databases of US primary law are included, along with the full text of a large number of North American law journals. Primary law and some journals from other jurisdictions can also be found—for the most part from Commonwealth or former Commonwealth countries.

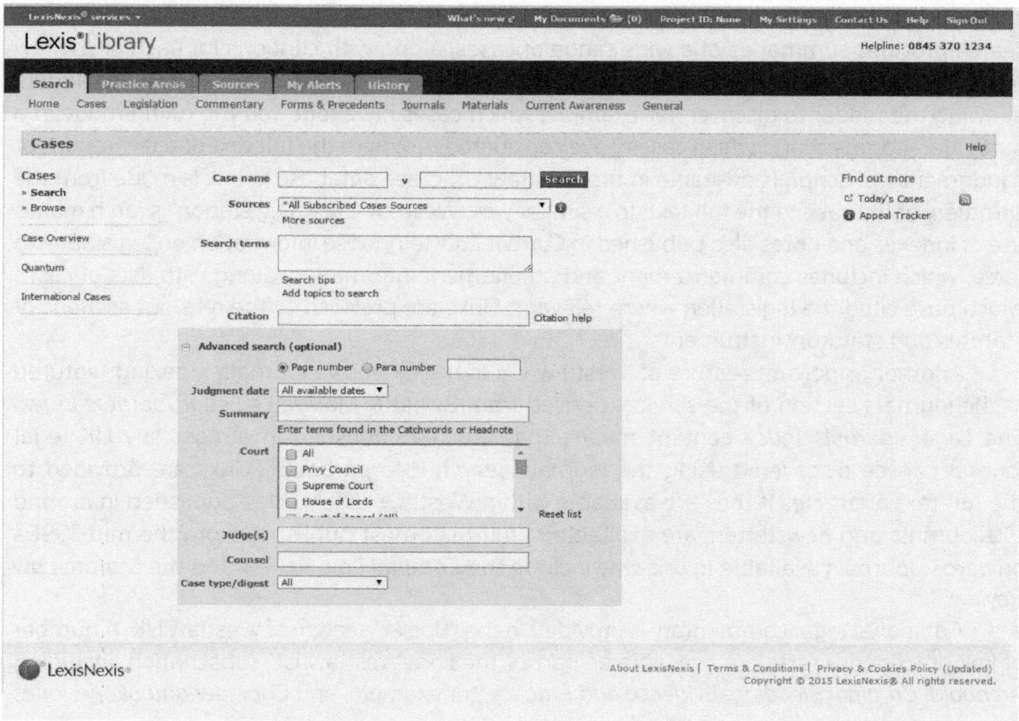

Fig 2.1
Lexis Library Cases Search

Additional searches can be made using the "Current Awareness" section of the Lexis Library. These include the ability to keyword search digests of recent cases, or to use the Lexis Journals Index to find recent articles.

The Lexis Library also has a companion Nexis (news and business) service, structured in much the same way as the Lexis Library. The news content of the service can be of particular benefit for legal research. The full text of all UK national newspapers is included, for the most part from the mid-1980s, along with many regional newspapers. International news sources are also included.

Westlaw UK

Westlaw UK uses the US-based Westlaw service to provide access to case law, legislation and journal databases provided by Sweet & Maxwell. As with the Lexis Library, a database of law in force in England and Wales is available, but full text coverage of law reports differs significantly. Like the Lexis Library, the full text of the *Law Reports* can be found in the cases section of the service, but unlike the Lexis Library, the full text of the *All England Law Reports* is not included. However, the full text of the *Weekly Law Reports* is present, along with the full text of over 30 specialist law reports. The specialist law reports, published by Sweet & Maxwell, are not available online elsewhere. 2.4

The Sweet & Maxwell content also means that Westlaw UK has the most comprehensive case finding database available for case law that applies to England and Wales. Using the indexes and brief case summaries published in print as *Current Law*, the Westlaw UK "Cases" search provides summaries of a wide range of cases, along with citations for each of the law report series that has published a report. Where relevant, brief case histories are also added, allowing the reader to discover, for example, which cases have followed the ruling made in a particular judgment and which cases have considered it. Where the full text of a law report, or a judgment transcript, is available in the Westlaw UK cases database, a link is made from the summary of the case to the full text. In a similar way, Westlaw UK's "Legislation" search makes use of indexes and notes also published in *Current Law* to provide information on legislation in force, which includes commencement and amendment information, along with lists of cases which have cited the legislation where relevant. Links are provided to the relevant sections of statutes and statutory instruments.

Another important feature of Westlaw UK is the extensive journals indexing featured in the journals section of the service, derived from Sweet & Maxwell's *Legal Journals Index*. The *Legal Journals Index* content means that articles published in almost any UK legal journal can be discovered using the journals search (see para.5.6). Links are provided to the full text of articles if they are available within Westlaw UK. Articles published in around 130 journals and newsletters are available in full text, most published from the mid-1990s onwards. Journals available in this way include the *Criminal Law Review* and the *Statute Law Review*.

Additional legal commentary is provided in the "Books" section of Westlaw UK. A number of key practitioner texts are available as part of the core Westlaw UK subscription, including *Archbold: Criminal Pleading, Evidence and Practice*, for example, and *Copinger and Skone Jones*

Fig 2.2
Westlaw UK Cases Search

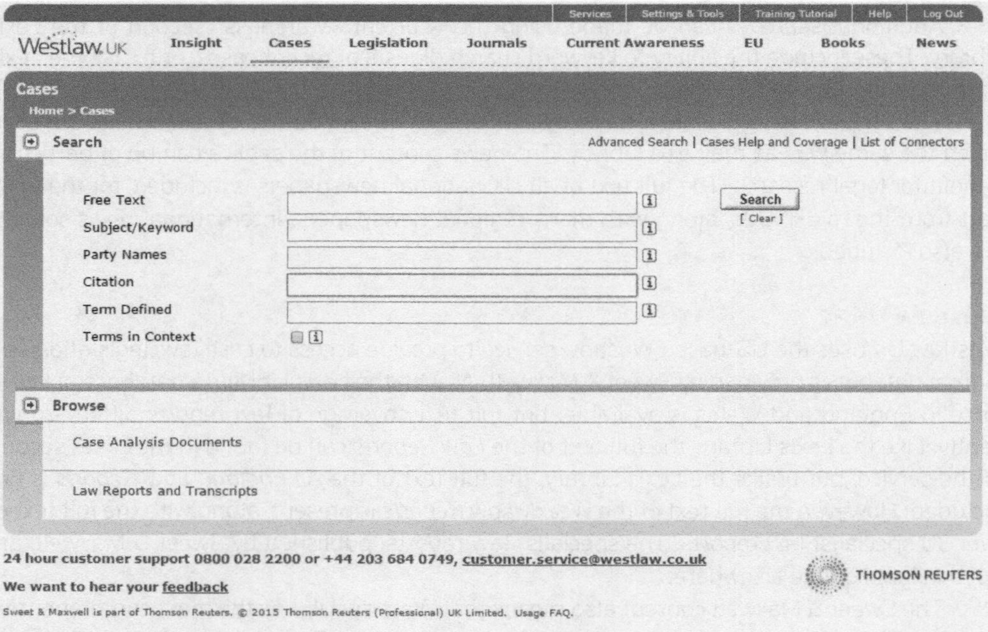

on Copyright. Your library may also have subscribed to a number of additional titles. These include *Chitty on Contracts* and *Clerk & Lindsell on Torts*.

The link with the US-based Westlaw service means that Northern American cases, legislation and journal articles can also be accessed from Westlaw UK using the "International Materials" link under "Services". A directory of sources gives a full listing of the law resources available. North American coverage is much the same as that provided by the Lexis Library.

Lawtel

Although aimed primarily at the legal profession, many university libraries provide access to Lawtel. Lawtel is essentially a current awareness digest service that provides brief case reports, usually within a day of a judgment being made. The case reports, which date back to the 1980s, are in turn linked to the full text of judgment transcripts as they become available. A number of additional features include a legislation search, which provides update notes on amendments and repeals made to sections of Acts, and an articles index, which provides summaries of articles from over 90 legal and potentially relevant non-legal journals. 2.5

The Lawtel service, like Westlaw UK, is a Thomson Reuters product, but it has retained its separate role and identity.

Justis Publishing

Your library may be able to provide access to one or more full text databases from Justis Publishing. These include online versions of the *Law Reports* and the *Weekly Law Reports* in which the text is presented in printer-ready PDF images, reproducing the pages of the original print versions. These have been attractive to libraries which do not have full archives of the original volumes, or to libraries aiming to fully replace print volumes with online versions. However, both the Lexis Library and Westlaw UK now also provide PDF versions of reported cases which reproduce the layout of the printed version of the report. Justis does though, also provide access to reports such as *CCH Tax Cases* and the *Irish Reports and Digests*. These may be available as individual Justis subscriptions. 2.6

Two unique legislation databases might also be available from your library. The UK statutes database contains the full unamended text of all Acts of Parliament made in England and Scotland from 1235 onwards, providing convenient access to historic legislation now repealed. The UK Statutory Instruments database provides the full text of statutory instruments made from 1671 onwards.

Your library may in addition have a subscription to the JustCite service. This provides access to an index of cases, legislation and journal articles containing links to the full range of full text sources available online. The service can work particularly well for case law. For each case indexed, a brief digest summary is provided, along with a listing of any later cases which considered the case and any journal articles providing significant discussion. The particular strength of the database is the provision within the index of full text links not just to the free online source of the judgment made in a case (see para.2.12), but also to any reported versions of the case available from the Lexis Library and Westlaw UK.

If available, JustCite may provide a valuable alternative to the Westlaw UK "Cases" search described in detail in para.3.15. JustCite users do not need to switch from Westlaw UK to the Lexis Library (or Justis) to find the full text of a law report.

Jordans Publishing

2.7 Jordans Publishing provide online versions of practitioner texts, case law, journals and legislation in a number of specialist legal areas. The Family Law Online service, for example, includes *Child and Family Law Quarterly*, the *Family Law Reports* and *Duckworth: Matrimonial Property and Finance*, along with relevant legislation. Specialist services such as these are more likely to be of interest to legal practitioners than university libraries. However, your library may well have subscriptions to online versions of individual journals and reports published by Jordans.

ACCESSING SUBSCRIPTION SERVICES

2.8 As already noted, subscription database services are web-based. This means that network access requires no more than a computer with an internet connection and a web browser. There is no specialist software that needs to be loaded or mastered.

However, you will only be able to use these services if your university law library or law school has paid a subscription. Typically access is licensed to staff and students of a university, either for a limited number of simultaneous users, or more usually, for unlimited access to any number of users. The licence will have been paid for on an annual basis with the result that no additional charge is made by the database provider for the connection time to the database.

Because subscription services are only available to licensed users, there must also, inevitably, be some method in place to ensure that the person accessing the service is indeed a student or staff member of a particular university. Two approaches are possible. One is based on the recognition of the university network by the service provider, allowing access to the relevant database service. The other approach is for the service provider to use an authentication system such as Athens or Shibboleth, which uses individual usernames and passwords to confirm that you are a student or staff member of a particular university. Shibboleth is a standard international authentication system which has largely replaced the UK-based Athens (or OpenAthens) system.

If the subscription service you are using works by recognising the university network ("IP recognition"), you will need to use your university ID and password to log on to the university network. You will not, however, be asked to enter a username and password to access the subscription service itself. Most online journals work in this way. This approach to authentication is almost always complemented by a university authentication system that allows "off campus" users to log on to a subscription service using a university network server. The server will request your university ID and password, and once you have entered those, you will be able to continue as if you were on the university network. There is no need to know the web address of the university server providing this service. The address will be included in standard links to databases and journals provided by the library catalogue and the library web pages. This has the important consequence that off-campus access will only be possible if you use links provided by your university.

If access to a subscription service is controlled by an authentication system such as Athens or Shibboleth, it will always be necessary to enter your university ID and password before you can use a subscription service. This will not, fortunately, be an additional ID and password. University systems allow the use of the same ID and password for both local network access and remote database access using Athens or Shibboleth. Logging on in this way has the advantage that various personalisation features for a service, including, for example, the ability to save searches, or add shortcuts to favourite resources, can be based on your university ID and password. Your university ID becomes the ID for your personal database account. Personalisation features for the Lexis Library, for example, work in this way.

It makes sense to use the links provided by your library to access subscription resources. However, the Shibboleth system also makes it possible to log in using links provided by the home pages of services such as the Lexis Library and Westlaw UK. To use these links, you must ensure that you choose options provided for academic users. There will be other login options provided for non-academic users. The login option for academic users will direct you to a long list of universities who are members of the "UK Access Management Federation". Selecting your own university directs your web browser to the university's local login page for Shibboleth access.

Fortunately authentication systems are usually linked by your university, so that if you are accessing subscription resources off campus, you are only asked for your username and password once in any online session. This means that if you log in first, for example, to a Justis database and then decide to move to Westlaw UK, you will not be asked for a username and password when you link to Westlaw UK. You are already recognised as a user with rights to access the service.

The most important point to remember is that all of the database resources paid for by your university should be available to you, both on and off campus. By using the correct web page links you can ensure that you are recognised as a valid user of a subscription service whether you are logging in from the library, an off-campus hall of residence, from home, or even the other side of the world.

Usernames and passwords

In most universities a single username and password combination enables a student to log on to both internal computing resources, such as a university email account, and university administration systems, as well as library subscription resources such as Westlaw UK and the Lexis Library. This is because usernames and passwords are validated locally, using university-based databases. Both username and password are usually given to you when you first register with the university. 2.9

In a small number of cases a different username and password will be needed for accessing remote services and you will be given separate account details. Your university library or computing service should inform you if you need to use an additional account.

Universities are also working towards the provision of a "single sign on" for all networked services. In a single sign on system, once you have logged on to the university network, you will not be asked again for usernames and passwords, whether you are using email accounts, accessing exam results, or using online subscription services.

Library search pages

Most university libraries provide search pages that allow you to search a range of library subscription services using a single keyword search. Sometimes these pages will be integrated into the library catalogue as an article search option. The initial search box is often also integrated into the library home page. 2.10

The search pages for these services are usually designed to look much like the search page of a web search engine. However, library searches do not work in the same way. Most work by searching a master "metadata" index of information drawn from data provided by journal publishers and others. Some library searches make direct, live, searches of the journal databases using the keywords you have entered. This older approach may require you first to select particular journal and index databases from a list, in order that the keywords you have entered can be passed on to the search interfaces of the databases selected.

In all cases, details of journal articles matching your keywords will be presented in a single results page. A link to the full text of a journal article will also be present if library subscriptions allow access.

As these library search pages make use of database indexing, they provide a valuable alternative to web search engines. Search results are more likely to closely match the keyword terms you have entered, and there will be fewer unexpected results. Options to search within broad subject categories can, in addition, significantly improve the relevance of search results. The integration of links to the full text of articles also spares you the need to make further searches of the library catalogue to check availability.

Unfortunately, the way the major subscription law services structure their databases means that they cannot be searched directly from library search pages. It is necessary instead to go to the home page of the relevant service. The various free sources of law on the internet noted in para.2.12 are also not usually included in library searches. As a result, library search pages provide a valuable approach to searching for journal articles (Ch.5), but do not provide a means of tracing cases and legislation.

DATABASE SEARCHING

2.11 Although the search pages of services such as Westlaw UK and the Lexis Library appear as web pages, and even though the results of a search are presented as a sometimes lengthy list of links to further web pages, when you search a subscription database you are not searching a website. The subscription services provide access to databases constructed from the fully indexed raw text of reports, statutes etc. This has consequences for the way these databases are best searched.

When a database of full text or bibliographic (reference) data is constructed, all uses of a word are automatically indexed and tagged according to their place in the document. Words are indexed as title words, for example, or as names appearing in the "parties" section of a case report. This enables searches to be restricted to words in the title or names in the parties section or "field" of the database. If a name, e.g. "Hart" is tagged as the name of a party to a case, for example, all cases in which someone called Hart is one of the parties will be listed in the computer index used for party names. If you search for Hart as the party to a case, the name you entered is matched against the database indexes and the relevant documents retrieved. The database index works at this level in much the same way as the index to this book, and the database search software is performing an operation that is equivalent to looking up a word in the index and seeing which pages contain relevant information.

> **TIPS** • *Break down your search query into single keywords and two-word phrases. Then combine keywords using "search operators" such as "AND" or "NEAR". Use "w/6" to specify that words should be near each other when using the Lexis Library or Westlaw UK.*

This indexing of words makes so-called "Boolean" searching a powerful way of retrieving information from a database. Two examples might help.

Suppose first, that you wish to search the journals section of Westlaw UK in order to find journal references relevant to the issue of provocation as a defence. You are particularly interested in linking the issue to domestic violence against women. Enter the words:

provocation AND domestic violence

in the "Free Text" area of the search page and click the search button. The search software will now retrieve all index entries that are linked both to the term "provocation" and the term "domestic violence". The significance of the "AND" (one of the "Boolean operators") is that it requests this linking of index entries to be made. The result is a list of references which contain both the word "provocation" and the words "domestic violence". (In many databases you need to use quotation marks to indicate that you wish "domestic violence" to be treated as a phrase.)

If you wanted to go further with this search, you might also consider that "domestic violence" is not the only phrase of potential interest that could occur in the title or summary of a journal article. Another significant Boolean operator that can help is "OR" which acts as a request to group the index entries for two different words. Using:

battered women OR domestic violence

will widen the scope to the references found to include those using either the phrase "battered women" or the phrase "domestic violence". As there are articles which use the term "battered women" but not "domestic violence", more references will be found. In this case it would be better to make two searches, one for both "provocation and domestic violence" and the other for "provocation and battered women".

Suppose now you wish to find cases that have discussed the way the word "charity" has been interpreted in English law. You have decided to look for judgments in which "charity" has been judicially interpreted and are going to search a full text database of case law, such as that provided by the cases search of either Westlaw UK or the Lexis Library. Here things can become a little more involved.

An initial consideration might be that because of the complexity of the English language, along with "charity", your keywords might also include, "sense", "usage", or "definition" as well as "interpretation". All these terms should be included in your search (either by repeating searches or using "OR"). Different forms of the same word can also be used. You might want to search for "define", "defines" and "defining" along with "definition" for example. Fortunately most databases allow a truncation symbol, which can help, so that "defin!" could cover all of the forms mentioned. Less fortunately, "definite" would also be included in the search, so use truncation with care.

Having thought about your search terms, also make sure that you use the symbol or "search operator" for the database that specifies that your keywords must be found close to each other in the long text of a judgment. Many databases allow "NEAR" to specify a standard proximity, the Lexis Library uses "w/" so that "charity w/6 definition" specifies that the two words must occur within six words of each other. Westlaw UK uses "/number" so that the same search would be presented as "charity /6 definition"

Putting these considerations together, a "good" search for judgments on the interpretation of charity, might consist of the following string of words, truncated words and search operators. The brackets ensure that all the alternatives are taken together in one search:

charit! w/6 (defin* OR sense OR usage)

Still other combinations are possible. Though convenient, there is no necessity to make a single complex search in quite this way. Brackets are also not always interpreted in the way you would wish. Simpler searches could be made and a results list built up by saving the results of each search individually.

The important point to remember is that Boolean searches provide a way of refining the accuracy and scope of your search. No single search is necessarily comprehensive. It is advisable to reconsider your search words and re-edit them as you read your search results and find, perhaps, much more than you had anticipated, or, indeed, much less. Be aware of the coverage of the database you are using, and don't be misled into thinking that any search is final or comprehensive.

Constructing searches in this way differs from the approach you would take if you were searching the internet using a search engine. The way in which results are presented is also different. A database usually lists the results containing your search words in reverse chronological order. A search engine lists a series of web links in which the pages carrying most prominently the word or words you used in your search are listed first. The words "AND" and "OR" also have a particular significance for databases which they do not have for search engines. These differences are worth remembering.

FREE SOURCES OF LAW ON THE INTERNET

2.12 The primary sources of law, the judgments made in the courts, and the statute law made by the UK's various legislative bodies, are not the property of legal publishers or subscription database providers. From the mid-1990s onwards, first the House of Lords and then the Court Service of England and Wales, began to put the full text of judgments onto their own websites; an example followed in both Scotland and Northern Ireland. During the same period the Office of Public Sector Information (OPSI), in its former guise as HMSO, began to place UK legislation on its own website. The recognition of the problems caused by this proliferation of public primary sources of law, then led, in 2000, to the creation of the BAILII website (para.2.15). The site brings together judgment transcripts from the different UK court services, enabling them to be searched from a single website, along with the various sources of UK legislation. A further significant development occurred in 2007, with the launch of the Statute Law Database by the Ministry of Justice. The database provided the first publicly accessible versions of amended primary legislation for the UK. This official publishing role was then transferred to the UK National Archives with the creation of the legislation.gov.uk website (para.2.13). The new website also took over the role of the OPSI website as the place of publication for UK legislation as enacted.

It should be noted though, that BAILII and the legislation.gov.uk website cannot provide some of the "value added" features provided by the commercial database suppliers. Results cannot be emailed, and printing can be inconvenient. There are also no hypertext links placed within the text of some documents. More importantly, neither are there the added headnotes and case summaries that are found in the commercially published law reports. Significant delays in the updating of primary legislation on the legislation.gov.uk website also mean that it remains the case that only the subscription database services can offer a completely current, amended text of legislation in force. Legislation.gov users need to check for amending legislation from prompts on the site and make the appropriate adjustments for changes themselves.

Legislation.gov.uk

The legislation.gov.uk website (at *http://www.legislation.gov.uk*) contains a wide range of UK legislation. Much of the primary legislation is available both as originally enacted and as later revised. However, secondary legislation is only available in its original form. The revision of the text of primary legislation is also incomplete. Revisions made by amending legislation after 2002 are not, for the most part, incorporated into the text. This can make the site difficult to use as links to later amended legislation need to be followed in order to work out the effect of changes. This should improve as efforts are made to bring the revised text of primary legislation up to date. 2.13

From 1991 onwards—the "baseline" date for the site—both original and revised versions of UK Acts of Parliament are available. Many Acts are also available for the period preceding 1991. Revised versions are available if the Act was in force in 1991. Some pre-1991 Acts are also available in their original form. The earliest of these date from 1801. All legislation is present as first published from 1988 onwards. Secondary legislation is available, unrevised, from 1987 onwards. A significant number of pre-1987 UK statutory instruments have also been added.

TIPS • *Always look for the "Advanced Search" when searching websites. Limit your search to the kind of document that interests you. Also specify e.g. that "All words" must be found in the pages searched.*

The revised versions of Acts have been updated with changes brought into force before 2002. Thereafter the position is more complicated. Roughly half of the Acts have been revised to the present, the remainder are lacking at least some of the amendments made from 2002 onwards. A "changes to legislation" link is present at the head of text of revised legislation if changes have not yet been incorporated into the main text.

Amendments made to legislation from 2002 onwards can also be discovered using the website's "Changes to Legislation" page. The page makes it possible to first specify the name of an Act and then discover all legislation which has made changes to that Act. Care is then needed to confirm the precise changes made to the sections and schedules of an Act.

Legislation can be found by title from the legislation.gov.uk home page. A number of useful search features can also be found on the "Advanced Search" page. These include the ability to search legislation by keyword. Searches can, in addition, be limited so that only legislation applying to particular jurisdictions within the UK will be found.

Fig 2.3
Legislation.gov.uk home page

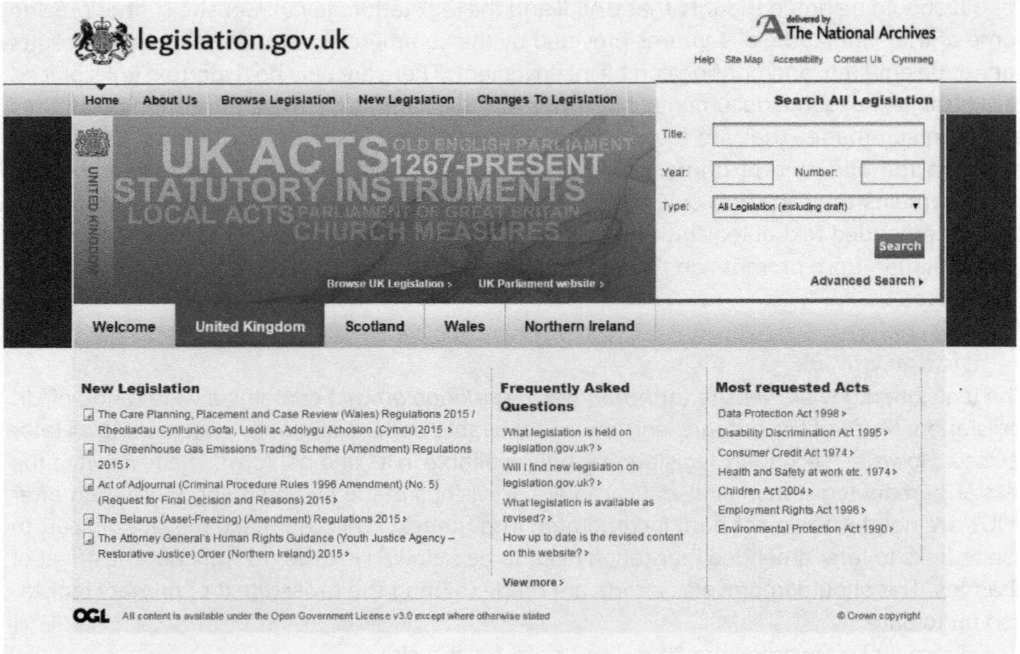

EUR-Lex

2.14 Free online access to case law in the UK has emerged gradually through a number of separate initiatives. The position is quite different for the EU. Within the institutional framework of the EU, the European Commission has acted as an official publisher, publishing and distributing print versions of the *Official Journal* of the EU and the *European Court Reports*. Part of the Commission's Europa website (para.8.2), the EUR-Lex website has extended this official publishing role, by providing free online access to both EU legislation and case law. All judgments made by the European Court of Justice are available and the website is the only source of revised "in force" versions of EU directives. As a result, Ch.8 of this book describes the use of EUR-Lex as the key resource for tracing EU legislation and case law, noting the use of online commercial services only where they provide a particularly useful alternative.

BAILII

2.15 The BAILII (British and Irish Legal Information Institute) website (at *http://www.bailii.org*) provides access to a series of databases derived from public sources of law. The site includes judgments drawn from official websites, or in the case of older England and Wales judgments, from official shorthand writers, to provide an extensive database of House of Lords, Court of Appeal and High Court judgments from 1996 onwards. Selected earlier judgments are also included from as early as 1838. The "Case Law Search" is particularly useful in this context, as it allows judgments to be found using law report citations. A wide range of UK tribunal decisions can also be found, dating for the most part from 2000. Some earlier decisions are available. The website is, in addition, a valuable source of judgments for Scotland, Northern Ireland and the

Republic of Ireland. The site should finally not be overlooked as a potential source of EU and European human rights case law, as it includes judgments of the European Court of Justice from 1954 onwards, and judgments of the European Court of Human Rights from 1960. PDF file and printable RTF versions of judgments, where available, greatly ease the viewing and printing of judgments which are otherwise presented as a single continuous web page.

The United Kingdom legislation included in BAILII corresponds to that available, both revised and unrevised, on the legislation.gov.uk website (para.2.13). Northern Ireland legislation and the Acts and statutory instruments of the Scottish Parliament can be found under links for Northern Ireland and Scotland.

The great advantage of the BAILII website is that all of these disparate sources are brought together in a standardised database format, easing searching. The database searching made possible by BAILII is also almost always an improvement on the search facilities available on the home site for the legislation or case law concerned. It is possible to search, for example, using Boolean searching ("AND", "OR" etc) and proximity searches enable the search to specify that keywords should be found close to each other in the full text of case law and legislation. BAILII was launched using systems and approaches developed by AUSTLII (Australasian Legal Information Institute) and this also means that primary sources of law for Commonwealth and former Commonwealth countries can be found from the site. BAILII's sister site CommonLII (at *http://www.commonlii.org*) brings together law from 60 Commonwealth and common law jurisdictions. It also provides access to an online version of the *English Reports* (para.3.12).

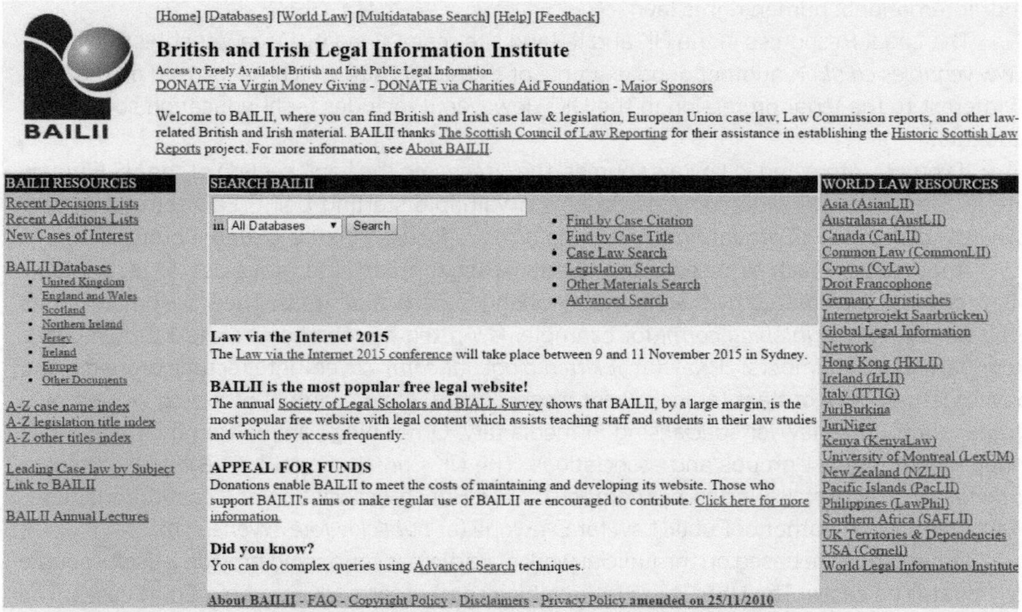

Fig 2.4
BAILII home page

SPECIALIST WEBSITES AND BLOGS

2.16 As you develop your legal research, you may well wish to move beyond the primary sources of law and the discussion and commentary provided by legal journals. Government and Parliamentary publications are covered in Ch.5. However, there are many other internet sites which may be of value beyond the sources of primary law, official publications and academic journals. If you are researching environmental law, for example, the websites of environmental organisations may well have material which could be of value to you. Medical and health law websites would have useful content if you are researching medical law, and so on.

One approach is to try putting relevant keywords into a web search engine. Another approach is to use websites which list useful sources of legal information by subject area. These are sites or web pages that act effectively as a directory of internet sources. The lawlinks site from the University of Kent (at *http://www.kent.ac.uk/lawlinks*) is a good example of a directory site with an academic focus. It provides lists of UK, EU and international sources of law, for example, along with subject listings of sources of law and relevant organisations. In this case, exploring the environmental law section of the website would prompt the discovery of such valuable environmental law sites as the Ecolex information service and the European Environmental Law Network pages from the Asser Institute in the Netherlands. Links to relevant organisations such as English Nature and Friends of the Earth can also be found.

Eagle-i (at *http://www.ials.sas.ac.uk/eagle-i.htm*) is another academic directory site supported by the Institute of Advanced Legal Studies. It provides listings of global law websites, providing a valuable starting point if you need to research beyond UK law. Again there is a listing of websites by subject area. Web sources are also listed by country and by international law topics. Listings are available for "International criminal law and war crimes" for example, and "International human rights law".

The Legal Resources in the UK and Ireland site maintained by Delia Venebles (at *http://www.venables.co.uk*) is another good example of a directory site, this time focused on material of interest to the legal profession in the UK. However, it includes legal education sources for students.

If you are interested in US law sources, the "Research the Law" section of the US Findlaw site (at *http://www.findlaw.com/casecode*) is a valuable starting point. Law.com (at *http://www.law.com*) and HG.org (at *http://www.hg.org*) are focused on the US legal profession.

Another approach to researching specialist legal areas is to make use of legal blogs. Many of these are created by practitioners working in particular areas. The UK Human Rights Blog (at *ukhumanrightsblog.com*), for example, is written by members to the 1 Crown Office Row barristers' chambers. IPKat (at *ipkitten.blogspot.com*) covers intellectual property and privacy issues. Jack of Kent (at *jackofkent.blogspot.com*) is an example of a blog written by a single individual, a lawyer specialising in media law. Other blogs are written by members of independent interest groups and associations. The UK Constitutional Law Blog (at *ukconstitutionallaw.org/blog*), is written by members of the British Association of Constitutional Law. Mark Elliott is the author of Public Law for Everyone (at *publiclawforeveryone.com*).

Other blogs are based on the judicial work of particular courts and provide a useful source for updates on cases. The UKSC blog (at *ukscblog.com*) reports UK Supreme Court cases. The ECJBlog.com provides reports of European Court of Justice cases, also carrying more general news items on the Court and other European legal developments. More systematic approaches to finding updates on recent cases are described in Ch.3 (para.3.22).

WHEN TO USE PRINT SOURCES

The reasons for using online sources are compelling. Sources of information which you may not otherwise be able to use will be available to you and you need never suffer the frustration caused by the discovery that the printed volume you sought on the library shelves is in use, missing or mutilated. More importantly, the availability of full text sources online means that sources of law can be searched in a way that simply was not possible when only print indexes were available. However, it should not be assumed that online sources are always better. For some tasks, such as checking a citation when the name and year of a case is already known to you, a print source can still be quick and easy to use. A fast, accurate result can be achieved, for example, by using the *Current Law Case Citator* (see para.3.16). More significantly, the full text of an Act of Parliament, or a House of Lords judgment, may also run to many pages. The typeface and layout of the printed versions, combined with the ability to scan and skip easily through the text, can make the printed publication much easier both to read and handle; especially when the alternative is a stack of pages gathered from a printer of a PDF file on a hard drive. There is also a significant time investment in getting to grips with an online source of information. The peculiarity of individual online services needs to be mastered, as does the search language associated with database searching. Of course, you cannot even begin, unless you have a network connection. 2.17

As a library user, you will also be faced with a limited choice of available sources. Just as the book and journal coverage of a library is limited by the funds available, so too is access to online subscription services. Very few libraries have access to anything like the full range of services. The complexity of linking subscription payments, user authorisation and valid web connections also means that sometimes library links to online resources fail. Where both print and online services are available, the choice generally depends on the particular resources to hand, the task you have in mind, and, of course, your own personal preferences.

Remember too, that some of the most significant legal resources are still found only in print form. The student textbooks and research monographs which make up much of a library collection are currently available, for the most part, only in print. This is still true of many of the authoritative practitioner texts. Some of the older journal literature in law is still also available only in print, though much is now available online (see para.5.2).

COMBINING PRINT AND ELECTRONIC SOURCES

It is important to place electronic resources in the wider context of your legal research. Online resources are an important part of the resources available to you, but you need to learn how to make use of these alongside printed resources. It is not simply the case that "online" means "modern" and "paper" means "old fashioned". Bear in mind that a student textbook usually provides your best starting point when you are new to a subject area. If you wish to find out about the impact of the Human Rights Act 1998 on statutory interpretation, for example, you need to clarify the basic issues. This is often best achieved with the help of a recent textbook 2.18

and some quality time to think about the core issues. You will find no shortage of textbooks in this area. Books published as "cases and materials" will offer a valuable quick reference as they contain extracts from leading cases and statute law. Only after you have looked at the textbook material will it probably make sense to go online using the journals search in Westlaw UK for example. Having studied the available textbook material, you will be ready to search for references to journal articles that have discussed and developed the issues you have identified in your basic preparation. Online access to case law might have its place as you search for judgments that have cited what you now know to be the key cases. Having traced journal articles and cases online, you may finally need to return to print sources and use the library catalogue to locate particular journals or law reports on the library shelves.

To make the best use of law library resources you must learn how to move comfortably between electronic and print sources. The ability to do so will result in better time management and better coverage of the material. The remaining chapters of this book, placing as they do, online resources beside those in print, are designed to enable you to switch research techniques as and when appropriate.

CD-ROMS

2.19 Many of the full-text products of the commercial legal publishers, including the *All England Law Reports*, the *Law Reports* series and UK Statutory Instruments, were first made available in CD-ROM form. The Westlaw UK databases first appeared on CD-ROM as Current Legal Information. In general, university libraries no longer carry major databases in this form, though they can still be useful for small organisations. However, CD-ROMs may be used in the library to provide improved search access to some of the key practitioner texts and looseleaf updating services (where they save on filing).

If you wish to use a CD-ROM held by your library you have to borrow the disc from an issue or information desk. As the CD-ROM requires particular search software to be loaded onto a computer before it can be used, you will be directed to a particular PC or workstation on which the search software is loaded. Alternatively the CD-ROM may be pre-loaded on a particular computer and you will need to locate the one that holds the CD-ROM database. This may or may not be located within the law library. Where CD-ROMs have been networked by your university, it may be possible for any machine on a university's local network to use the CD-ROM database, though again the particular machine may need to have CD-ROM search software pre-loaded. When in doubt ask for advice from the library staff about what is located where in the library.

3
Law reports

INTRODUCTION

Law reports are one of the basic (or "primary") sources of English law. Traditionally, the common law develops through the practical reasoning of the judges. This is based on the particular facts of the case in question, social forces and previous judicial reasoning when it has a bearing on the case being heard. Legal principles stated in earlier decisions are given effect in later cases by the operation of the doctrine of precedent, which is described in detail in most introductory texts to the English legal system. The successful development of the common law depends largely upon the production of reliable law reports which carry not only the facts, issues and decision, but also, most importantly, the legal principles upon which the judgment is made. Currently, the senior judiciary spend most of their court time considering the scope and application of particular Acts of Parliament. 3.1

A law report re-prints the full text of a judgment, i.e. the statement of facts and judicial reasoning made by judges in a case and adds additional material. This consists of a summary of the legal issues, lists of other cases cited, legislation referred to, and other key features of the case (see para.3.6).

Only a very small proportion of cases decided by the courts is reported in the law reports. Just because a case is widely reported in the media, it does not follow that it will appear in a law report. A case is selected for reporting if it raises a point of legal significance. Judgments made in appeal cases which are not reported, though publicly available, are referred to as "unreported judgments". Unreported judgments can nonetheless be cited in court cases where it is felt that relevant legal issues are raised. Typescript transcripts of judgments and judgments held on online databases have been referred to in court cases for some time.

Older unreported judgments remain difficult to trace, but judgments made since 2000, though still "unreported", can easily be found online using the BAILII website (para.2.15). The system of "neutral" citation (para.3.4) has also made it easier to cite unreported judgments. However, despite the relative ease with which recent unreported judgments can be found and cited, the element of selection provided by the law reports, and the additional explanatory material included, has meant that law reports continue to be the major primary source of case law in the English legal system. Throughout your legal study you will make constant use of law reports, occasionally supplemented by unreported judgments, usually those made in significant recent cases which have not yet been reported. It is worth remembering, though, that if you do not have access to a particular recent law report, the judgment made in the case reported is almost certainly available online. For the great majority of 19th and 20th century cases, you will have to rely on law reports.

THE HISTORY OF LAW REPORTS

3.2 Law reports have existed, in one form or another, since the reign of Edward I. These very early law reports are known as the *Year Books*. If you wish to see a copy, reprints of a number of these *Year Books* are available in the series of publications published by the Selden Society, in the Rolls Series and in facsimile reprints issued by Professional Books.

After the Year Books had ceased, collections of law reports published privately by individuals began to appear. These reports, the first of which were published in 1571, were normally referred to by the name of the reporter or compiler. For this reason, they are collectively referred to as the *Nominate Reports* and they vary considerably in accuracy and reliability. Few libraries will have a complete collection of these old reports and if you do obtain a copy, you may find that the antiquated print makes it difficult to read. Fortunately, the great majority of these *Nominate Reports* can be found in at least one of three reprint series: the *English Reports*, the *Revised Reports* and the *All England Law Reports Reprint* series. The most comprehensive of the three series is the *English Reports*, which is examined in detail later in the chapter (para.3.12).

In 1865, a body called the Incorporated Council of Law Reporting commenced publication of the *Law Reports*, a single series of reports covering all the major courts. These reports were rapidly accepted by the legal profession as the most authoritative version of law reports and, as a result, most of the earlier series published by individuals ceased publication in 1865 or soon after. Judgments in the *Law Reports* have been checked by the relevant judges before publication and are cited in court in preference to any other series. The *Law Reports* series is described in more detail in para.3.10.

Today, there are over 50 different series of law reports for England and Wales. The *Weekly Law Reports* and the *All England Law Reports*, like the *Law Reports*, cover a wide range of topics and are aimed at the lawyer in general practice. There are also a large number of law reports which cover a specialised area of the law, such as the *Criminal Appeal Reports* and the *Road Traffic Reports*.

A case may be reported in more than one series of law reports. For example, a short report may appear in *The Times* newspaper (under the heading "Law Report") a day or so after the judgment is given. A summary or a full report may be published in some of the weekly legal journals, such as the *New Law Journal* and the *Solicitors Journal*, or a case note may discuss the significance of the new judgment. Several months later, the case may be published in one or both of the two general series of law reports which appear weekly, the *All England Law Reports* and the *Weekly Law Reports*, and in specialist law reports and journals (e.g. *Tax Cases*, the *Criminal Law Review*). Some time later, a final, authoritative version checked by the judges concerned may be published in the *Law Reports*. Thus, if your library does not hold the series of law reports given in the reference you have, it is worth checking whether the case is reported elsewhere (see para.3.14).

CITATION OF LAW REPORTS

Lawyers often use abbreviations when referring to the sources where a report of a case can be found. These can appear confusing at first, but constant use will rapidly make you familiar with the meaning of most of the abbreviations used. References to cases (called citations) are structured as shown in the following example: 3.3

Giles v Thompson[1] [1993][2] 2[3] W.L.R.[4] 908[5]

1 the names of the parties involved in the case;
2 the year in which the case is reported. Square brackets indicate that the date is an essential part of the citation. Some series of law reports number the volumes serially from year to year, so the reference is sufficient even if the year is omitted. Round brackets are used if the date is not essential but merely an aid;
3 the volume number, i.e. the second volume published in 1993. Where only one volume is published in a year, the volume number is omitted unless it is essential for finding the correct volume;
4 the abbreviation for the name of the law report or journal;
5 the page number on which the case begins.

In this example, the case of *Giles v Thompson* will be found in the 1993 volumes of the *Weekly Law Reports* (abbreviated to W.L.R.). There are three volumes of the *Weekly Law Reports* containing the cases reported in 1993. The case referred to will be found in the second volume, at p.908.

If you wish to draw attention to a particular phrase or section in the judgment, you should write out the citation for the case, followed by "at" and the page number where the section or phrase is printed, hence:

Giles v Thompson [1993] 2 W.L.R. 908 at 910

Since 2001 reports published by Sweet & Maxwell have been cited using a case number rather than a page number. For example:

Nestlé v Mars [2005] 3 C.M.L.R. 12.

This refers to case 12 of Vol.3 of the *Common Market Law Reports*. The report begins on p.259 of Vol.3.

If a neutral citation has not been added to a reference to a case, citation practice for the Oxford University Standard for Citation of Legal Authorities (OSCOLA) is to add an abbreviation for the court at the end of the law report citation. The *Giles v Thompson* case would then be cited:

Giles v Thompson [1993] 2 W.L.R. 908 (HL)

Neutral citations

In 2001 the High Court and Court of Appeal adopted a neutral, or common, form of citation for all cases. The use of such citations rapidly became standard for all UK courts. These "neutral" citations do not distinguish between print and online media and are independent of any of the 3.4

published law reports. This form of citation has been adopted in order to make it easier to cite and to trace unreported judgments. The neutral form of citation for *Stellato v Ministry of Justice*, for example, is:

Stellato v Ministry of Justice [2010] EWCA Civ 1435

"*EWCA Civ*" is the standard abbreviation for the Court of Appeal (Civil Division) for England and Wales. The number 1435, placed without brackets after EWCA Civ, tells you in addition, that the judgment is judgment number 1435 for 2010.

Other abbreviations for England and Wales courts are EWCA Crim for the Court of Appeal (Criminal Division) and EWHC (Ch) for the High Court Chancery Division. Note that the abbreviations for the different divisions of the High Court follow the case number, e.g.:

Goldsmith v O'Brien [2015] EWHC 510 (Ch)

Rather than give page references, neutral citations use numbers in square brackets to indicate the paragraph of a judgment, e.g.:

Stellato v Ministry of Justice [2010] EWCA Civ 1435 at [40]–[42].

Standard practice is also to place the neutral form of citation ahead of any other citations. *Stellato v Ministry of Justice* has been reported in the *All England Law Reports*, so the case would be cited as follows:

Stellato v Ministry of Justice [2010] EWCA Civ 1435; [2011] 3 All E.R. 251

You are likely to encounter neutral citations for House of Lords and the UK Supreme Court judgments frequently. The neutral citation for a House of Lords judgment, for example, is as follows:

Serco Ltd v Lawson [2006] UKHL 3

Neutral citations were assigned by the House of Lords for the period 2001 to 2009. If you are using BAILII (para.2.15) you will see that neutral citations have also been retrospectively assigned to judgments found in the database that pre-date 2001. These are judgments added by BAILII to improve public access to 20th century, and even some 19th century, case law.

The UK Supreme Court handed down its first judgment in 2009. A neutral citation for a Supreme Court judgment is as follows:

Gohill v Gohill [2015] UKSC 61

HOW TO FIND THE MEANING OF ABBREVIATIONS

3.5 A variety of different reference sources enable you to check the meaning of abbreviations. The most extensive is the Cardiff Index to Legal Abbreviations (at *http://www.legalabbrevs.cardiff.ac.uk*). If you are faced with an abbreviation for a law report or journal which you do not recognise, the website's abbreviations search finds matching law publications using a database compiled from a wide range of legal abbreviations. Either exact or close matches can be sought, making it possible to search for the meaning of an abbreviation even if you are not sure of the initial letter. A particular advantage of an online index is the ability it provides to search for the preferred abbreviation of a journal or law report. This can be useful if you have noted the full title of a law report or journal, but are unsure how to abbreviate it for citation purposes.

The *Current Law Monthly Digest* provides a convenient print source for current UK abbreviations. A list of abbreviations of reports and journals cited in *Current Law* (para.3.16) can be found near the front of each issue. *The Digest* (para.3.17) prints a list of abbreviations near the front of Vol.1 which can help with older abbreviations. Most law library reference shelves also have Raistrick's *Index to Legal Citations and Abbreviations*. Some of the most commonly used abbreviations are listed in Appendix III of this book.

FORMAT OF LAW REPORTS

Figure 3.1 gives a typical example of the first page of a law report. The citation is *Cleveland Petroleum Co Ltd v Dartstone Ltd and Another* [1969] 1 All E.R. 201. Several key points in the illustration are numbered. 3.6

1. The names of the parties. In a civil case, the name of the plaintiff (the person bringing the action) comes first, followed by the name of the defendant. The small letter "v" between the names is an abbreviation of the Latin "versus" but when speaking of a civil case, you say "and" not "versus". A criminal case, on the other hand, might appear as *R. v Smith*. R. is the abbreviated form for the Latin words Rex (king) or Regina (queen). The charge against Smith, the accused, is brought on behalf of the Crown and this case would be said as "the Crown against Smith".
2. The name of the court in which the case was heard, the names of the judges (M.R.: Master of the Rolls; L.JJ.: Lords Justices) and the date on which the case was heard.
3. A summary of the main legal issues of the case. You are advised not to rely on this, as it is not necessarily complete or accurate.
4. The headnote, which is a brief statement of the case and the nature of the claim (in a civil case) or the charge (in a criminal case). Again, do not rely on the publisher's précis but instead read the case.
5. The court's ruling is stated, with a summary of reasons.
6. In certain reports, e.g. the *All England Law Reports*, the major legal points are cross-referenced to *Halsbury's Laws* and *The Digest*.
7. A list of cases which were referred to during the hearing.
8. A summary of the history of the previous proceedings of the case. The final sentence explains where in the report you can find the details of the facts of the case.
9. The names of the counsel (the barristers) who appeared for the parties. Q.C.s (Queen's Counsel) are senior counsel.
10. The start of the judgment given by Lord Denning M.R.

Fig 3.1
First page of a law report from the *All England Law Reports*

First page of a Law Report from the All England Reports. The illustration is taken from the online version available from the Lexis Library.

[1969] 1 All ER 201

Cleveland Petroleum Co Ltd v Dartstone Ltd and Another [1]

COURT OF APPEAL, CIVIL DIVISION

LORD DENNING MR, RUSSELL AND SALMON LJJ [2]

26 NOVEMBER 1968

Trade—Restraint of trade—Agreement—Petrol filling station—Solus agreement—Lease by garage owner to petrol supplier—Underlease to company to operate service station—Covenant in underlease for exclusive sale of supplier's products—Assignment of underlease by licence granted by supplier—Interim injunction to restrain breach of covenant.

3

S the owner in fee simple of a garage, leased the premises to the plaintiffs for 25 years from 1 July 1960. The plaintiffs granted an underlease to COSS by which COSS covenanted, inter alia, to carry on the business of a petrol filling station at all times and not to sell or distribute motor fuels other than those supplied by the plaintiffs. After several assignments the underlease was assigned to the defendants who undertook to observe and perform the covenants. The defendants thereupon challenged the validity of the ties. The plaintiffs issued a writ claiming an injunction restraining the defendants from breaking this covenant. The plaintiffs obtained an interim injunction against which the defendants appealed.

4

Held—The appeal would be dismissed, the tie was valid and not an unreasonable restraint of trade because the defendants, not having been in possession previously, took possession of the premises under a lease and entered into a restrictive covenant knowing about such covenant, and thereby bound themselves to it (see p 203, letters *c*, *f* and *g*, post).
Dicta in *Esso Petroleum Co Ltd v Harper's Garage* (Stourport) ([1967] 1 All ER at pp 707, 714, and 724, 725) applied.
Appeal dismissed. [5]

Notes

As to agreements in restraint of trade, see 38 *Halsbury's Laws* (3rd Edn) 20, para 13; and for cases on the subject, see 45 *Digest* (Repl) 443–449, *271–297*. [6]

Case referred to in judgment

-Esso Petroleum Co Ltd v Harper's Garage (Stourport) [1967] 1 All ER 699, [1968] AC 269, [1967] 2 WLR 871, Digest (Repl) Supp. [7]

Interlocutory Appeal

This was an appeal by the defendants, Dartstone and James Arthur Gregory, from an order of Eveleigh J, dated 1 November 1968, granting an interim injunction restraining the defendants from acting in breach of a covenant contained in an underlease made on 1 July 1960 between the plaintiffs, Cleveland Petroleum Co and County Oak Service Station and assigned to the defendants on 30 August 1968. The facts are set out in the judgment of Lord Denning MR. [8]

Raymond Walton QC and M C B Buckley for the defendants. [9]
A P Leggatt for the plaintiffs.

26 November 1968. The following judgments were delivered.

LORD DENNING MR. [10]

This case concerns a garage and petrol station called County Oak service station, at Crawley in Sussex. Mr Sainsbury was the owner in fee simple. On 1 July 1960, there were three separate transactions: First, Mr Sainsbury granted a lease.

FINDING A LAW REPORT

A law report citation (para.3.3) provides the most direct route to finding a law report. As there is often more than one reported case between the relevant parties, the citation provides the means of identifying the report for a specific case. You might have the following reference, for example: 3.7

Hill v Chief Constable of West Yorkshire [1989] A.C. 53

To find the relevant report, search using the citation "[1989] A.C." This will ensure that you find the House of Lords case referred to, and not, for example, the earlier Court of Appeal case between the two parties, *Hill v Chief Constable of West Yorkshire* [1988] Q.B. 60. Case citations are essential if you are searching online and the party names are common, or are family law cases where letters are used for the purposes of anonymisation. An example would be:

A v X [2015] EWHC 2080 (Fam), [2015] Fam. Law 1192

Searching online using citations is explained in para.3.8. Paragraph 3.9 explains how to use citations for print reports, noting in particular how to find reports in recently printed unbound issues of law reports.

It is worth bearing in mind, as explained in para.3.2, that the same case can be reported in different law report series. If you are unable to find the particular law report you have a citation for, the Westlaw UK "Case Analysis" displays alternative reports for a case (para.3.15). The print volumes of the Current Law Case Citator (para.3.16) can also be used to find alternative citations.

Finding a law report online

As explained in Ch.2, most UK law reports are available from either the Lexis Library (para.2.3), or Westlaw UK (para.2.4). Your library may also have a subscription to the JustCite service (para.2.6) which searches for cases from all available online services. 3.8

To use any of these sources to find a law report, use the "Citation" search box. In both the Lexis Library and Westlaw UK, this can be found under "Cases". Suppose you wish to find the report referred to below:

Hill v Chief Constable of West Yorkshire [1989] A.C. 53

Enter the citation without brackets or abbreviations, as these are not necessary for the search, i.e. "1989 ac 53". Neutral citations (para.3.4) can also be used to find published law reports for a case. As with law report citations, remove citation brackets when searching.

Remember that neither the Lexis Library, nor Westlaw UK can provide access to all published law reports. If you have a citation for a report published in the *All England Law Reports*, for example, and search Westlaw UK using an *All England Law Reports* citation (All E.R.), the report published in the *All England Law Reports* will not be found. However, alternative reports of the case are likely to be available.

Specialist reports are rarely found in more than one online service, which can be more of a problem. In the absence of a JustCite search for online sources for a case, be prepared to check the Lexis Library, Westlaw UK, Justis, or any other available source. The library catalogue may also have entries confirming online access for specialist law reports, such as *Family Law Reports* or *Property, Planning and Compensation Reports*.

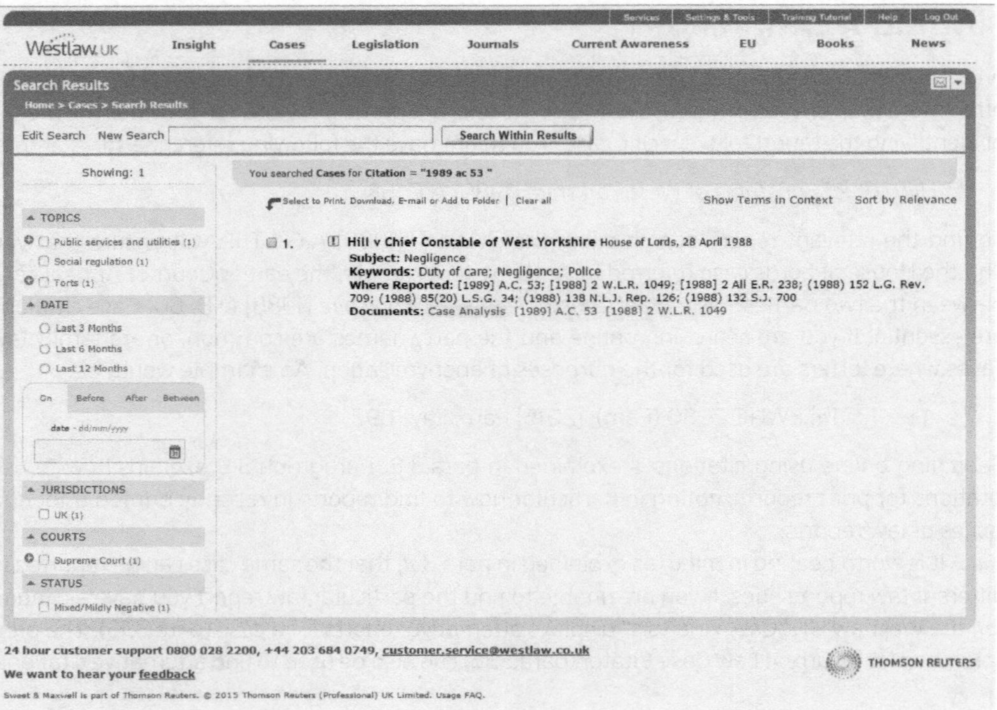

Fig 3.2 Westlaw UK Citation Search Results Page

The key source for finding very old law reports online is the *English Reports*, as explained in para.3.11.

Finding a law report in print

3.9 To find a print law report using the report citation, you first need to decipher the abbreviation used for the law report (para.3.5) and then search the library catalogue for the location of the bound volumes as explained in paras 1.7–1.9. To continue with the example used above:

Hill v Chief Constable of West Yorkshire [1989] A.C. 53

The abbreviation "A.C." stands for the *Law Reports' Appeals Cases*. This is the name of the report found on the bound volumes and the name needed to search the library catalogue. Entries for law reports are not always easy to find in library catalogues and the bound volumes of law reports may also be shelved in a special designated area, so be prepared to ask library staff for help to find the print collection of law reports. Law reports are usually shelved in a standard sequence, starting with the *Law Reports*, shelved in order described in para.3.10, followed by the *Weekly Law Reports*, the *All England Law Reports* and any specialist law reports held in print by your library.

Once you have located the bound volumes of the relevant law report, the law report citation can be used to locate the volumes or volumes for the relevant year. The page number given is the number of the first page of the report in the relevant printed volume.

Recent print issues of law reports are held in a separate area. Again, be prepared to ask library staff for help in locating recent unbound issues of law reports.

To find a law report in a recent issue, check the citation range given at the top of the front cover of each unbound issue. These show the citations that will eventually be used for the bound volumes of the law report. An unbound issue of the *All England Law Reports* might show the following for example:

[2015] 4 ALL E.R. 169–246 Part 3, 7 October 2015

This indicates that this issue (Part 3) will eventually form pages 169–246 of the third bound volume of the *All England Law Reports* for 2015. A report with the citation [2015] 4 ALL E.R. 169 will be the first report printed in the issue.

Reports of all four series of the *Law Reports* are published in each monthly unbound issue of the *Law Reports*, with the relevant citations shown for all four series shown on the front cover. The publication of reports in the unbound issues of the *Weekly Law Reports* is a little more confusing. Three bound volumes are produced each year, and each weekly issue contains some cases which will eventually appear in Vol.1 of the bound volumes for that year, and some cases which will subsequently appear in either Vol.2 or Vol.3. The front cover of each issue shows the contents and the volume in which these pages will eventually appear. Part 36 for 2015 has the following citation entries on the front cover:

- [2015] 1 W.L.R. 4307–4340;
- [2015] 3 W.L.R. 803–908.

This means that Part 36 contains pages 4307–4340 of what will eventually form Vol.1 of the *Weekly Law Reports* for 2015, and pages 803–908 of what will eventually form Vol.3. You may wonder why the publishers have chosen this method of publishing the issues. The reason is that the cases in Vols 2 and 3 will be republished, after being checked by the judges and with a summary of counsel's arguments, in the *Law Reports*. Those cases appearing in Vol.1, however, will not reappear in the *Law Reports*.

THE LAW REPORTS SERIES

The publication known as the *Law Reports*, which first appeared in 1865, was originally published in 11 series, each covering a different court. The rationalisation of the court structure since that time has reduced this to four series. These are: 3.10

- Appeal Cases (abbreviated to A.C.);
- Chancery Division (Ch.);
- Queen's Bench Division (Q.B.); and
- Family Division (Fam.).

This is the order in which the bound volumes are usually arranged on the library shelves. As noted in para.3.9 above, each monthly issue of the *Law Reports* contains reports from all four series of the *Law Reports*, although they are bound as separate series.

The location on the shelves of the various earlier series often reflects their relationship to the present four series, for example, the historical predecessors of the present Queen's

Fig 3.3
Table of the *Law Reports*

Law Reports

Table of the Law Reports

The mode of citation is given in brackets. In the first, second and third columns, dots (. . .) are put where the number of the volume would appear in the citation. In the fourth column square brackets([ ]) are put where the year would appear in the citation.

1866–1875	1875–1880	1881–1890	1891–present
House of Lords, English and Irish Appeals (L.R. ... H.L.) House of Lords, Scotch and Divorce Appeals (L.R. ... H.L.Sc. or L.R. ... H.L.Sc. and Div.) Privy Council Appeals (L.R. ... P.C.)	Appeal Cases (...App.Cas.)	Appeal Cases (...App.Cas.)	Appeal Cases ([ ]) A.C.)
Chancery Appeal Cases (L.R. ... Ch. or Ch. App.) Equity Cases (L.R. ... Eq.)	Chancery Division (...Ch.D.)	Chancery Division (...Ch.D.)	Chancery Division ([ ]) Ch.)
Crown Cases Reserved (L.R. ... C.C., or, ... C.C.R.) Queen's Bench Cases* (L.R. ... Q.B.) Common Pleas Cases (L.R. ... C.P.) Exchequer Cases‡ (L.R. ... Ex.)	Queen's Bench Division (...Q.B.D.) Common Pleas Division (...C.P.D.) Exchequer Division (...Ex.D.)	Queen's Bench Division (...Q.B.D.)	Queen's (or King's) Bench Division ([ ] Q.B. or K.B.)†
Admiralty and Ecclesiastical Cases (L.R. ... A. & E.) Probate and Divorce Cases (L.R. ... P. & D.)	Probate Division (...P.D.)	Probate Division (...P.D.)	Probate Division ([ ]P.) Since 1972 Family Division ([ ]Fam.)

* Note that there is also a series called Queen's Bench Reports in the old reports (113–118 E.R.).

† After 1907 this includes cases in the Court of Criminal Appeal, later the Court of Appeal, in place of the previous Court for Crown Cases Reserved.

‡ Note that there is also a series called Exchequer Reports in the old reports (154–156 E.R.).

(Reproduced from G. Williams, *Learning the Law* (12th ed.), p. 40.)

Bench Division (called the King's Bench Division when a King is on the throne) were the Court for Crown Cases Reserved, the Court of Common Pleas and the Court of Exchequer. These are therefore usually shelved before the Queen's Bench Division reports (because they are its predecessors) but after the Appeal Cases and Chancery Division reports. The same arrangement is applied with the other three current series (i.e. reports of the predecessors of the present courts are filed at the beginning of each series).

Figure 3.3 shows the way in which the complete series of *Law Reports* are arranged on the shelves in most libraries. The abbreviations used to denote each series are shown, and also the dates during which each series appeared.

Citations for the *Law Reports* have varied over the years as the system of numbering the reports changed. Until 1891, for example, each volume in the various series had its own individual number, running sequentially through the years. The date in the citation is therefore in round brackets, to show it is not essential to the reference. For the *Law Reports* after 1891, however, the date is in square brackets, since the year must be quoted in order to locate the correct volume. The other slight complication in the citation of the *Law Reports* is the use of the abbreviation L.R. (for *Law Reports*) which is placed before the volume number in citation of *Law Reports* before 1875, e.g. *Rylands v Fletcher* (1868) L.R. 3 H.L. 330.

Figure 3.3 also clarifies the use of abbreviations and brackets for the *Law Reports*. It is worth noting, however, that the abbreviation H.L. stands for *Law Reports: English and Irish Appeal Cases* and not, as you might guess, *Law Reports: House of Lords*.

The *Law Reports* are available online from Westlaw UK (para.2.4), the Lexis Library (para.2.3) and Justis (para.2.6).

Older Law Reports

We have concentrated upon the modern series of law reports because these are the reports which you will be using most frequently. However, from time to time you will need to look at older cases, that is, those reported in the first half of the 19th century or even several centuries earlier. Reports of older cases can be found in several series: the *English Reports*, *Revised Reports*, the *Law Journal Reports*, the *Law Times Reports* and the *All England Law Reports Reprint* series. We shall now look at some of these series in more detail. 3.11

The reports published privately by individuals (and known as the *Nominate Reports*) ceased publication around 1865, when the *Law Reports* were first published. If the date of the case you want is before 1865, you are most likely to find it in a series known as the *English Reports*. The *English Reports* reprinted the original *Nominate Reports* in a uniform series of volumes, annotating the reprinted text with the page and volume numbers of the original reports.

Many libraries have the *English Reports* in print form. The reports are also available online, either from Justis Publishing (para.2.6), the HeinOnline journal archive, or the CommonLII website (at *http://www.commonlii.org*). Justis and HeinOnline are both subscription sources. If your library has a subscription, searching for cases is straightforward using either source if you have the names of parties, the citation of the original report (the "nominative" citation), or the citation for the report as it appeared in the *English Reports*. In both cases, names of parties, or the citation you have, can be entered into the relevant search box to retrieve the text of the report as published in the *English Reports*. Search options for the free CommonLII site are

Fig 3.4
Table of Cases in the *English Reports*

Table of Cases in the English Reports

	424 DAN	Index of Cases		
	Ⓐ Ⓑ		Ⓒ	
→	Daniel *v.* North, 11 East, 372		**103**	1047
	——*v.* Phillips, 4 T. R. 499		**100**	1141
	——*v.* Pit, Peake Add. Cas. 238		**170**	257
	——*v.* Pit, 6 Esp. 74		**170**	834
	——*v.* Purbeck, W. Kel. 97		**25**	510
	——*v.* Purkis, W. Kel. 97		**25**	510
	——*v.* Purkurst, 2 Barn. K. B. 214, 220	**94**	457,	461
	——*v.* Russell, 14 Ves. Jun. 393; 2 Ves. Jun. Supp. 376	33 572;	**34**	1139
	——*v.* Skipwith, 2 Bro. C. C. 155		**29**	89
	——*v.* Sterlin, 1 Freeman, 50		**89**	39
	——*v.* Thompson, 15 East, 78		**104**	774
	——*v.* Trotman, 1 Moo. N. S. 123		**15**	649
	——*v.* Turpin, 1 Keble, 124		**83**	852
	——*v.* Ubley, Jones, W. 137		**82**	73
	——*v.* Uply, Latch, 9, 39, 134	82 248,	264,	312
	——*v.* Upton, Noy, 80		**74**	1047
	——*v.* Waddington, Cro. Jac. 377		**79**	322
	——*v.* Waddington, 3 Bulstrode, 130		**81**	111
	——*v.* Warren, 2 Y. & C. C. C. 290		**63**	127
	——*v.* Wilkin, 7 Ex. 429		**155**	1016
	——*v.* Wilkin, 8 Ex. 156		**155**	1300
	——*v.* Wilson, 5 T. R. I.		**101**	1
	Daniel's Case, 2 Dy. 133 b		**73**	291
	——Trust, *In re*, 18 Beav. 309		**52**	122

slightly more limited. Reports can be browsed alphabetically by the name of the first party, or by year. Links are also provided for a name search and a general database search. In all cases, the report is presented as a PDF file. The HeinOnline download version can also be used for copying and pasting extracts from the reports.

The text of the reports themselves can be confusing though if you are not aware of the way in which the *English Reports* are organised in print. The chart to the *English Reports* reproduced in the following section shows how citations to the original nominate reports, with their standard abbreviations, are related to volumes in the *English Reports*.

How to use the English Reports in print

3.12 If you know the name of the case, look it up in the alphabetical index of the names of cases, printed in Vols 177–178 of the *English Reports*. The abbreviation for the name of the original nominate reporter is printed beside the name of the case along with the volume and page number of the report series in which the case originally appeared. The number printed in bold type next to this is the volume number in the *English Reports* where the case will be found, and this is followed by the page number in that volume:

Fig 3.5 Chart to the *English Reports*

Chart to the English Reports

Table of English Reports

Old Reports.	Volume in English Reports.	Abbreviations.	Period Covered (approximate).	Series.
Dow & Clark, 1 & 2	**6**	Dow & Cl.	1827–1832	H.L.
Dowling & Ryland	**171**	Dowl. & Ry. N.P.	1822–1823	N.P.
Drewry, 1–3	**61**	Drew.	1852–1859	V.C.
Drewry 4	**62**			
Drewry & Smale, 1 & 2	**62**	Drew & Sm. or Dr. & Sm.	1860–1865	V.C.
Dyer, 1–3	**73**	Dy.	1513–1582	K.B.
East, 1–6	**102**			
→ **East, 7–11**	**103**	East.	1801–1812	K.B.
East, 12–16	**104**			
Eden, 1 & 2	**28**	Eden.	1757–1766	Ch.
Edwards	**165**	Edw.	1808–1812	Ecc. Adm. P. & D.
Ellis & Blackburn, 1–3	**118**			
Ellis & Blackburn, 4–7	**119**	El. & Bl.	1851–1858	K.B.
Ellis & Blackburn, 8	**120**			
Ellis, Blackburn & Ellis	**120**	El. Bl. & El.	1858	K.B.
Ellis & Ellis, 1	**120**	El. & El.	1858–1861	K.B.
Ellis & Ellis, 2 & 3	**121**			
Eq. Cases Abridged, 1	**21**	Eq. Ca. Abr.	1667–1744	Ch.
Eq. Cases Abridged, 2	**22**			
Espinasse, 1–6	**170**	Esp.	1793–1807	N.P.

Daniel v North[a]   11 East, 372[b]   **103**[c] 1047

a name of the case;

b volume, name of the original reporter, page number in the original report, i.e. the original report of this case appeared in Vol.11 of *East's Reports* p.372;

c the reprint of the report appears in Vol.103 of the *English Reports* at p.1047.

You will see that Vol.103 of the *English Reports* has the volumes and names of the *Nominate Reports* which are to be found in that volume printed on the spine. Page 1047 appears in its normal position at the top outer corner of the page whilst the volume and page number of the original report are printed at the inner margin.

Sometimes you may only have a citation (reference) to the original nominate report, e.g. 3 Car. & P. (*Carrington and Payne*); 2 Barn. & Ald. (*Barnewall and Alderson*). This reference is often printed in an abbreviated form. You do not know the name of the case, so you are unable to look it up in the index to the *English Reports*. Let us suppose, for example, that you have come across a reference to (1809) 11 East 372. Because the date is before 1865, you know that it is likely to be found in the *English Reports*; but you do not know the name of the case. How do you find it? If the name of the report has been abbreviated, e.g. 3 Car. & P., you will need to use the *Cardiff Index to Legal Abbreviations* or look in Raistrick's *Index to Legal Citations and Abbreviations* (see

Fig 3.6 Example Page from the *English Reports*

11 EAST, 371. AMBROSE *v.* REES 1047

before; but they could not agree on the person to be substituted, and therefore the original appointment stood as before.

Per Curiam. Rule absolute.

AMBROSE *against* REES. Wednesday, June 14th, 1809. Notice having been given for the trial of a cause at Monmouth, which arose in Glamorganshire, as being in fact the next English county since the st. 27 H. 8, c. 26, s. 4, though Hereford be the common place of trial; the Court refused to set aside the verdict as for a mis-trial, on motion; the question being open on the record.

Marryat opposed a rule for setting aside the verdict obtained in this cause, upon the ground of an irregularity in the trial. The venue was laid in Glamorganshire, and the cause was tried at Monmouth, as the next English county where the King's writ of venire runs (*b*); but it was objected that it ought to have been tried at Hereford, according to the general custom that all causes in which the venue is laid in any county in South Wales should be tried at Hereford. But the rule being that the cause should be tried in the next English county, and Monmouth being in fact the next English county to Glamorganshire, and more conveniently situated for the trial of the cause, there seems no solid ground for impeaching the validity of the trial; though the practice relied on is easily accounted for by the consideration that Monmouthshire was originally a Welch county, and till it became an English county in the 27th year of Hen. 8, Herefordshire was in fact the next English county to Glamorgan. And there is no reason for setting aside this verdict on the ground of surprize; for the defendant had not merely a notice of trial in the next English county, generally, which might have misled him by the notoriety of the **[371]** practice, but a specific notice of trial at Monmouth, to which he made no objection at the time.

Abbott, in support of the rule, relied on the known practice which had always prevailed, as well since as before the Statute 27 H. 8; and referred to *Morgan* v. *Morgan* (*a*), where the question arose in 1656, upon an ejectment for lands in Brecknockshire, which was tried at Monmouth; and afterwards judgment was arrested, on the ground of a mis-trial, as it ought to have been tried in Herefordshire; for that Monmouthshire was but made an English county by statute within time of memory; and that trials in the next English county of issues arising in Wales have been time out of mind and at the common law; so that a place newly made an English county cannot have such a trial. And he observed, that if this trial were good, all the judgments in causes out of Glamorganshire tried at Hereford have been erroneous.

Lord Ellenborough C.J. If the question appear on the record, then the defendant cannot apply in this summary manner. And as he did not object at the time, we shall not relieve him upon motion.

Per Curiam. Rule discharged.

[372] DANIEL *against* NORTH. Wednesday, June 14th, 1809. Where lights had been put out and enjoyed without interruption for above 20 years during the occupation of the opposite premises by a tenant; that will not conclude the landlord of such opposite premises, without evidence of his knowledge of the fact, which is the foundation of presuming a grant against him; and consequently will not conclude a succeeding tenant who was in possession under such landlord from building up against such encroaching lights.

[Considered and applied, *Wheaton* v. *Maple* [1893], 3 Ch. 57; *Roberts* v. *James*, 1903, 89 L. T. 286. For *Rugby Charity* v. *Merryweather*, 11 East, 375, n., see *Woodyer* v. *Hadden*, 1813, 5 Taunt. 138; *Wood* v. *Veal*, 1822, 5 B. & Ald. 457; *Vernon* v. *St. James's, Westminster*, 1880, 16 Ch. D. 457; *Bourke* v. *Davis*, 1889, 44 Ch. D. 123.]

The plaintiff declared in case, upon his seisin in fee of a certain message or dwelling-house in Stockport, on one side of which there is and was and of right ought to be six windows; and stated that the defendant wrongfully erected a wall 60 feet high and 50 in length near the said house and windows, and obstructed the light and

(*b*) Vide 1 Term Rep. 313. (*a*) Hard. 66.

para.3.5) to find the meaning of the abbreviation. You then turn to the *Chart to the English Reports*. This may be displayed near the *English Reports*, or it may be a slim volume shelved with the *English Reports* themselves. The Chart contains an alphabetical list of the names of all the reporters whose work has been reprinted in the *English Reports*, showing which volume their work appears in. The Chart indicates that Vols 7–11 of *East's Reports* are reprinted in Vol.103 of the *English Reports*. If you open Vol.103 at random, you will see that, at the top of each page (at the inner margin) the volume and page numbers of the original report are printed. Find the volume and page reference which most nearly corresponds to your reference. There is no entry at the top of the page for Vol.11 of *East's Reports*, p.372, but there is an entry, at the top inner margin, for p.371. Figure 3.6 shows the text of the relevant *English Reports* page. "11 East, 371" is displayed at the top of the page. There are also numbers printed, in square brackets, in the body of the text. These indicate when the page numbers in the original report changed. For instance, in the original Vol.11 of *East's Reports*, p.371 began with the words "practice, but a specific notice of trial at Monmouth . . .". Page 372 began with the case of *Daniel v North*.

Other older law reports

If the *English Reports* are not available in your library, you may find the case you need reprinted in the *Revised Reports*. The *Revised Reports* has similar coverage to the *English Reports* but is not as comprehensive. 3.13

The *All England Law Reports Reprint* series is another useful source for old cases between 1558 and 1935. The cases are reprinted from the reports which originally appeared in the *Law Times Reports*, which commenced in 1843, and from earlier reports. The *Reprint* series contains some 5,000 cases selected principally upon the criterion that they have been referred to in the *All England Law Reports* and in *Halsbury's Laws of England*. Online access to the full text of the *Reprint* series is available from the Lexis Library (para.2.3). The *Reprint* cases can be searched alongside more modern cases, or searches restricted to *Reprint* cases only. There is an index volume to the printed series containing an alphabetical list of cases and a subject index of the cases included in the reprint.

Two other series of 19th century cases are also referred to regularly: the *Law Journal Reports* and the *Law Times Reports*. The *Law Journal Reports* cover the period 1823–1949. These print volumes can be complicated to use because two volumes were usually published each year, both bearing the same volume number. One volume printed the cases heard in common law courts, the other printed equity cases. You will need to check both volumes, unless you know whether the case you want is equity or common law. To add to the difficulty, the volume numbering and the method of citation changed during the course of its publication. The first nine volumes (1823–1831) are known as the *Old Series* (L.J.O.S.). References to the *New Series* (1833–1949) omit the letters N.S. Citations give the abbreviation for the court in which the case was heard. It is therefore necessary to decide if the court was a court of common law or equity, so that you consult the correct volume. For example, the reference 16 L.J.Q.B. 274 is a reference to Vol.16 of the *Law Journal* (New Series) in the common law volumes (since Queen's Bench was a court of common law), at p.274 of the reports of Queen's Bench. Volume 16 contains law reports from several different courts. Each court's reports have a separate sequence of page numbers. You are looking for p.274 in the sequence of Queen's Bench reports.

The *Law Times Reports* (L.T.) cover the period 1859–1947. Prior to this, the reports were published as part of the journal entitled *Law Times* and these are cited as the *Law Times, Old Series* (L.T.O.S.) which ran from 1843–1860. You may find this *Old Series* is shelved with the Journals, not with the law reports.

HOW TO FIND REPORTS OF A CASE

3.14 Perhaps you wish to know whether a particular case has been widely reported. Or is the case of specialist interest, or perhaps not reported at all. Is the case name you have that of an "unreported judgment"? More straightforwardly, you might have a reference which has proved inaccurate. How can you find out where a report of the case appears?

The easiest way of tracing a case by name is to use the Westlaw UK "Cases" search (para.3.15), especially if you think your case was probably decided in or after 1947. Only brief entries are available for earlier cases. *The Digest* (para.3.17) can help find older cases. In addition, most series of law reports have their own indexes to cases. The JustCite service from Justis Publishing (para.2.6), if available, is an effective alternative to the Westlaw UK cases search. It provides much the same information on cases as Westlaw UK, with the additional advantage that links are provided to the appropriate location of the online text of the reports and judgments cited. Links are provided from the JustCite record for a report to Westlaw UK, the Lexis Library, and various free-to-access judgment sites. The Westlaw UK Cases search can only link to the full text of reports and judgments available within Westlaw UK. JustCite also includes links for cases from Commonwealth and other common law countries not found by the Westlaw UK "Cases" search.

How to use the Westlaw UK Cases search

3.15 The Westlaw UK "Cases" search is particularly useful if you wish to trace reported versions of a case. The search uses a database which contains information on all reported England and Wales cases since 1947, taken from the print volumes of *Current Law*, along with keywords and citations for earlier cases where they have been cited by *Current Law*. In addition, the database links directly to cases reported in the *Law Reports* from 1864 onwards.

To use the search, select the "Cases" tab on the Westlaw UK home page and enter the case names you have in the "Party Names" search box. If both party names are known the "v" citation convention can be used to retrieve all cases featuring the two names e.g.:

"Douglas v Hello"

A results list showing brief details of matching cases is then displayed. A number of separate cases have been reported for *"Douglas v Hello"* and the results list will include, for example:

Douglas v Hello! Ltd (No.1)

> **TIPS** • *The full name of both parties does not need to be entered when searching for a case using party names. Enter the most distinctive elements, e.g. "Factortame", not "Secretary for State for Transport Ex p. "Factortame".*

The "No.1" in brackets has been added to distinguish this case from a number of subsequent related cases, e.g. *Douglas v Hello! Ltd (No.9)*. You may need to check to ensure that you are looking at the right case.

As noted in para.3.3, cases which use initials for party names to protect anonymity can cause particular problems. A search for *"R v A"*, for example, finds literally hundreds of

Fig 3.7 Example Case Analysis from the Westlaw UK Cases Search

Kennedy v Information Commissioner

Also known as:

Kennedy v Charity Commission

Supreme Court

26 March 2014

Case Analysis

Where Reported

[2014] UKSC 20; [2015] A.C. 455; [2014] 2 W.L.R. 808; [2014] 2 All E.R. 847; [2014] E.M.L.R. 19; [2014] H.R.L.R. 14; (2014) 158(13) S.J.L.B. 37; Times, April 2, 2014; Official Transcript

Case Digest

Subject: Administrative law **Other related subjects:** Human rights; Charities

Keywords: Charity Commission for England and Wales; Exempt information; Freedom of expression; Freedom of information; Inquiries

Summary: The Freedom of Information Act 2000 s.32(2) provided an absolute exemption from any duty of disclosure under the Act of documents created by a public body or placed in its custody for the purposes of an inquiry conducted by that body. That exemption continued until the documents became historical records. The European Convention on Human Rights 1950 art.10 did not require s.32(2) to be interpreted differently.

Abstract: The appellant journalist (K) appealed against a decision (*[2012] EWCA Civ 317, [2012] 1 W.L.R. 3524*) that the respondent Charity Commission was not required to disclose under the Freedom of Information Act 2000 documents concerning an inquiry it had conducted.

The Commission had refused disclosure on the basis that the documents were exempt from disclosure under s.32(2) and it was not required to disclose them until they became historical records 30 years after their creation.

K argued that the exemption only subsisted for the duration of the relevant inquiry; if a natural construction of s.32(2) did not produce that result, the European Convention on Human Rights 1950 art.10 required it to be read down to produce that result.

Held: Appeal dismissed.

(Lords Wilson and Carnwath dissenting as to the effect of art.10) (1) The critical phrase in s.32, "for the purposes of ..." was repeated in relation to and placed at the end of each head of documents identified. Read naturally, it qualified each head. To read it as referring back to the initial words of each sub-section was far-fetched. Further s.63(1), dealing with historical records, mentioned s.32: the natural inference was that it was contemplated that information falling within s.32 would continue to be exempt for 30 years. The scheme of the Inquiries Act 2005 was different from that which applied under the 2000 Act in respect of a Charity Commission inquiry; in any event, the position under the 2005 Act could not affect the construction of the earlier Act. Section 32 had potential matches in the cases database. A citation becomes essential unless the case name has been extended to include further identification, e.g. *R. v A (Complainant's Sexual History)*. The full phrase in brackets can be added to ensure that a match is found for the particular case you are looking for. If you are fairly sure of the keywords likely to be used in a case, an alternative is to use the "Subject/Keyword" search which can be found under "Advanced Search".

Selecting the "Case Analysis" link for a case from the brief details provided in your search results displays a page of information headed by a list of citations for the case. As already noted, a significant case is likely to be reported in a number of law reports. *Kennedy v Information Commissioner*, for example, has been reported, among other places, in the *Law Reports*, as [2015] A.C. 455, and in the *Entertainment and Media Law Reports* as [2014] E.M.L.R. 19. The citations listed in the Westlaw UK Case Analysis for the case is shown in fig.3.7. The neutral citation for the case is also included, [2014] UKSC 20. This is not a citation to a law report (see para.3.4).

If the full text of the law report is available from the Westlaw UK, the relevant citation will be shown as a hyperlink. This opens a reproduction of the law report text within Westlaw UK. Asterisked numbers placed within the screen text mark the start of the printed pages and enable precise quotations to the print volumes be traced. Where cases cited within the report are available from Westlaw UK, citations are again shown as hyperlinks.

The "Official Transcript" placed at the end of the law report citations can be helpful if Westlaw UK does not have the full text of a law report online. However, if your library has a subscription to the Lexis Library (para.2.3), or to Justis (para.2.4), it makes sense to search those services for a full law report, once a citation has been confirmed.

The Westlaw UK "Cases" search also provides a significant amount of additional information about a case which can be of value even if the full text or a report or judgment is not available.

Summaries are provided for all of the cases reported after 1947. In addition a "Case History" section of the case analysis page shows a list of cases which have followed, for example, the decision made by the case in question, or been "distinguished" from it. See para.7.18 for more on tracing the judicial history of the case. The case analysis page also lists citations for journal articles which have commented on the case.

How to use the Current Law Case Citators

3.16 The print volumes of the *Current Law Case Citator* each have an alphabetical list of the names of cases which have been published or quoted in court between the dates specified on the spine. If you have an idea of the approximate date, and easy access to the *Citator* volumes, they provide a quick and easy way to trace a citation. The *Citator* is published in a number of parts:

1. The *Current Law Case Citator* bound volumes covering cases which were reported or cited in court in the years noted on the spine, e.g. 1947–1976, 1991–2001, 2002–2004;
2. A paperback issue of the *Current Law Case Citator* including references to cases reported or cited since the last bound volume and before the end of the preceding year; and
3. The *Current Law Monthly Digest*. To find cases reported in the current year, look in the Table of Cases in the most recent issue of the *Monthly Digest*. The December issue of the previous year's *Monthly Digest* can be used to find cases in that year, if the cumulative supplement has not yet been published.

The different parts of the *Citator* may at first seem confusing. It is best to look through the citators in chronological order, as above, in order to ensure that you have looked in all the relevant issues.

You may find your library has copies of the *Scottish Current Law Case Citator* for the periods 1948–1976 and 1977–1988. Despite its name, the Scottish version does contain all the English cases but, in addition, it lists Scottish cases in a separate alphabetical sequence at the back of the volume. The two publications have now merged and the *Current Law Case Citator* volumes since 1989 have included Scottish cases. Part 1 of the *Citator* now lists all the England, Wales and Northern Ireland cases, while the Scottish cases are listed in Pt 2. Make sure you look for your case in the right section!

In each of the citators, the cases are listed in alphabetical order. Cases which start with a single letter, e.g. *S. v Cox*, are at the beginning of that letter of the alphabet; criminal cases starting with *R. v* are at the beginning of the letter R section. If the title of the case is *Re Smith*, or *Ex p. Smith*, look under Smith. When you have traced the case you require, you will find an entry similar to the following:

> *Biles v Caesar* [1957] 1 W.L.R. 156; 101 S.J. 108; [1957] 1 All E.R. 151; [101 S.J. 141; 21 Conv. 169], C.A. . . . . *Digested*, 57/1943: *Followed*, 59/1834: *Applied*, 68/2181; 69/2037

The entry for *Biles v Caesar* in the 1947–1976 volume shown here gives you a complete "life history" of the case for the years covered by the volume. Like the Westlaw UK Case Locator (para.3.15) it shows you where and when the case was originally reported and where you can find journal articles commenting on the case; there are also citations relevant to its subsequent judicial history (see para.7.18).

The entry for *Biles v Caesar* gives the following information:

(1) After the name of the case (*Biles v Caesar*) there is a list of three places where you can find a full report of the cases:
   (a) [1957] 1 W.L.R. 156—for the year 1957 in the first of the three volumes of the *Weekly Law Reports* at p.156;
   (b) (1957) 101 S.J. 108—for the year 1957 in Vol.101 of the *Solicitors Journal* at p.108 (this, as the name suggests, is a journal, shelved with other journals);
   (c) [1957] 1 All E.R. 151—for the year 1958 in the first volume of the *All England Law Reports* at p.151.
(2) The entries which are enclosed in square brackets in the printed volume—[101 S.J. 141; 21 Conv. 169]—are references to articles or comments in law journals where the case is discussed in some detail. If you select Vol.101 of the *Solicitors Journal*, or Vol.21 of *The Conveyancer*, you see articles discussing the case of *Biles v Caesar*.
(3) The C.A. after the references to the case tells us that it is a Court of Appeal Decision. If the decision of the court of first instance was reported, references to these reports would have been included after the C.A.
(4) The word Digested followed by the figures 57/1943 indicates that you will find a digest (a summary) of the case in the 1957 volume of the *Current Law Year Book* (see para.7.13). Every item in the 1957 volume has its own individual number; you

will find that item 1943 is a summary of the facts and decisions in the case of *Biles v Caesar*.

You may also wish to know whether the decision given in a particular case has been subsequently approved, i.e. whether the case has been quoted with approval by another judge in a later case. By 1976, when the print *Citator* volume was published, the case of *Biles v Caesar* has been quoted in three other cases—in 1959, when the decision was followed, and in 1968 and 1969 when the courts applied the decision in the *Biles* case to two other cases, following the doctrine of precedent. You can find the names of the cases in which *Biles* was referred to by looking in the 1959 *Current Law Year Book*, at item 1834, and in the 1968 and 1969 Year Books, at the item numbers given.

If you are using the *Citator* and, as in the above example, you find a reference to your case in the *Citator* for 1947–1976, it is still advisable to check through the more recent *citators* to find the present status of the judgment. You can find out whether since 1976, for example, the case has been taken to a higher court or the decision has been approved or overruled in other judgments.

How to trace a case in The Digest

3.17 Older English and Scottish cases can also be traced in print using *The Digest* (formerly known as the *English and Empire Digest*), as can many cases heard in Irish, European and Commonwealth courts. *The Digest* consists of the main work (around 70 volumes), several *Continuation Volumes*, a *Cumulative Supplement*, a *Consolidated Table of Cases* and a *Consolidated Index*. *The Digest* is in its third edition which is called the *Green Band Reissue* because of the green stripe on the spine. All of the Green Band Reissue volumes have been updated and reprinted at least once. They are now in their 2nd or 3rd reissue and the reissue is stated on the spine. The date of reissue of any volume is printed on the title page inside the front cover.

To trace a particular case in *The Digest*, go first to the four-volume *Consolidated Table of Cases*. This contains an alphabetical list of the cases summarised in *The Digest* and gives a reference to the volume in which the case can be found. Figure 3.8 shows the entry in the *Consolidated Table of Cases* for the case of *Bell v Twentyman*. This case is included in Vols 19(1), 35(3) and 36(1) of *The Digest*, since it is relevant to the law of easements, negligence and nuisance. At the front of each of these volumes, there is another Table of Cases which refers you to the case number (or page number in older volumes—see the heading at the top of the column) where you can find a summary of the case and a list of citations where the full report can be found. If, for example, you wished to find a summary of the negligence aspects of the case of *Bell v Twentyman*, you would now look up the name of the case in the Table of Cases at the front of Vol.35(3). Alongside the name of the case is the number 378, which refers you to case number 378 in that volume. The entry is shown in fig.3.9. The case number is given in bold, followed by a summary of the case and references to where the full text of the report can be found. The case of *Bell v Twentyman* was reported in a number of series. To find the meaning of the abbreviations used, look in the list of abbreviations in the *Cumulative Supplement*. The *Consolidated Table of Cases* is updated and reprinted every two years. To find the latest cases, you will need to look in the annual *Cumulative Supplement*. There is a Table of Cases at the

Fig 3.8
Example Page from *The Digest* Consolidated Table of Cases

Bell v Jarvis (Sheriff) (1850) (CAN) **42(1) Shrffs**
Bell v Johnson (1861) **22(2) Evid**
Bell v Johnston Bros Ltd (1917) (CAN) **35(4) Negl**
Bell v Jutting (1817) **1(3) Agcy; 29(1) Insce**
Bell v Keesing (1888) (NZ) **3(1) Arbn; 7(3) Bldg Conts**
Bell v Kennedy (1868) **11(2) Confl**
Bell v Klein (No 3) (1955) **18 Discy**
Bell v Klein (No 5) (1955) (CAN) **22(2) Evid**
Bell v Krohn (1931) (CAN) **1(4) Agcy**
Bell v Kymer (1814) **43(2) Ship**
Bell v Lafferty (1894) (CAN) **7(1) B of Sale**
Bell v Lee (1883) (CAN) **37(2) Powers**
Bell v Lever Bros Ltd (1932) **20(1) Empt; 34(2) Mistake; 37(1) Pldg**
Bell v Light (1867) (CAN) **27(1) H & W**
Bell v London & North Western Ry Co (1852) **8(3) Chos**
Bell v London & South Western Bank (1874) **7(3) Bldg Soc**
Bell v Long (1928) (CAN) **21(2) Exon**
Bell v Lothiansure Ltd (in liq) (1990) (SCOT) **29(2) Insce**
Bell v Love (1883) **34(1) Mines**
Bell v McCubbin (1989) **2 Agric**
Bell v McDougall (1882) (CAN) **4(3) Bkpcy**
Bell v McKindsey (1865) (CAN) **17(1) Deeds**
Bell v McLean (1868) (CAN) **42(1) Shrffs**
Bell v Maklin (1887) (CAN) **40(2) S Land**
Bell v Manning (1865) (CAN) **6 B of Exch**
Bell v Mansfield (1893) (AUS) **42(1) Ship**
Bell v Marsh (1903) **21(2) Estpl**
Bell v Marsh (1951) (CAN) **19(1) Esmt**
Bell v Matthewman (1920) (CAN) **23(1) Exors**
Bell v Midland Ry Co (1861) **17(2) Damgs; 19(1) Esmt; 36(1) Nuis**
Bell v Miller (1862) (CAN) **3(2) Arbn**
Bell v Miller (1877) (AUS) **29(1) Insce; 29(2) Insce**
Bell v Milner (1957) (CAN) **9(2) Coys**
Bell v Moffat (1880) (CAN) **6 B of Exch**
Bell v Montreal Trust Co (1956) (CAN) **45 Stats**
Bell v Murray (1833) (SCOT) **27(3) H & W**
Bell v Nangle (1841) (IR) **17(1) Deeds**
Bell v Nash (1994) (CAN) **44(1) Solrs**
Bell v National Forest Products Ltd, Luttin, Porter (1964) (CAN) **26(1) Guar**
Bell v National Provincial Bank of England Ltd (1904) **27(5) Inc T**
Bell v Nevin (1866) **36(2) Prtnrs**
Bell v New Zealand Rugby Football Union (1931) (NZ) **12(2) Contr**
Bell v Nicholls, Ex p Richards (1919) (CAN) **21(2) Exon**
Bell v Nixon (1816) **29(1) Insce**
Bell v North Staffordshire Ry Co (1879) **37(3) Prac & Proc**
Bell v Northern Constitution Ltd (1943) (NI) **32(1) Libel**
Bell v Northwood (1886) (CAN) **45 Sp Pfce**
Bell v Norwich (Bp) (1565) **19(2) Eccl**
Bell v Oakley (1814) **18 Distr**
Bell v Ogilvie (1863) (SCOT) **44(1) Solrs**
Bell v Ontario Human Rights Commission and McKay (1971) **16 Cr Pract**
Bell v Ontario Human Rights Commission and McKay (1971) (CAN) **1(1) Admin L**
Bell v Ottawa Trust & Deposit Co (1897) (CAN) **5(1) Bkpcy**
Bell v Park (1914) (IR) **52 Wills**
Bell v Parke (1860) (IR) **32(1) Libel**
Bell v Patent (1903) (CAN) **33 Mags**
Bell v Peter Brown & Co (a firm) (1990) **32(2) Limit of A; 44(1) Solrs**
Bell v Petry (1897) (NZ) **27(1) H & W**
Bell v Phyn (1802) **36(2) Prtnrs; 52 Wills**
Bell v Pitt (1956) (AUS) **19(1) Esmt**
Bell v Plumbly (1900) **46(1) Stk Exch**
Bell v Port of London Assce Co (1850) **22(2) Evid**
Bell v Portland Shire (1876) (AUS) **1(2) Admin L**
Bell v Postlethwaite (1855) **3(2) Arbn**
Bell v Puller (1810) **43(1) Ship**
Bell v Quebec Corpn (1879) **49(2) Water**
Bell v Raisbeck (1844) **23(1) Exors**
Bell v Riddell (1882) (CAN) **27(1) H & W**
Bell v Riddell (1884) (CAN) **12(2) Contr**
Bell v Robinson (1824) **18 Distr; 25 Fam Arr**
Bell v Robinson (1909) (CAN) **5(2) Bkpcy**
Bell v Rogers (1914) (CAN) **6 B of Exch**
Bell v Rokeby (1905) (CAN) **1(4) Agcy**
Bell v Ross (1885) (CAN) **5(1) Bkpcy**
Bell v Rowe (1901) (AUS) **12(2) Contr**
Bell v Roy Estate (1993) (CAN) **50 Wills**
Bell v Ry Comr (1861) (AUS) **2 Animals**
Bell v Sarvis (1903) (CAN) **50 Wills; 51 Wills**
Bell v Schultz (1912) (CAN) **39(3) S Goods; 46(2) Tort**
Bell v Scott (1922) (AUS) **40(2) S Land**
Bell v Secretary of State for Defence (1986) **16 Cr Pract 39(2) Royal F**
Bell v Shuttleworth (1841) **6 B of Exch; 12(3) Contr 26(1) Guar; 30 Jdgmts**
Bell v Simpson (1857) **4(2) Bkpcy**
Bell v Skelton (1831) **23(2) Exors**
Bell v Smith (1826) **22(2) Evid**
Bell v Spelliscy (1932) (CAN) **23(1) Exors**
Bell v Spereman (1726) **38(3) Recrs**
Bell v Stanley Industrial Consultants Ltd (1996) (CAN **20(1) Empt**
Bell v Stewart (1842) (IR) **6 B of Exch**
Bell v Stocker (1882) **27(1) H & W**
Bell v Stockton etc Tramway Co (1887) **39(1) R Traf**
Bell v Stone (1798) **32(1) Libel**
Bell v Sunderland Bldg Soc (1883) **35(2) Mtge**
Bell v Tainthorp (1834) **30 Juries**
Bell v Tape (1837) (IR) **11(3) Const L**
Bell v Taylor (1836) **44(2) Solrs**
Bell v Thatcher (1675) **32(1) Libel**
Bell v Thompson (1934) (AUS) **2 Animals**
Bell v Tilden Car Rental Inc (1997) (CAN) **35(3) Negl**
Bell v Timiswood (1812) **23(1) Exors**
Bell v Toronto Transportation Commission (1926) (CAN **18 Discy**
Bell v Travco Hotels Ltd (1953) **29(1) Inns**
Bell v Turner (1874) **22(2) Evid**
Bell v Turner (1877) **48(2) Trusts**
Bell v Twentyman (1841) **19(1) Esmt; 35(3) Negl; 36(1) Nui**
Bell v Union Bank (1923) (NZ) **3(3) Bank**
Bell v Walker & Debrett (1785) **13(1) Coprt**
Bell v Wardell (1740) **17(1) Custom; 46(1) Time**
Bell v Welch (1850) **12(1) Contr; 26(1) Guar**
Bell v Wermore (1880) (CAN) **21(2) Exon**
Bell v Westmount Town (1899) (CAN) **8(3) Comwlth**
Bell v Wetmore (1880) (CAN) **17(2) Damgs; 27(2) H & W**
Bell v White (1857) (CAN) **7(1) Bounds**
Bell v Whitehead (1839) **13(1) Coprt**
Bell v Wilson (1865) **17(1) Deeds; 34(1) Mines**
Bell v Wilson (1866) **34(1) Mines**
Bell v Wilson (1900) (CAN) **32(1) Libel**
Bell v Windsor & Annapolis Ry Co (1892) (CAN) **8(1) Car**
Bell v Wright (1895) (CAN) **44(2) Solrs**
Bell v Wyndham (1865) **25 Fish**
Bell v Young (1855) **4(1) Bkpcy**
Bell (or Young or Farrell) v Arnott (1857) (SCOT) **3(1) Arb**

Fig 3.9
Example Page from
The Digest Vol 35(3)

1 GENERAL PRINCIPLES OF THE LAW OF NEGLIGENCE Case **384**

goods by order, delivered them at a booking-office, with the customer's address, and booked them, to be forwarded to him, not specifying any particular conveyance, and no particular mode of transmission having been pointed out by the customer.

Quaere: whether the consignor could maintain an action against the office-keeper for a negligent loss of the goods while under his charge.

Gilbart v Dale (1836) 5 Ad & El 543; 2 Har & W 383; 1 Nev & PKB 22; 6 LJKB 3; 111 ER 1270

ANNOTATION **Apld** Mid Ry v Bromley (1856) 17 CB 372

378 No negligence without duty

In case for an injury to plaintiff's reversionary interest by defendant's obstruction of a water-course on his land and thereby sending water upon and under the house and land in the occupation of plaintiff's tenant, defendant pleaded, that the obstruction was caused by the neglect of plaintiff's tenant to repair a wall on the demised land, that in consequence it fell into the watercourse, and caused the damage, and that within a reasonable time after defendant had notice he removed it: *Held* to be a bad plea, it not showing any obligation on the tenant to repair the wall merely as terre-tenant. *Quaere*: whether it would have been good if it had.

Bell v Twentyman (1841) 1 QB 766; 1 Gal & Dav 223; 10 LJQ B 278; 6 Jur 366; 113 ER 1324

ANNOTATION **Distd** Taylor v Stendall (1845) 5 LTOS 214

379 No negligence without duty

A declaration in case stated, by way of inducement, that plaintiff was possessed of a dwelling-house as tenant to defendant, and that defendant, at the request of plaintiff, promised to fit up a cellar for a wine cellar, with brick and stone bins; and then charged that it became the duty of defendant to use due care in fitting up the same, but that he did not, and that the slabs gave way, and broke plaintiff's wine bottles. It was proved that defendant did fit up a wine cellar with brick and stone bins; but that plaintiff afterwards required more bins to be made, and defendant consented to have the partitions carried up to the roof of the cellar. The workmen, however, by plaintiff's directions, erected the new partitions upon the centre of the slabs which covered the bins first made, and the slabs then gave way. It was proved that those slabs would have been strong enough to bear the weight of empty bottles; but some of the witnesses thought not that of full bottles: *Held* under these circumstances no breach of duty was shown, defendant having only undertaken to fit up a wine cellar with brick and stone bins, and not one of any particular character.

Richardson v Berkeley (1847) 10 LTOS 203

380 No negligence without duty

The declaration stated that defendants were possessed of a mooring anchor, which was kept by them fixed in a known part of a navigable river, covered by ordinary tides, that the anchor had become removed into, and remained in, another part of the river covered by ordinary tides, not indicated, whereof defendants had notice, and although they had the means and power of refixing and securing the anchor, and indicating it, they neglected so to do, whereby plaintiffs' vessel, whilst sailing in a part of the river ordinarily used by ships, ran foul of and struck against the anchor, and was thereby damaged, etc: *Held* bad, for not showing that defendants were privy to the removal of the anchor, or that it was their duty to refix it and to indicate it.

Hancock v York, Newcastle & Berwick Ry Co (1850) 10 CB 348; 14 LTOS 467; 138 ER 140

381 No negligence without duty

Negligence creates no cause of action unless it expresses a breach of a duty (*Erle, CJ*).

Dutton v Powles (1862) 2 B & S 191; 31 LJQB 191; 6 LT 224; 8 Jur NS 970; 10 WR 408; 1 Mar LC 209; 121 ER 1043, Ex Ch

382 No negligence without duty

Plaintiff, a carman, being sent by his employer to defendants for some goods, was directed by a servant of defendants to go to the counting house. In proceeding along a dark passage of defendants in the direction pointed out, plaintiff fell down a staircase, and was injured: *Held* defendants were not guilty of any negligence; for if the passage was so dark that plaintiff could not see his way, he ought not to have proceeded; and if, on the other hand, there was sufficient light, he ought to have avoided the danger.

Wilkinson v Fairrie (1862) 1 H & C 633; 32 LJ Ex 73; 7 LT 599; 9 Jur NS 280; 158 ER 1038

ANNOTATIONS **Apld** Lewis v Ronald (1909) 101 LT 534 **Consd** Campbell v Shelbourne Hotel Ltd [1939] 2 KB 534

383 No negligence without duty

Skelton v London & North Western Ry Co no 828 post

384 No negligence without duty

Plaintiffs, merchants at Valparaiso, received through defendants a telegram purporting to come from London and addressed to them, ordering a large shipment of barley. No such message was ever in fact sent to plaintiffs. The misdelivery of the message was caused by the negligence of defendants, and occasioned heavy loss, to plaintiffs, in consequence of a fall in the market price of barley. In an action to recover the amount of this loss: *Held* there was no duty owing by defendants to plaintiffs in the matter, either by contract or law, and therefore no action would lie.

front of the volume, which indicates where in the *Cumulative Supplement* a summary of the case can be found. For more information on *The Digest*, refer to para.7.14.

Tracing a case through print indexes to law reports

In addition to the *Current Law Case Citators* and *The Digest*, there are a number of indexes to the cases in individual series of law reports. For instance, the *All England Law Reports* has published a volume containing a list of all the cases in the *All England Law Reports Reprint* series (see para.3.13), which covers selected cases between 1558 and 1935. In addition, there are three volumes containing the *Consolidated Tables and Index 1936–2014*. Volume 1 contains a list of all the cases included in the *All England Law Reports* between these dates. The reference given is to the year, volume and page number. Volumes 2 and 3 contain a subject index. 3.18

If you know that the case you are looking for is old, you can turn to the index in Vols 177 and 178 of the *English Reports*, and this will tell you if the case is printed in the *English Reports* (see para.3.12). Several other series of law reports also publish indexes and these can be useful if you know that a case is reported in a particular series but you have not got an exact reference.

The indexes to the *Law Reports* are very useful for all but the most recent cases. From 1865 to 1949, a series of *Law Reports: Digests* were published. These contain summaries of the cases reported in the *Law Reports*, in subject order, and a list of cases is usually included. From 1950 this has been published as the *Law Reports Consolidated Index*, usually referred to as the *Red Index*. Five bound volumes, each covering cases in a 10-year period, have been published for the period 1951–2000. Indexes have also been published for 2001–2005, 2006–2010 and 2011–2014. An annual paperback index was also published, containing cases indexed to the end of the previous year. From 2015, the *Pink Index*, formally issued at intervals during the year, is issued as an annual volume. The main arrangement of all the indexes is by subject, but there are two alphabetical lists. The list of Cases Reported, at the front of each volume, covers recently reported cases, whilst the separate list of Cases Judicially Considered, at the back of the volume, gives information on older cases which have been mentioned in court during the period covered by the index. In addition to cases published in the *Law Reports* and the *Weekly Law Reports*, the Red and Pink indexes also include cases published, in the *All England Law Reports*, the *Criminal Appeal Reports*, the *Lloyd's Law Reports*, the *Local Government Reports*, the *Industrial Cases Reports*, and the *Road Traffic Reports* and *Tax Cases*.

RECENT REPORTS AND JUDGMENTS

The law is constantly changing, with new cases being reported daily. Therefore be prepared to consult recent reports and judgments. This is essential if you are to remain aware of new developments in the law. Recent reported cases can be browsed using the "Cases" section of the Lexis Library (para.2.3) or Westlaw UK (para.2.4). To do this using Westlaw UK, for example, use the "Law Reports and Transcripts" link under the "Browse" heading to see recent reports from the law reports held in full text by Westlaw UK. However, law reports are published a few months after the judgment has been handed down in a case. 3.19

The most up-to-date reports are published by *The Times* newspaper. These reports appear ahead of the major law report series, but, unlike them, do not reproduce the full text of judgments. This need not be a problem. Transcripts of judgments made in a very wide range of cases are now available online, sometimes within hours of the judgment being handed down. Where cases have provoked coverage in the newspapers and other media, the availability of judgments on the internet makes it possible to examine the legal issues by going directly to the full text.

Supreme Court judgments can be found on the Supreme Court website (at *https://www.supremecourt.uk*). As these are the judgments of the court of final appeal, they are the most influential recent judgments available online. Judgments from 2009 can be found on the "Decided Cases" page of the website. The judgments can be found either by neutral citation or case name, but it is not possible to search the full text of the judgments, as they are only held as PDF files. The BAILII site (para.3.20) provides the best approach for keyword searching recent Supreme Court judgments. However the Supreme Court site features useful press summaries for each judgment, noting the background to the appeal, the decision made and the reasons for the judgment.

Judgments of the Judicial Committee of the Privy Council can be found on the "Decided Cases" page of the Judicial Committee website (at *https://ww.jcpc.uk*). The Judicial Committee of the Privy Council is the court of final appeal for some Commonwealth and former Commonwealth countries and for UK overseas territories.

Until relatively recent years, the Court Service website was also an important source for recent judgments. Now retitled Her Majesty's Courts and Tribunals Service, the Service no longer makes judgments directly available. Instead, anyone seeking an England and Wales court judgment needs to use either BAILII or Casetrack (see para.3.20 below).

How to find judgments

3.20 If you are looking for an extremely recent Supreme Court judgment, perhaps one made the previous day, it makes sense to look for the judgment on the Supreme Court website as noted in para.3.19. However, the wider coverage of the BAILII website makes it the most useful starting point for recent judgments. Most UK universities also provide access to the Casetrack service, which provides access to a rapidly updated database of judgments. Some universities subscribe, in addition, to Lawtel, which combines summaries of judgments with access to the full text.

The BAILII website (at *http://www.bailii.org*) provides a convenient way of finding all recent UK judgments as they bring together judgments from Her Majesty's Courts and Tribunals Service, the Supreme Court and the Privy Council. Judgments from Scotland and Northern Ireland courts are also included. BAILII databases are listed by jurisdiction. Courts are then listed within each jurisdiction. Judgments can be viewed either alphabetically or by year and month by selecting the link for a particular court. Select "England and Wales", for example, and "Court of Appeal (Civil Division) Decisions" to see the relevant judgments. Select "United Kingdom" to see Supreme Court and Privy Council judgments.

However, unless you are looking for a very recent judgment, the BAILII "Case Law Search" provides the most effective means of finding judgments on the website. A link is provided from the BAILII home page to the full search screen. Searches can be made by case name or citation using the search screen, and all UK jurisdictions searched in a single operation. More general keyword or "exact phrase" searches are also possible. If you wish to restrict a search to a particular court this can be done by selecting the court using the tick boxes placed below the main search area.

The Casetrack service (at *http://www.casetrack.com*) provides direct access to Smith Bernal transcripts of judgments made in the Court of Appeal, the Administrative Court and the High Court, along with searchable links to Supreme Court and Privy Council judgments. Judgments from Scottish courts are also included. As Smith Bernal is the official reporter to the Court of Appeal and the Administrative Court, judgments from these courts can be made available very quickly, sometimes within hours of being handed down. As a result judgments not yet available on BAILII may be available from Casetrack. The database can be searched by case name, date and keyword. Searches can also be further restricted to subject areas. Access to the database is limited to registered users, so you will need to request a username and a password from your law library (Casetrack does not use either the Shibboleth authentication system generally used by UK universities, or the older Athens authentication system—see para.2.8).

As the UK's leading current awareness service for law, Lawtel (para.2.5) provides another effective way of searching for recent judgments, though by no means all university libraries subscribe. The range of judgments available is again wide, and judgments are loaded onto Lawtel databases as soon as they become available. The brief summaries of judgments provided by Lawtel are a particular advantage, making it possible to quickly grasp the key points of a case.

It should be emphasised, however, that the greatest benefit of the availability of judgments online, lies in the opportunity it gives the student to find recent judgments which are already known to be of legal significance. The ability to search through large numbers of judgments is not in itself a particular benefit to the law student. Some of the judgments will be reported later, but many will not. About a third of Court of Appeal cases will be reported. As noted in the introduction to this chapter, the aim of law reporting is to make available those cases that raise a point of legal significance. It is unusual for cases which raise a significant legal issue to go unreported.

TIPS • *Use the "neutral citation" (para.3.4) if known when searching for recent judgments, e.g. [2011] UKSC 45. (The citation can be used with paragraph numbers in square brackets when quoting from a judgment.)*

SUMMARY: HOW TO FIND A CASE

1. If the date is unknown:
   use the Westlaw UK "Cases" search, JustCite, or the *Current Law Case Citator*.
2. If the case is thought to be very old, search
   the *English Reports,* or the
   All England Law Reports Reprint series online, or use the
   The Digest Consolidated Table of Cases,
3. If the case is thought to be very recent and unreported, use one of the databases described in para.3.19 and para.3.20.
4. If the case is thought to be a reported UK case, use:
   the Westlaw UK "Cases" search,
   or the *Current Law Monthly Digest in print;* the indexes of the *Law Reports*, the *Weekly Law Reports* and the *All England Law Reports* provide further print alternatives.

HOW TO TRACE JOURNAL ARTICLES AND COMMENTARIES ON A CASE

3.21 You may want to find journal articles written about a case, or trace comments on a recent court decision. Such articles and comments usually explain the significance of the case and relate it to other relevant decisions. Sometimes writers who disagree with a decision made in a case may suggest that the case provides a justification for a substantive change in the law.

If you have used the Westlaw UK "Cases" search to find a case (para.3.15), or the *Current Law Case Citator* (para.3.16), you may already have been alerted to the existence of journal articles providing comment and analysis. Brief journal citations appear at the end of the "Case Analysis" entry for a case provided by Westlaw UK. These will be linked to the full text of the article if it is available within Westlaw UK. In the *Current Law Case Citator*, journal articles appear in square brackets after citations for law reports.

Not all cases attract comment in journals. Significant cases may be referenced many times. *Douglas v Hello! Ltd (No.1)* has been discussed to date in over 80 journal articles. Some of the articles will be very brief, others extensive, running to many pages. Case comment from legal journals may appear before a case is fully reported; more extensive academic discussions may be available relatively soon after a case is reported. The case *Kennedy v Information Commissioner* mentioned in para.3.15 was reported in 2014 and early in 2015. Two reasonably substantial articles commenting on the case appeared soon after it was reported. One of these is listed by Westlaw UK as:

J.R. 2014, 19(3), 180–187

This refers to an article published in *Judicial Review* which discussed the case in issue 3 of Vol.19, the volume for 2014, starting at p.180. The most recent case comment appeared in the *European Human Rights Law Review* and is listed as

E.H.R.L.R. 2015, 1, 57–65

Sources explaining the meaning of abbreviations are noted in para.3.5. These can be useful if you need to check a library catalogue to see if a university library holds a particular journal (para.1.9).

Note that the Westlaw UK references do not use a standard citation form. The standard form for the 2015 article would be:

[2015] 1 E.H.R.L.R. 57

However, the Westlaw UK "Cases" search and the *Current Law Case Citator* provide only the briefest information about a journal article. This can be a problem if you wish to assess the potential value of the article. More information can often be found using the Westlaw UK "Journals" search, or the Lawtel "Articles Index". Both services provide brief summaries of articles indexed.

To search for articles on a case using the Westlaw UK "Journals" search, first select the "Advanced Search" from the "Journals" search page. The citation for the case which interests you (or the party names) can then be entered in the relevant search box. Brief details of any potentially relevant journal articles are displayed once the search has been made, along with link under "Documents" to the summary of the article found in the *Legal Journals Index* (see para.5.8). This will not necessarily be the same list of articles as that found in the "Case Analysis" for the case, as indexing for the *Legal Journals Index* is carried out separately. The article summaries can be very brief, especially for older articles, but are usually more than sufficient as an aid to assessing the focus and nature of an article. The summary for the *European Human Rights Law Review* article cited above, states, for example, that it:

> "Comments on recent Supreme Court jurisprudence that has reaffirmed the importance of the common law as a source of individual rights protection. Discusses why: (1) the Human Rights Act 1998 initially led to judicial neglect of constitutional common law rights; and (2) there has been a recent resurgence of interest in common law rights protection. Analyses the relationship between the rights protected by the common law and the European Convention on Human Rights 1950."

The keywords associated with the *Legal Journals Index* entry can also be useful. If the full text of an article is available, a "Full Text Article" link is displayed alongside the "Legal Journals Index" link.

The Articles Index contained in the Lawtel service (para.2.6) provides an effective online alternative to the journals search on Westlaw UK. Although fewer articles are indexed than is the case for Westlaw UK, the summaries provided are somewhat more extensive. Articles are indexed from 1988. To search for case comment on Lawtel, select the "Articles and Press" link from the navigation bar, then select "Articles" to search the Articles Index. Case names can be entered in the "Case Law Cited" box.

If you are simply looking for any comment on a recent case likely to be of general interest, a more direct approach can be adopted. The relevant print issues of weekly journals such as the *New Law Journal* or the *Solicitors Journal* may be kept on the library shelves. These always carry notes and comments on recent cases. The journals can also be browsed using the Journals section of the Lexis Library (para.2.3). Key specialist journals such as *Public Law* and the *Criminal Law Review also* carry notes and comments on recent cases. Recent print issues are unlikely to be kept on library shelves, but can be browsed online. See Ch.5 for more on using journals online.

> **TIPS** • *Use both the Westlaw UK "Cases" search (look for the "Case Analysis") and the "Journals" "Advanced Search" when tracing journal articles on a case. Different articles can be listed.*

HOW TO FIND UPDATES ON RECENT CASES

A number of online services provide brief summaries of new cases. These enable the legal profession to identify the key features of recent judgments that might be of interest. Cases can be reviewed quickly, without the need to read through the judgments. The brief summaries provided by these services may sometimes be the only text available that notes the content of a judgment. 3.22

Updating services are provided by the *All England Reporter* section of the Lexis Library (para.2.3), the free Cases Search provided by the Incorporated Council of Law Reporting, Lawtel (para.2.5), and the Westlaw UK "Cases" search (para.3.15). These are explained below.

The value of the print issues of the *Current Law Monthly Digest* is also noted. These provide update summaries of reported cases.

The *All England Reporter* from the Lexis Library is one of the most wide-ranging sources for summaries of new judgments; most appearing soon after the judgment is made. Some of the judgments will later be reported in the *All England Law Reports*, but many will not. The cases that will be reported later are marked with an asterisk against the case name.

To access the *Reporter* database, first select "Cases" from the Lexis Library home page, then "Browse". Select the *Reporter* database to display a list of cases. The most recent are shown first. Although relatively brief, the summaries provided give the key facts for each case. Subject keywords are also added.

A summary can be cited using the *All England Reporter* reference number and the month of the judgment, e.g.:

R. v Nasir [2015] All E.R. (D) 104 (Sep)

The "Current Awareness" tab in the Lexis Library provides an alternative approach to finding updates on cases using a keyword search. Select "General Case Digest" from the "Sources" dropdown menu choice. Then enter your keywords to find brief summaries of cases listed in chronological order, with the most recent shown first.

A more selective alternative to the *All England Reporter* database, or the Lexis Library Current Awareness search, is provided by the Incorporated Council for Law Reporting. The "Case Search" available from the ICLR website (at *http://www.iclr.co.uk*) provides digests of cases that will later be reported in the *Weekly Law Reports*. This has the distinct advantage of ensuring that the cases summarised on the database raise questions of legal significance. The "Case Summaries" search on the "Case Search" page can be used to search for summaries of recent cases using both subject keywords and date limits. Publication reference links can then be selected to view keywords and summaries from the ICLR. The summaries can be cited using a W.L.R. digest number as follows:

FAS v Bradford Metropolitan District Council and another [2015] W.L.R. (D) 396

Not all libraries provide access to Lawtel, but Lawtel's "Case Law" search provides another rapidly updated source of summaries of judgments. An advantage of the Case Law search is that the case report summaries provided are always linked to the full text of judgments. A similar result can be achieved using the Westlaw UK "Cases" search. Select the "Advanced Search" from the case search page, then set one of the standard date limits, e.g. "28 days" and click to search. Brief details of recent cases are displayed along with links to summaries contained in the "Case Analysis" page. Subject keywords (e.g. "Privacy") can also be entered to find new reported cases of interest in a particular subject area.

Though these services are highly effective, the availability of online summaries of recent judgments can nonetheless be a mixed blessing, especially when the database providing the summaries is as wide-ranging as Lawtel's Case Law service or the *All England Reporter*. Though the specialist practitioner, or legal academic, may be able to sift through case summaries and decide which raise legal issues of significance, this is not easily accomplished by the law student. Finding information and interpreting it are two separate tasks involving different skills and levels of expertise.

Updates on recent reported cases, though less immediate, are more likely to yield new cases that might be important. The *Current Law Monthly Digest* prints summaries of cases under major subject headings (along with notes of journal articles and new legislation). A Cumulative Table of Cases in each monthly issue enables cases to be traced by name for the current year. The relevant month and entry item number is noted against each case.

EUROPEAN HUMAN RIGHTS CASE LAW

The Human Rights Act 1998 incorporated into UK law the principles of the European Convention for the Protection of Human Rights and Fundamental Freedoms. Although the Convention had been of potential relevance to the law of the UK before the Human Rights Act, the Act requires that courts take Convention case law into account in all cases where it might be considered relevant, greatly increasing its importance to UK domestic law. As a result, knowing how to find and cite European Convention case law has become an essential skill for students of UK law. **3.23**

The European Convention is a treaty agreed by the Member States of the Council of Europe—not to be confused with the European Union, though many of its 47 Member States are also members of the EU. The UK ratified the Treaty in 1951 and it came into force in 1953. The Convention established both the European Court of Human Rights and the European Commission of Human Rights and both bodies have played a role in the creation of Convention case law. The role of the European Commission is now subsumed into that of the European Court. The Council of Europe website (at *http://www.coe.int*) provides a themed approach to the areas of activity of the Council under the general headings "Human Rights", "Democracy" and "Rule of Law". Explanatory information is available along with key legal texts including the relevant sections of the European Convention.

European Convention case law consists of both judgments and decisions. Judgments are made by the full sessions of the European Court of Human Rights, sitting in Strasbourg. Decisions are admissibility decisions which determine whether a case should proceed to a full hearing of the European Court. Before 1998 admissibility decisions were made by the European Commission of Human Rights. Decisions are now made by a committee of the European Court of Human Rights itself. Both judgments and decisions are relevant to the interpretation of the European Convention and must be taken into account under the Human Rights Act 1998.

All applications to the European Court of Human Rights are given an application number consisting of five digits plus two digits for the year the application was lodged. Where a case is unreported, this application number can be used to cite both judgments and decisions, e.g.:

Boyle v the United Kingdom (App.no.55434/00) ECtHR, 8 January 2008

specifies the judgment made in the case:

Boyle v the United Kingdom (dec.) (App.no.55434/00) ECtHR, 28 October 2005

specifies the decision made in the same case.

The citation format following the Council of Europe's specification is slightly different from that given above. The judgment would be cited as:

Boyle v the United Kingdom (No.55434/00), 8 January 2008.

Fig 3.10
First Page of an ECHR Judgment

CONSEIL DE L'EUROPE

COUNCIL OF EUROPE

COUR EUROPÉENNE DES DROITS DE L'HOMME
EUROPEAN COURT OF HUMAN RIGHTS

FOURTH SECTION

CASE OF BOYLE V. THE UNITED KINGDOM

(Application no. 55434/00)

JUDGMENT

STRASBOURG

8 JANUARY 2008

FINAL
08/04/2008

This judgment will become final in the circumstances set out in Article 44 § 2 of the Convention. It may be subject to editorial revision.

Tracing European Convention case law

3.24 The full text of European Convention case law can be found on the European Court of Human Rights website (at *http://www.echr.coe.int*). Judgments and decisions are held in the HUDOC database, in the "Case-Law" area of the website. The database contains all judgments made by the European Court of Human Rights since 1959 and all admissibility decisions made since 1986. Some decisions are also available for the period 1955 to 1986.

If you have the application number for a case, use the full number in the "Application Number" search box of the HUDOC database, to retrieve a link to the full text (e.g. "44875/98"). Tick boxes allow judgments, decisions or both to be selected for searching. Resolutions of the Committee of Ministers of the Council of Europe are also included, though these are not often cited in legal discussion.

If you do not have the application number for a case, the name of the case can be entered under "Case Title" (e.g. "B.B." or "Hobbs"), along with the respondent state (e.g. "United Kingdom"). The use of abbreviations in case titles and the need to have an exact case name can cause problems. It may be necessary to try likely subject keywords in the "Text" box to find a case.

Though the HUDOC database is the official online source for European Court of Human Rights case law, judgments (though not decisions) from the Court are also available from the BAILII database (para.2.15). The judgments are listed by year and can be found under the "Europe" heading on the BAILII home page (at *http://www.bailii.org*). Particular judgments can also be located using the BAILII "Case Law" search. Tick the "European Court of Human Rights" box below the search area to limit the search to the relevant case law. Party names can be used in the "Case name" search, but be careful to enter the names exactly as cited by the Court (e.g. "*X, Y and Z v the United Kingdom*"). Application numbers need to be entered in the "Exact phrase" search box.

BAILII also adds a citation following the UK neutral citation model. The Boyle judgment cited in para.3.23 is cited in BAILII as [2008] E.C.H.R. 15.

Printed judgments and decisions

Judgments made before 1996 were published by Carl Heymanns Verlag in *Series A* of the Publications of the Court. Each judgment has a number within the series, so that a full standard citation is as follows: 3.25

Soering v the United Kingdom (1989) Series A no.161

References to paragraph numbers may follow (e.g. para.65).

The text of individual judgments was also printed by the Council of Europe and distributed to libraries up until 1997. Some law libraries which do not hold the *Series A* text of a judgment may have retained these individually printed transcripts. Confusingly, they have their own numbering system. This is not used in citation.

From 1996 onwards selected judgments and decisions have been published (again by Heymanns Verlag) as *Reports of Judgments and Decisions*, and cited as e.g.:

Robins v the United Kingdom ECHR 1997–V

Pages and paragraph numbers may again be added to the citation.

Decisions made between 1974 and 1995 were published by the Council of Europe as *Decisions and Reports* (DR). These are cited as follows:

Hewitt and Harman v the United Kingdom (1989) 67 D.R. 88

Here, 67 specifies the volume number and 88 the first page of the report. Only a few law libraries hold the full *Decisions and Reports* series, which can be a problem as the HUDOC database does not contain all decisions made before 1986. Decisions made between 1960 and 1974 were published by the Council of Europe as *Collection of Decisions of the European Commission on Human Rights* (C.D.). These are rarely cited.

Other sources of European human rights law

3.26 Most of the human rights cases cited in UK courts have been reported in either the *European Human Rights Reports* (E.H.R.R.) or *Butterworths Human Rights Cases* (B.H.R.C.). Digests are also available in the *European Human Rights Law Review* (E.H.R.L.R.). These are commercial publications available both in print and online. The full text of the *European Human Rights Reports* and the *European Human Rights Law Review* are available online from Westlaw UK (para.2.5). *Butterworths Human Rights* Cases is available online from the Lexis Library (para.2.3). Citations from these publications use the standard format for UK law reports and journals. As with other Sweet & Maxwell law reports, the *European Human Rights Reports* from 2001 onwards are referenced using a case number rather than a page number, e.g.:

Boyle v United Kingdom (2008) 47 E.H.R.R. 19

Here the reference is to case 19 of the 2008 reports volume. Summaries and extracts of reports are also included in the *European Human Rights Reports*, and these are referenced as e.g.:

Brinks v Netherlands (2005) 41 E.H.R.R. SE5

Some admissibility decisions are reported in a separate section of the E.H.R.R. and are cited as E.H.R.R. C.D.

Although the *European Human Rights Reports* concentrates on European Convention case law, *Butterworths Human Rights Cases* is more wide ranging, including cases from other common law countries which may be of relevance to the human rights law of the UK. Cases might be reported from the Constitutional Court of South Africa for example, or the United States Supreme Court. These appear alongside reports of UK cases.

Textbooks on UK human rights law also refer to cases from the Court of Justice of the European Union (para.8.13) where these concern European Convention principles.

Summaries of European Court of Human Rights cases have also been published in book form. Vincent Berger's *Case Law of the European Court of Human Rights* for example was published in three volumes and covers the period 1960 to 1993. Peter Kempees' *Systematic Guide to the Case Law of the European Court of Human Rights* covers the period 1960 to 1998 in four volumes, arranging summaries according to the relevant article or articles of the European Convention within each volume.

TIPS • *Use Westlaw UK and the Lexis Library to search for ECHR cases reported in UK law reports. These are the cases most often cited in UK legal discussion. All ECHR judgments can be found on the BAILII website.*

The *Human Rights Information Bulletin*, produced by the Council of Europe 1978 to 2012, is a source for summaries of older judgments and can be found on the "Publications" section of the Council of Europe website. The European Court of Human Rights has also issued case-law information notes since 1999 which contain brief summaries of judgments arranged by Convention article. These can be found in the "Case-Law" section of the website (at *http://www.echr.coe.int*).

TRIBUNALS

The establishment of the welfare state led to the creation of a large number of tribunals. They were set up to resolve disputes over entitlement to welfare benefits. Subsequently, other areas, such as problems between landlords and tenants, and between employer and employees because of unfair dismissal, became subject to resolution through tribunals. Tribunals can be extremely busy, hearing many thousands of cases each year, but only a small number of cases are eventually reported in the law reports. Some law reports, such as the *Industrial Cases Reports* and *Immigration Appeals*, carry reports of appeals from the tribunal to an appeal court, but the vast majority of cases heard by tribunals are not reported. Some other law reports which include tribunal decisions are noted in para.3.29. 3.27

Relatively recent tribunal decisions can, however, be found on the GOV.UK website (at *https://www.gov.uk*). Content for the website is provided by the HM Courts and Tribunals Service, and can be found in the HM Courts and Tribunals Service section of the GOV.UK site (search for "HM Courts and Tribunals Service" using the home page search box to find the relevant pages). Links to the various tribunals for which the HM Courts and Tribunals Service is responsible can be found in the "What we do" area of the GOV.UK page. This may change as this section of the GOV.UK site is currently under development.

Many of the tribunals are listed under "First Tier Tribunal" and "Upper Tier Tribunal" headings, following the structure created by the Tribunals, Courts and Enforcement Act 2007. Appeals against decisions made by government departments and other bodies are heard initially by the relevant tribunal in one of the chambers of the First Tier Tribunal. The Asylum Support Tribunal, for example, considers appeals against decisions made by the UK Border Agency. The Upper Tribunal hears appeals from the First Tier Tribunal and consists of four chambers: the Administrative Appeals Chamber, the Immigration and Asylum Chamber, the Lands Chamber and the Tax and Chancery Chamber. The Upper Tribunal (Administrative Appeals) Chamber, for example, considers decisions made by a number of First Tier tribunals, including those belonging to the Social Entitlement Chamber and the Health, Education and Social Care Chamber.

A number of other tribunals listed on the HM Courts and Tribunals web page are not part of the First Tier Tribunal or the Upper Tribunal. The most important of these are the Employment Tribunal and the Employment Appeal Tribunal.

Decisions for the tribunals listed on the GOV.UK site can be found under a "previous decisions" heading for the relevant tribunal. Decisions are available for all four chambers of the Upper Tribunal from 2008 onwards, but only some tribunals constituting the First Tier.

The standard abbreviation for the Upper Tribunal is "UKUT". An abbreviation for the relevant chamber is also added after the decision number. An Administrative Appeals Chamber decision, for example is cited:

NC v Secretary of State for Work and Pensions (ESA) [2015] UKUT 147 (AAC)

Employment Appeal Tribunal citations incorporate the appeal number as follows:

A v West Midlands Police (Harassment) [2015] UKEAT/0313/14/JOJ

The BAILII website (at *http://*www.bailii.org) provides a more straightforward presentation of tribunal decisions than that provided by official websites. Tribunals are listed under the "United Kingdom" heading and decisions can be found by year or party name. The BAILII "Case Law" search can also be restricted to find results from tribunal databases only.

The BAILII site includes decisions from all four chambers of the Upper Tribunal, along with appeals from the Health Education and Social Care Chamber and the General Regulatory Chamber of the First Tier Tribunal. Employment Appeal Tribunal decisions are also available from 1976 onwards.

Social welfare law

3.28 Law libraries have collected social welfare tribunal decisions, sometimes from the 1950s onwards. The most important current social welfare decisions are now taken by the Upper Tribunal (Administrative Appeals) Chamber and, as noted in para.3.27 above, these date from 2008. Earlier decisions taken by the Social Security and Child Support Commissioners can be found on the BAILII website (at *http://www.bailii.org*) from as early as 1972.

Between 1976 and 1990, bound volumes of reported decisions were published by HMSO, the last appearing in 1993 as Reported Decisions of the Social Security Commissioner Vol.13, 1989–1990. Reported decisions between 1948 and 1976 were published in the seven volumes of the Reported Decisions of the Commissioner under the Social Security and National Insurance (Industrial Injuries) Acts, known as the Blue Books because of their colour.

Commissioners' decisions were cited using a standard series abbreviation and all reported decisions since 1950 bore the prefix R. For example, the prefix R(U) indicated a Commissioner's decision on unemployment benefit, and R(P) a decision on entitlement to pensions. Within each series, reports are cited by the report number and the year: R(U) 7/62 indicates a reported unemployment benefit decision, case No.7 of 1962. The following abbreviations were in use:

- R(A) Attendance Allowance
- R(CS) Child Support
- R(DLA) Disability Living Allowance
- R(DWA) Disability Working Allowance
- R(F) Family Allowances and Child Benefit
- R(FC) Family Credit
- R(FIS) Family Income Supplement
- R(G) General—miscellaneous (maternity benefit, widow's benefit, death grant, etc.)
- R(I) Industrial Injuries
- R(IS) Income Support
- R(M) Mobility Allowance
- R(P) Retirement Pensions

- R(S) Sickness and Invalidity Benefit
- R(SB) Supplementary Benefit
- R(SSP) Statutory Sick Pay
- R(U) Unemployment Benefit

Unpublished decisions were prefaced by C instead of R. For example, CP3/81 is a reference to an unpublished 1981 Commissioner's decision on pensions and CSB 15/82 is an unreported decision on supplementary benefits. The year in "starred" cases (1987–2001) is given in full, e.g. CDLA 1347/1999.

Reported cases from 1948–1950 had a different method of citation. They were prefixed by C, followed by a letter (not enclosed in brackets) representing the area of law covered. Thus, CI denotes an early decision on industrial injuries. The cases were numbered in sequence.

Reported decisions of other tribunals

The wide range of tribunals makes a complete guide to reported decisions impossible within the available space. What follows is selective. 3.29

Immigration appeals are covered by *Immigration Appeal Reports*, published by TSO. VAT and Duties Tribunals Reports were published by TSO up to 2009.

Many Lands Tribunal cases appear in the *Property, Planning and Compensation Reports* and in the *Estates Gazette* and the *Estates Gazette Law Reports*. The latter series also covers leasehold valuation tribunals. Barry Rose published a series of volumes entitled *Lands Tribunal Cases*.

Most reported cases, in subjects other than welfare law, appear in standard series of law reports and are conventionally cited. *Current Law* contains references to many tribunal decisions, under appropriate subject headings, and provides a summary for each one. Looseleaf encyclopedias frequently refer to both published and unpublished decisions in the appropriate subject.

The *Industrial Tribunal Reports*, published until 1978, now form part of the *Industrial Cases Reports*. These contain many cases heard by the Employment Appeal Tribunal and many E.A.T. decisions also appear in the *Industrial Relations Law Reports*.

4
Legislation

INTRODUCTION

4.1 When a Bill (para.6.6) has been approved by both Houses of Parliament and has received the Royal Assent, it becomes an Act of Parliament. The Act is made available on the legislation.gov.uk website (at *http://www.legislation.gov.uk*) and the first printed version is available from TSO, usually within a few days of receiving the Royal Assent.

There are two types of Acts. Public General Acts deal with public policy and apply to the whole population, or a substantial part of it. Local and Personal Acts, on the other hand, affect only a particular area of the country, or a named organisation or group of individuals. This chapter will concentrate on Public General Acts, which you are more likely to use regularly. Local and Personal Acts will, however, be examined in para.4.25.

THE STRUCTURE OF AN ACT

4.2 A copy of the Anti-Slavery Day Act 2010 is reproduced below. This is an unusually short Act, as most Acts are many pages in length. All Acts are structured in the same way, although some of the parts described below are not included in every Act.

The parts of an Act (see the illustration) are:

1. Short title.
2. Official citation (see para.4.3).
3. Long title. This may give some indication of the purpose and content of the Act.
4. Date of Royal Assent.
5. Enacting formula. This is a standard form of words indicating that the Act has been approved by Parliament.
6. Main body of the Act. This is divided into sections, which are further divided into subsections and paragraphs. When referring to a section, it is usual to abbreviate it to "s." Subsections are written in round brackets. You would therefore write section 2, subsection 1 as s.2(1).
7. Date of commencement. A specific date may be set for the Act to come into force. Alternatively, the Act may give a Minister of the Crown the power to bring it into force at a later date. This will be done through a commencement order, which is a form of delegated legislation. If there is no commencement section at the end of an Act, it comes into force on the date of the Royal Assent.

Fig 4.1
Anti-Slavery Day Act

Anti-Slavery Day Act 2010 [1]

2010 CHAPTER 14 [2]

An Act to introduce a national day to raise awareness of the need to eradicate all forms of slavery, human trafficking and exploitation; and for connected purposes [3]

[4] [8th April 2010]

BE IT ENACTED by the Queen's most Excellent Majesty, by and with the advice and consent of the Lords Spiritual and Temporal, and Commons, in this present Parliament assembled, and by the authority of the same, as follows:-- [5]

1 Anti-Slavery Day [6]

(1) The Secretary of State shall by order made by statutory instrument specify a date which shall be observed each year as Anti-Slavery Day.

(2) The purpose of Anti-Slavery Day shall be to--

(a) acknowledge that millions of men, women and children continue to be victims of slavery, depriving them of basic human dignity and freedom;

(b) raise awareness amongst young people and others of the dangers and consequences of slavery, human trafficking and exploitation and encourage them to be proactive in the fight against it;

(c) draw attention to--

(i) the progress made by government and those working to combat all forms of slavery, human trafficking and exploitation, and

(ii) what more needs to be done.

(3) In this Act "slavery" includes--

(a) trafficking for sexual exploitation,

(b) child trafficking,

(c) trafficking for forced labour, and

(d) domestic servitude.

NOTES

Initial Commencement

Royal Assent

Royal Assent: 8 April 2010: (no specific commencement provision). [7]

Extent

This Act does not extend to Scotland: see s 2(2).

2 Short title and extent

(1) This Act may be cited as the Anti-Slavery Day Act 2010.

(2) This Act extends to England and Wales. [8]

8. Extent. Acts of Parliament usually apply to the whole of the UK, unless specified otherwise in an extent section.

Schedules and tables are sometimes included at the end of an Act. They may contain detailed provisions not included elsewhere in the Act or may summarise and clarify the effect of the Act. They help to prevent the main body of an Act becoming too cluttered with detail and are used in the same way as appendices in a book. Until 2001 the text of an Act also included helpful marginal notes, explaining the contents of a section.

Citation of statutes

4.3 Statutes (or Acts) are commonly referred to by a shortened version of their title (the short title) and the year of publication, e.g. the Theft Act 1968. Every Act published in a year is also given its own individual number and Acts may also be cited by the year in which they were passed and the Act (or chapter) number. Thus the Theft Act was the 60th Act passed in 1968 and is cited as 1968, c. 60. "Chapter" is abbreviated to "c." when written, but it is spoken in full.

The present system of citing statutes by their year and chapter number began in 1963. Before that date, the system was more complicated. Prior to 1963, statutes were referred to by the year of the monarch's reign (the "regnal year") and the chapter number. For example, a citation 3 Edw. 7, c. 36 is a reference to the Motor Car Act 1903, which was the 36th Act passed in the third year of the reign of Edward VII.

A session of Parliament normally commences in the autumn and continues through into the summer of the following year. A "regnal year" is reckoned from the date of the sovereign's accession to the throne and a session of Parliament may therefore cover more than one regnal year. In the case of Queen Elizabeth II, who came to the throne in February, the first part of a Parliamentary session, from the autumn until February, falls into one regnal year, whilst the latter part of the session of Parliament falls into a different regnal year. Statutes passed before February bear a different regnal year to those passed after the anniversary of her accession to the throne. Two examples make this clearer:

1. The Children and Young Persons Act 1956 received the Royal Assent in March 1956, when the Queen had just entered the fifth year of her reign. It was the 24th Act to receive the Royal Assent during the Parliament which commenced sitting in the autumn of the fourth year of her reign, and which continued in session during the early part of the fifth year of her reign. The Act is therefore cited as 4 & 5 Eliz. 2, c. 24.
2. By contrast, the Air Corporations Act 1956 was passed during the following session of Parliament and it received the Royal Assent in December 1956, when the Queen was still in the fifth year of her reign. Since, at that time, there could be no certainty that the Queen would still be on the throne in two months' time or that Parliament would still be in session in February, when she would be entering the sixth year of her reign, the statute was cited as 5 Eliz. 2, c. 3 (i.e. the third Act passed in the Parliament held in the fifth year of the reign). When the Queen subsequently survived to enter her sixth year, the statute would henceforth be referred to as 5 & 6 Eliz. 2, c. 3.

Both these Acts are to be found in the 1956 volumes of the statutes, which contain all the Acts passed during that year, regardless of the session of Parliament in which they were passed.

Until 1939, the volumes of the statutes contained all the Acts passed in a particular session of Parliament. After that date, the annual volumes contain all the statutes passed in a calendar year. This can give rise to some confusion. For instance, the volume for 1937 contains the statutes passed in the parliamentary session which extended from November 1936 to October 1937. Thus, some Acts which actually bear the date 1936 are included in the 1937 volume. The volume for 1938 includes some statutes passed in December 1937 (which one might normally expect to find in the 1937 volume). The simple rule with older Acts is: if it is not in the volume you expect to find it in, look in the volumes on either side of it!

Citation of the names of monarchs and their regnal years

The names of the monarchs are abbreviated as follows: 4.4

Anne	Ann.
Charles	Car., Chas. or Cha.
Edward	Edw. or Ed.
Elizabeth	Eliz.
George	Geo.
Henry	Hen.
James	Ja., Jac. or Jas.
Mary	Mar. or M.
Philip and Mary	Ph. & M. or Phil. & Mar.
Richard	Ric. or Rich.
Victoria	Vict.
William	Will., Wm. or Gul.
William and Mary	Wm. & M., Will. & Mar. or Gul. & Mar.

Lists (or calculators) translating regnal years into the equivalent calendar years can be found on a number of websites, including the JustCite Knowledge Base (at *http://www.justcite.com/kb*) under "Search". A list of the regnal year of monarchs showing the equivalent calendar year can also be found at the back of *Osborn's Concise Law Dictionary*.

MODERN STATUTES

Acts of Parliament are published in print in the red-bound volumes of the Public General Acts & Measures. They also appear online on the legislation.gov.uk website (at *http://www.legislation.gov.uk*), which contains the original text of all Acts from 1988 onwards, along with PDF file versions of the original text of many earlier Acts. These are the official sources of statutes (para.4.6). However, a number of alternative sources for statutes are also available. Which source to use may not be obvious. The following considerations can help ensure that you choose an appropriate source for modern statute law. 4.5

First, you should consider whether you need to consult the current amended text of an Act. Is it important that you are consulting law in force? If so, you should consider using one of the sources introduced in para.4.12. These include subscription services such as Westlaw UK (para.4.14) or the Lexis Library (para.4.13), also the print volumes of *Halsbury's Statutes of England* (para.4.16). The legislation.gov.uk website (para.4.15) is the only free online source of law in force. However, web page alerts need to be checked if you are using legislation.gov.uk in order to ensure that legislation is read as currently in force.

If it is important to see the full text of legislation as originally enacted, then turn to the sources noted in the following sections.

Having decided this, it is useful to consider whether you need to consult a particular section of an Act, or the Act as a whole; online sources are usually best if you wish to find a particular section of an Act (especially if you already have the relevant section number). This could be done using one of the subscription sources of law in force noted above, or a free public source of legislation as enacted. This might be the legislation.gov.uk website (para.4.6) or the BAILII website (para.4.8).

If you wish to gain an understanding of an important piece of legislation taken as a whole, it is worth turning to print editions. Important legislation can be extensive, making it difficult to read and review an entire Act on screen. Your library is likely to have the print volumes of both *Public General Acts & Measures* (para.4.6) and *Current Law Statutes* (para.4.11). These are sources of statutes as originally enacted. *Halsbury's Statutes of England* (para.4.16) is the only print source for statutes in force.

An additional advantage of some print editions is the inclusion of often extensive annotations, which can help direct your understanding of legislation. Both *Current Law Statutes* and *Halsbury's Statutes of England* provide annotations.

There are also books devoted to particular key Acts of Parliament. These can be particularly helpful as they combine detailed comment with a reprinted version of the Act itself. Relevant secondary legislation is usually included. Extracts of parliamentary debates and government white papers might also be found. *Blackstone's Guide to the Human Rights Act 1998* (7th edn 2015) is an example. Student textbooks which reprint key legislation in particular areas may also be available in your library. These are not always annotated. *Blackstone's Statutes on Criminal Law 2015-2016* is an example of such a reprint volume.

Official sources of statutes as originally enacted

4.6 The legislation.gov.uk website lists Public General Acts on its "Browse Legislation" page (at *http://www.legislation.gov.uk/browse*). There are also links to Northern Ireland, Scotland and Wales legislation. Acts are listed chronologically (i.e. in chapter number order), but can be selected by year and sorted by title. If you are sure of the title of an Act, a title search box is available. It will be necessary to include the year of the Act to your search, as many Acts can share the same title words (e.g. "Education Act"). Selecting the title of an Act displays a table of contents page listing the section titles of the revised version of an Act. This can be changed to display the contents of the original version. A link for an "Original Print PDF" of the Act is also displayed. This reproduces the Act as printed by TSO, providing a useful way of both reading and selectively printing from the Act. Sections of an Act are otherwise displayed as separate (and sometimes lengthy) web pages, which are not designed for printing. As noted in para.2.3 above, all Acts passed by Parliament from 1988 onwards are available on the legislation.gov.uk website. A great many pre-1998 Acts can also be found, in both web page and PDF file versions, but coverage for the 19th century and early to mid-20th century is limited. New Acts are added to the legislation.gov.uk within 24 hours of the publication of the Act in printed form.

Acts are printed individually on demand by TSO, the publisher responsible for most UK official print publishing, after they receive the Royal Assent. Bound annual volumes are later published as the official *Public General Acts & Measures* of 2012, 2013 etc. This series of volumes has been published since 1831 (originally under the title *Public General Acts*). There are now a number of volumes for each year. At the front of the annual volumes there is a list of all the Acts passed during the year, in alphabetical order, showing where they are to be found in the bound volumes. There is also a list in chapter number order giving the same information. The General Synod Measures of the Church of England are printed in full at the back of the annual volumes of the *Public General Acts*. A list of Local and Personal Acts published during the year is also printed in the annual volume, although the texts are not included. Most law libraries keep the bound annual volumes, few would keep any individually published Acts.

Alternative sources for the official text of statutes

The BAILII website (para.4.8) reproduces the full text of the post-1987 statutes available on the legislation.gov.uk website, along with revised versions of pre-1988 statutes. The revised statutes do not incorporate any post-2001 amendments. The layout of the BAILII website, along with its more straightforward keyword searching, means that the site can be easier to use than the legislation.gov.uk site. However the mixture of unamended and amended legislation on the BAILII site can make it confusing to use. 4.7

Complete historical coverage online of UK statutes as originally enacted is only offered by Justis UK Statutes (para.4.9). This is a subscription service and not all law libraries can provide access. There are also two print series which reprint the text of statutes as originally enacted. *Law Reports: Statutes* (para.4.10) reproduces the *Public General Acts & Measures* text in a smaller, more easily handled, format. *Current Law Statutes* (para.4.11) prints the same text with additional annotations. Most law libraries will have one or both of these print series.

BAILII United Kingdom Statutes

Statutes can be found on the BAILII website (at *http://www.bailii.org*), under the "United Kingdom" heading. Acts can be found by year of enactment and also alphabetically, using a single A–Z listing for all of the Acts on the site. If you are unsure of the year of an Act, this makes the BAILII site a little easier to use than the legislation.gov.uk alternative. However, prior to 2011, each Act is only reproduced on the site as a single continuous web page. You need to be sure that you want the entire text of an Act before you click to print. From 2011 onwards, PDF page versions of Acts are available. As is the case in the legislation.gov.uk website, the section names in the list of sections near the start of most Acts are hyperlinked to the relevant section. Northern Ireland, Scotland and Wales legislation is also available. 4.8

It is important to bear in mind that only the post-1987 statutes are provided in their complete, unamended form. As noted in para.4.7 above, earlier statutes are provided as in force in 2001. This is because the text of the earlier statutes was derived from the Statute

Law Database, a database of amended legislation which has since been incorporated into the legislation.gov.uk website.

Justis UK Statutes

4.9 The Justis UK Statutes service is the only complete source of United Kingdom statute law available online, containing the full text of all Acts of Parliament from 1235 onwards. It is one of a number of Justis subscription services (see para.2.6), so you need to check if your law library can provide access. Though the text of statutes is presented as enacted, a particular feature of the database is the ability it provides to trace the path of amendment and repeal from one statute to another. For each statute, any amending legislation is presented as a family tree, with the relevant links leading you from statute to statute. Justis UK Statutes is the best source available for tracing the historical development of statute law. As with other subscription services, Acts are presented section by section, making printing easier than is the case with the BAILII website. PDF facsimiles of Acts as they were originally published are also included.

Law Reports: Statutes

4.10 The Incorporated Council of Law Reporting published a series called *Law Reports: Statutes*, until relatively recently, alongside the *Law Reports* and the *Weekly Law Reports*. However, the series did not continue beyond the last annual volume for 2010. The series was published in the same Royal Octavo page size and publishing format as the *Law Reports*. Both unbound parts and annual volumes were issued. The page size adopted meant that the bound volumes of the *Law Reports: Statutes* were appreciably easier to manipulate than the large folio volumes of *Public General Acts & Measures*. As a result a number of law libraries have held (and are likely to retain) the reprint series as well as *Public General Acts & Measures*.

Current Law Statutes Annotated

4.11 *Current Law Statutes Annotated* reprints the full text of all Public General Acts with additional annotations. Recent Acts are kept in a Service File in chapter number order. An alphabetical list of the Acts at the front of the Service File can help you find a particular Act. If the Act you want to look at is not listed, it means that it has not yet been published in this series.

The annotations give a detailed account of the background to the Act, including references to discussions on the Bill in the Houses of Parliament as reported in *Hansard*. They also include a summary of the contents of the Act, as well as definitions and explanations of the meaning of individual sections of the Act. The annotations are in smaller print to avoid confusion with the Act itself. Although the annotations have no official standing, they can be extremely useful.

The information in the Service File is reissued during the year in bound volumes. *Current Law Statutes Annotated* covers all Public General Acts since 1948, when the series commenced publication. Private Acts have been included since 1993. The series has been known as *Current Law Statutes Annotated* since 2005. For most of its publication history it has been known simply as *Current Law Statutes*, apart from a brief period between 1991 and 1993 when it was also titled *Current Law Statutes Annotated*.

SOURCES OF STATUTES AS CURRENTLY IN FORCE

The Lexis Library "Legislation" search (para.4.13), the Legislation search from Westlaw UK (para.4.14) and legislation.gov.uk (para.4.15) all provide online access to statutes as currently in force. The volumes of *Halsbury's Statutes of England* (para.4.16) provide a print alternative. Though both the Lexis Library and Westlaw UK are subscription sources, they are likely to be available in most UK universities. Legislation.gov.uk is a free online resource. However, as noted in para.4.5, alerts need to be checked for updating the legislation. As a result, the Lexis Library and Westlaw UK are preferable alternatives for statutes currently in force. 4.12

It is important to keep in mind the difference between the amended text of legislation provided by these sources and the unamended text of statutes as originally enacted provided by the sources noted in para.4.6 and para.4.7. A simple example might help.

If you look for the text of the Dangerous Dogs Act 1991 using any source of law in force, you will find that some of the text is printed between square brackets. This is text "inserted" under the provisions of another, later, Act; in this case the Dangerous Dogs (Amendment) Act 1997. This is one of the many Acts whose sole purpose is to revise the provisions of an earlier Act. Sometimes complete new sections are added. These have letters attached to their numbers in order to retain the numbering of the original Act. The text of the Dangerous Dogs Act 1991, for example, now contains a section "4A" inserted by the later amending Act (see the illustration below). This new section makes a significant change to the law on the destruction of dangerous dogs. Note that the amended Dangerous Dogs Act 1991 is still the Act to turn to find the relevant legislation on dangerous dogs. It is not superseded by the later Act.

Sections or subsections of an Act can also be "deleted" by later amending legislation. This is shown by the presence of three dots against the subsection. For some Acts, only a single section or part of a section remains in force. This is true of the oldest Acts still in force. Examples can be found if you search for the various Treason Acts in databases of law in force; the earliest one still partly in force dates from 1351.

When using online sources of statutes in force to find legislation, it is also important to check that you have the correct title and year for an Act, including the relevant year. There is only one Human Rights Act for example, but many Education Acts. If you type "Education Act" in the Westlaw UK Legislation search and search for statutes, the result will be a long results list, displaying around 150 separate statutes that match "Education Act". There are even more that include "Education" somewhere in the title.

Once the title of a particular Act has been selected, a search results page opens, displaying the various sections of the Act as a series of discrete database items. Sections of Acts are the basic units of databases of legislation, because in most legal discussion, it is particular sections of Acts that need to be referred to, not the Act as a whole. Making sections the basic database unit also means that links can be created, for example, that take you directly from a reference to legislation in a judgment, to the full text of a section of an Act in a legislation database. The text of law reports available online from the Lexis Library and Westlaw UK is linked to legislation in precisely this way. It is sections of Acts, rather than whole Acts, that can be emailed, printed or saved directly from the

> **TIPS** • *Always enter the exact title of legislation (including the year) when searching databases of legislation in force. Check the title using other sources (e.g. print indexes and textbooks) if you are not sure.*

Fig 4.2
Section 4A of the Dangerous Dogs Act 1991 (reproduced from Westlaw UK)

Dangerous Dogs Act 1991 c. 65

This version in force from: **May 13, 2014** to **present**

(version 3 of 3)

The text of this provision varies depending on jurisdiction or other application. See parallel texts relating to:

England and Wales | Scotland

England and Wales

[**4A.— Contingent destruction orders.**

(1) Where—

(a) a person is convicted of an offence under section 1 above or an aggravated offence under [section 3(1)] [2] above;

(b) the court does not order the destruction of the dog under section 4(1)(a) above; and

(c) in the case of an offence under section 1 above, the dog is subject to the prohibition in section 1(3) above.

the court shall order that, unless the dog is exempted from that prohibition within the requisite period, the dog shall be destroyed.

(2) Where an order is made under subsection (1) above in respect of a dog, and the dog is not exempted from the prohibition in section 1(3) above within the requisite period, the court may extend that period.

(3) Subject to subsection (2) above, the requisite period for the purposes of such an order is the period of two months beginning with the date of the order.

(4) Where a person is convicted of an offence under [section 3(1)] [3] above, the court may order that, unless the owner of the dog keeps it under proper control, the dog shall be destroyed.

(5) An order under subsection (4) above—

(a) may specify the measures to be taken for keeping the dog under proper control, whether by muzzling, keeping on a lead, excluding it from specified places or otherwise; and

(b) if it appears to the court that the dog is a male and would be less dangerous if neutered, may require it to be neutered.

(6) Subsections (2) to (4) of section 4 above shall apply in relation to an order under subsection (1) or (4) above as they apply in relation to an order under subsection (1)(a) of that section.] [1]

database (though PDF versions of whole Acts are available). Notes of amending legislation and relevant secondary legislation are also placed at the end of each section of an Act, not at the end of the Act as a whole.

The Lexis Library Legislation search

UK Statutes can be found using the Lexis Library "Legislation" search. A tick box is pre-selected so that only Acts, rather than Acts and statutory instruments, are searched. A "Sources" box can also be used to restrict the search specifically to "UK Parliament Acts", or to select other available legislation sources, e.g. Scottish Parliament Acts. 4.13

Enter the title of the Act you wish to find in the title search box, adding the year, if known. It helps greatly to have both an exact title and the year of an act, as noted in para.4.11. If the year of an Act is not specified in the Legislation search, the results list displays all sections of all Acts matching, e.g. "Dangerous Dogs". If you only have incomplete details, and more than one Act matches the title keywords entered, check the "Results Groups" displayed in the left hand column of the search results. The full titles and dates of the Acts matching the details you have entered are listed in the "Results Groups" section, allowing individual Acts to be selected. Sections are then only displayed for that Act.

The "Find out more" box displayed in a column beside the text of each section of an Act is a particular strength of the Lexis Library. The "Commentary" link, for example, links directly to any references to the section that might be found in *Halsbury's Laws of England* (para.7.3). Other links include "Is it in force?", which displays commencement information for the section, and "Find related cases". The link for the *Halsbury's Statutes Citator* displays a hyperlinked list of any amending legislation for the section. A PDF file version of the whole Act as in force is also available with annotations for each section noting amending and subordinate legislation.

Westlaw UK Legislation search

Statutes can be searched by title directly from the Westlaw UK home page. More search options are available from the "Legislation" search. These include the possibility of searching for "historic versions" of Acts. These are versions of an Act at a particular, specified, point in time. This can be helpful, for example, if you are studying the decision made in a particular case and wish to consult legislation in force at that time. Historic versions can be found for the period from 1991 onwards. Use the "Advanced Search" within "Legislation" to specify the in force date you wish to use. 4.14

To find Acts as currently in force, use the "Act/SI Title" search box, including the year on the Act in the title if known. If you do not have the year of an Act, all Acts matching your title words are displayed. Once a particular Act is selected the sections of the Act are displayed as individual screen pages. If you wish to view or print an entire Act, the "PDF of entire Act" link found alongside the standard print, save and email options, opens a new window containing a PDF file. As is the case with the Lexis Library, the PDF version shows the Act as in force with annotations for each section noting amending and subordinate legislation.

A screen column, alongside the results display for a particular Act, contains an "Overview Document" showing commencement information, amendments and repeals. Any journal articles discussing the Act as a whole are also noted here.

Legislation.gov.uk

4.15 To find a statute using the legislation.gov.uk website (at *http://www.legislation.gov.uk*), enter the title and year of the Act in the appropriate search boxes on the legislation.gov.uk home page. The search can also be restricted to Public General Acts using the "Type" dropdown selection. The "Advanced Search" adds some useful additional search options. A search for statutes can be restricted, for example, by "Geographical Extent" so that legislation is found as it applies to England and Wales, Scotland, or Northern Ireland (along with all possible combinations of jurisdictions). A "Point in Time" search can also be used to find versions of revised legislation in force at any point in time from 1991 onwards.

The results page for an Act displays the latest revised version available, presenting each section as a separate web page. The "Print Options" link at the top of the results page can, in addition, be used to view PDF versions of the section displayed, or the whole Act, much as is the case with the Lexis Library and Westlaw UK.

However, the text of the statutes on the legislation.gov.uk website is not necessarily presented in its current, fully revised form. The main text has been revised for amendments made to the end of 2002, but by no means all amendments made since 2002 are incorporated into the text of the statutes. If there are still outstanding changes that need to be incorporated, a "Changes to legislation" box is displayed at the top of each section of an Act. A "View outstanding changes" link within the box can then be used to see links to amending legislation.

It is also possible to use legislation.gov.uk to check for all changes made to a particular Act using the "Changes to Legislation" search page. First, enter the Act which interests you in the "Changes that affect" box, then select "Get results" to see a table of all changes to the Act made since 2002 with a note of the kind of change made, e.g. "text amended". A "made by" search form can also be used to isolate changes made by a particular amending Act.

Halsbury's Statutes of England

4.16 *Halsbury's Statutes* differs from the other annotated series of statutes available in print. These reproduce Acts as they were originally printed. The purpose of *Halsbury's Statutes* is to provide the correct and amended text of all legislation in force, whatever the date of Royal Assent. It includes all Public General Acts in force in England and Wales, although the texts of some Acts of limited importance are not printed. The text of each Act is accompanied by notes which provide, for example, details of amendments and relevant case law.

The bulk of *Halsbury's Statutes* consists of over 50 volumes, arranged alphabetically by subject. Volume 1 contains the Acts dealing with agriculture, fisheries and food, whilst Vol.2 contains the law of animals and so on. The current volumes are reissues of the fourth edition of Halsbury's Statutes first published between 1985 and 1992. Legislation post-dating the main volumes appears in the *Current Statutes Service* binders. The annual *Cumulative Supplement* summarises and explains the effect of new Acts, statutory instruments and case law on existing legislation and this in turn is kept up to date by a looseleaf *Noter-Up* service. Some library subscriptions may not include the *Current Statutes Service Binder* and looseleaf *Noter-Up*.

If you know the name of an Act, the easiest way to find it in *Halsbury's Statutes* is by looking in the Alphabetical List of Statutes in the front of the annual paper-covered *Consolidated Index* volume. An example page from the Alphabetical List is shown in fig.4.3. The entry tells you the volume number (in bold type) and the page number in *Halsbury's Statutes* where you will find the full text of the Act. If the volume number in the Alphabetical List of Statutes is followed by (S), you will find the Act printed in the looseleaf *Current Statutes Service* under the volume and page number given. Some Acts are not printed in full in one place, but are divided up, each portion of the Act being printed under the most appropriate subject title. If you want to look at the complete text of an Act which has been split up this way, it may be easier to find the Act in one of the other publications outlined above.

If you want to find the text of a very recent Act, look in the Alphabetical List of Statutes which appears in the first volume of the *Current Statutes Service* under the heading "Contents". The entries give the volume number and page where the text of the Act will be found in the *Current Statutes Service* binders.

Once you have located your Act, either in the main volumes or in the *Current Statutes Service* binders, you will find the official text of the Act. Following each section there are the notes, in smaller type, giving the meaning of words or phrases used, referring to cases on the interpretation of that section and providing details of any amendments which have been made to the text of the Act since it was first passed. You will also find references to statutory instruments which have been passed under the authority granted by that Act. At the beginning of each Act, you are informed when it became law and provided with a summary of the main provisions of the Act. An example page from Vol.19 (2A) of *Halsbury's Statutes* is shown in fig.4.4.

It is important to check that the information on the Act is still up to date (i.e. it has not been amended or repealed). To do this, you will need to consult both the *Cumulative Supplement* and the looseleaf *Noter-up* service.

An example can help show how this works. Suppose you want to know whether there have been changes to the Trade Marks Act 1994 since it was passed. You have looked in the Alphabetical List of Statutes (see fig.4.3) and found the relevant part of the text of the Act in Vol.19 (2A) (see fig.4.4). To find out if this Act has been amended since Vol.19 (2A) was published, turn first to the *Cumulative Supplement* and look at the entries for Vol.19 (2A). The *Cumulative Supplement* lists, volume by volume and page by page, changes which have occurred in the law since each of the main volumes was published. There are a number of entries showing changes to the Trade Marks Act 1994. These include amending legislation and new statutory instruments issued under authority granted by the Act.

The information in the *Cumulative Supplement* is up to date to the end of the preceding year. For more recent changes to the Act, you should consult the looseleaf *Noter-up* service under the appropriate volume and page number. This will tell you of any changes in the law in the last few months.

SUMMARY: FINDING UP-TO-DATE INFORMATION ON AN ACT USING HALSBURY'S STATUTES

1. Look for the name of the Act in the Alphabetical List of Statutes in the paper-covered *Consolidated Index* volume. This will refer you to the appropriate volume (in bold type) and page number. An (S) following the volume number refers you to the *Current Statutes Service*.

Fig 4.3 Example page from the Alphabetical List of Statutes in *Halsbury's Consolidated Index*

Alphabetical List of Statutes	**Treason**
Tokyo Convention Act 1967	**4(1)**, 84
Tonga Act 1970	**10(1)**, 1230
Torts (Interference with Goods) Act 1977	**45 (2008R)**, 1562
Tourism (Overseas Promotion) (Scotland) Act 1984	**9**, 381
Tourism (Overseas Promotion) (Wales) Act 1992	**9**, 440
Town and Country Planning Act 1954	**34(1)**, 191
Town and Country Planning Act 1959—	
ss 22–24, 26, 29, 30, 57, 59, Sch 4	**25(1)**, 559
ss 45, 57, 59	**34(1)**, 220
Town and Country Planning Act 1990	**34(2)**, 2
Town and Country Planning (Scotland) Act 1997	**34(2)**, 800
Town Development Act 1952	**34(1)**, 176
Town Gardens Protection Act 1863	**32**, 20
Town Police Clauses Act 1847—	
ss 1–4, 21, 23–29, 37, 38, 40–66, 68	**36**, 368
ss 1–4, 31	**35(1)**, 47
Town Police Clauses Act 1889	**36**, 491
Towns Improvement Clauses Act 1847	**35(1)**, 40
Trade Descriptions Act 1968	**39(1)**, 86
Trade Marks Act 1994	**19(2A)**, 993
Trade Union and Labour Relations (Consolidation) Act 1992	**16**, 214
Trade Union Reform and Employment Rights Act 1993	**16**, 640
Trading Schemes Act 1996	**9**, 442
Trading with the Enemy Act 1939	**3**, 231
Traffic Calming Act 1992	**38(1)**, 413
Traffic Management Act 2004	**38(2)**, 406
Tramways Act 1870	**36**, 445
Transport Act 1962	**36**, 625
Transport Act 1968	**36**, 764
Transport Act 1978	**36**, 1014
Transport Act 1980	**36**, 1022
Transport Act 1981—	
ss 5–18, 40–43, Schs 2–5, Sch 12, Pts I, II	**39(2)**, 425
ss 35, 41–43	**37**, 96
Transport Act 1982—	
ss 8–15, 17, 20–26, 70–76, Schs 5, 6	**37**, 145
ss 66, 76	**39(2)**, 511
Transport Act 1983—	
ss 1, 2, 6–9, 12, Schedule	**37**, 178
ss 11, 12	**16**, 175
Transport Act 1985	**37**, 437
Transport Act 2000—	
ss 1–107, 273–280, Schs 1, 2, 5–7, 9, Sch 31, Pt I	**4(1)**, 553
ss 108–109C, 112–141, 143, 144, 145A–150, 153–155, 157, 160–199, 215, 227, 240, 241, 244, 247, 248, 250, 253, 254, 260, 263, 268, 272–280, Schs 10, 12, 25, 26, 28, 29, 31	**38(2)**, 91
Transport and Works Act 1992	**38(1)**, 414
Transport Charges &c (Miscellaneous Provisions) Act 1954—	
ss 6, 8, 12–15	**39(2)**, 115
ss 8, 10, 12–15	**36**, 597
Transport (Finance) Act 1982	**37**, 142
Transport for London Act 2008	**26(2)**, 898
Transport Holding Company Act 1972	**36**, 941
Transport (London) Act 1969	**25(1)**, 864
Transport Police (Jurisdiction) Act 1994	**38(1)**, 792
Transport (Wales) Act 2006—	
ss 1–10, 12–17	**38(2)**, 676
ss 11–17	**4(1)**, 719
Travel Concessions (Eligibility) Act 2002	**38(2)**, 342
Treason (1495)	**12(1)**, 78
Treason Act 1351	**12(1)**, 75
Treason Act 1695	**12(1)**, 82
Treason Act 1702	**10(1)**, 131
Treason Act 1814	**12(1)**, 92
Treason Act 1842	**12(1)**, 107

Fig 4.4 Example page from *Halsbury's Statutes*

Trade Marks Act 1994, s 43 *1041*

43 Renewal of registration **[937]**

(1) The registration of a trade mark may be renewed at the request of the proprietor, subject to payment of a renewal fee.

(2) Provision shall be made by rules for the registrar to inform the proprietor of a registered trade mark, before the expiry of the registration, of the date of expiry and the manner in which the registration may be renewed.

(3) A request for renewal must be made, and the renewal fee paid, before the expiry of the registration.

Failing this, the request may be made and the fee paid within such further period (of not less than six months) as may be prescribed, in which case an additional renewal fee must also be paid within that period.

(4) Renewal shall take effect from the expiry of the previous registration.

(5) If the registration is not renewed in accordance with the above provisions, the registrar shall remove the trade mark from the register.

Provision may be made by rules for the restoration of the registration of a trade mark which has been removed from the register, subject to such conditions (if any) as may be prescribed.

(6) The renewal or restoration of the registration of a trade mark shall be published in the prescribed manner.

NOTES

Sub-s (1): May be renewed It was stated in Chapter 4, para 4.31 of the White Paper *Reform of Trade Marks Law* (Cm 1203) (September 1990) that the Government did not intend to introduce an arrangement requiring the proprietor of a registered trade mark to furnish proof of use in order to renew the registration.

Sub-s (1): At the request of the proprietor As to acts done by authorised agents, see s 82 post.

Sub-s (1): Renewal fee As to the payment of fees in respect of applications and registration, etc under this Act, see s 79 post.

See also the second paragraph of the note "Application fee; class fees" to s 32 ante.

Sub-s (2): Rules The Secretary of State may make rules for the purposes of any provision of this Act authorising the making of rules with respect to any matter; see s 78(1)(a) post. See further the note "Rules under this section" below.

Sub-s (2): Expiry of the registration As to the duration of registration, see s 42 ante.

Sub-s (3): Months See the note to s 25 ante.

Sub-s (3): Prescribed This means prescribed by rules made by the Secretary of State; see s 78(1)(b) post. See further the note "Rules under this section" below.

Sub-s (5): Shall remove the trade mark from the register As to the register of trade marks, see ss 63–65 post. As to appeals from decisions of the registrar (including acts of the registrar in exercise of a discretion), see ss 76, 77 post.

Transitional provisions See s 105, Sch 3, para 15(2), (3) post.

Additional information See the Introductory Note(s) to this Act.

Rules under this section
Trade Marks Rules 2008, SI 2008/1797, as amended as noted to s 4 ante.
As to the power of the Secretary of State to make rules, generally, under this Act, see s 78 post.
Further information may be found in the appropriate title of *Halsbury's Statutory Instruments*.

Definitions
"publish": s 103(1)
"the register": s 63(1)
"registered trade mark": s 63(1)
"the registrar": s 62
"registration": s 63(1)
"trade mark": s 1

2. If the Act is very recent, consult the Alphabetical List of Statutes at the front of Vol.1 of the *Current Statutes Service*.
3. Look up the Act in the appropriate volume, or the *Current Statutes Service*, and note the volume number and the page which contains the relevant information.
4. Look to see if there is an entry for your volume and page number in the *Cumulative Supplement*. If there is an entry, there has been a change in the law. Whether or not there is a relevant entry in the *Cumulative Supplement*, you should now turn to the *Noter-up* service (see below).
5. Finally, look for any entries for your volume and page number in the *Noter-up* service. Read this information (if there is any) in conjunction with the information in the main volume and the *Cumulative Supplement*.

Remember the stages:

- main volume;
- *Cumulative Supplement;*
- *Noter-up* service;

and consult them in that order.

TRACING COMMENCEMENTS, AMENDMENTS AND RELEVANT CASE LAW

4.17 The full provisions of an Act do not necessarily all come into force on the same day. The dates of commencement for some sections may differ from those of others. As a result, it is sometimes important to check the commencement date of an individual section of an Act in order to discover the day on which that section came into force, or is due to come into force.

The Westlaw UK "Legislation" search (para.4.18) and the statute law pages of the *Current Law Legislation Citator* (para.4.19) provide the useful means of tracking both commencement dates, amendments and repeals. Both sources have the additional advantage that they draw on the extensive indexing of cases and journal articles which supports both Westlaw UK and the print citator volumes of *Current Law*. However, *Is it in Force?* provides a useful alternative, both in print and online from the Lexis Library if you wish to check commencement dates for legislation. Details of amending legislation can be found using *Halsbury's Statute Citator*.

Is it in Force? can be found online in the "Commentary" section of the Lexis Library service as *Halsbury's Is it in Force?* and in print as a single annual volume associated with *Halsbury's Statutes of England* (para.4.16). Both sources list commencement dates for statutes passed since 1980 by year and then alphabetically by title. Commencement dates are noted by section if there is no single date of commencement for the Act. The online version of *Is it in Force?* has the advantage that commencement dates are added as Acts receive the Royal Assent. The print volume only lists Acts previous to the year of publication. Updates are available in the *Noter Up* service binder of *Halsbury's Statutes*. The *Cumulative Supplement* and *Noter Up* services of *Halsbury's Statutes* also enable you to find out if a statute has been repealed or amended.

If you are interested in a specific section of an Act, the *Is it in Force?* content is more usefully obtained online by first searching for the relevant section using the Lexis Library "Legislation" search (para.4.13). The "Find out more" box associated with that section then provides access, not only to the relevant information contained in *Is it in Force?*, but also to information on amendments provided by *Halsbury's Statutes Citator*.

Lawtel (para.2.5), if available, provides an additional online means of checking commencement dates of law in force, along with details of repeals and amendments. Lawtel's "Legislation" search provides a "Statutory Status Table" for an Act which lays out amendments and commencements section by section.

It might also be important to legal research to gain an understanding of the way an Act has been amended. This necessitates an understanding of the particular impact of one Act on another. This is complicated by the fact that not all amendments are made using amendment Acts such as the Dangerous Dogs (Amendment) Act 1997. Changes can be much harder to track. How has the Children and Families Act 2014, for example, affected the provisions of the Education Act 1996? Online sources of the full text of law in force (para.4.12) could be used to discover this information, but displaying the text of a series of sections of Acts and checking amendments could prove tedious. Fortunately, the "Changes to Legislation" which forms part of the legislation.gov.uk website (para.4.15) can be used to specify the title of the original Act along with the title of the more recent amending legislation. The numbers of sections repealed and amended in the original Act are then listed.

TIPS • *Use the "Changes in Legislation" search on the legislation.gov.uk website to trace how an Act has amended earlier legislation.*

How to use the Westlaw UK Legislation search

To check commencement dates, amendments and relevant case law using the Westlaw UK Legislation search, first search for the Act which interests you as noted in para.4.14, using the full title and year. When a particular section of an Act is displayed, a "Legislation Analysis" link alongside the legislation text provides further links to commencement information and a list of any amending legislation, along with a list of cases citing the particular section displayed. **4.18**

If you search for information on the Dangerous Dogs Act 1991 (the example used in para.4.12) and select the entry for section 4A, the "Legislation Analysis" provides a table of amendments noting all amending legislation. This confirms that the in force version of section 4A (version 2) shows the section as amended by the Dangerous Dogs (Amendment) Act 1997 and the Control of Dogs (Scotland) Act 2010, which added the text of the section as it applies in Scotland. The Anti-social Behaviour, Crime and Policing Act 2014 also deleted words in two sections. Section 4A was added to the original Dangerous Dogs Act 1991, so there are effective dates for the amending legislation, but no commencement date is given. Related legislation is shown in the penultimate heading.

The "Cases Citing" heading of the Legislation Analysis notes 12 cases which have cited the section. Key cases are listed first, the most recent being *R. (on the application of Ali) v Chief Constable of Merseyside* [2014] EWHC 4772 (Admin), [2015] Crim.L.R. 645. There are no journal citations at this level, but the "General Materials" link displayed alongside all sections of the Act lists 14 journal articles citing the Act.

Fig 4.5 Cases Citing section from the Westlaw UK Legislation Analysis page

Key Cases Citing

s. 4A

R. (on the application of Ali) v Chief Constable of Merseyside
[2014] EWHC 4772 (Admin); (2015) 179 J.P. 333; [2015] Crim. L.R. 645 (QBD (Admin))

R. (on the application of Hooker) v Ipswich Crown Court
[2013] EWHC 2899 (Admin) (DC)

R. v Singh (Navdeep)
[2013] EWCA Crim 2416 (CA (Crim Div))

Kelleher v DPP
[2012] EWHC 2978 (Admin); (2012) 176 J.P. 729; [2013] A.C.D. 21 (QBD (Admin))

R. v Davies (Grant David Robert)
[2010] EWCA Crim 1923; (2010) 174 J.P. 514 (CA (Crim Div))

R. v Baballa (Moses)
[2010] EWCA Crim 1950; [2011] 1 Cr. App. R. (S.) 50 (CA (Crim Div))

All Cases Citing

s. 4A

R. (on the application of Ali) v Chief Constable of Merseyside
[2014] EWHC 4772 (Admin); (2015) 179 J.P. 333; [2015] Crim. L.R. 645 (QBD (Admin))

R. (on the application of Hooker) v Ipswich Crown Court
[2013] EWHC 2899 (Admin) (DC)

Brough v St Helens MBC
[2013] EWHC 4747 (Admin) (QBD (Admin))

R. v Singh (Navdeep)
[2013] EWCA Crim 2416 (CA (Crim Div))

R. (on the application of Sandhu) v Isleworth Crown Court
[2012] EWHC 1658 (Admin); (2012) 176 J.P. 537 (DC)

Kelleher v DPP
[2012] EWHC 2978 (Admin); (2012) 176 J.P. 729; [2013] A.C.D. 21 (QBD (Admin))

How to use the Current Law Legislation Citator

The *Current Law Legislation Citator* enables you to track changes to legislation in print, using a series of bound volumes listing references to amending legislation. Commencement orders can also be traced. The first volume details changes to Acts (of whatever age) that took place between 1947 and 1971. A number of other volumes cover the changes made in following years (again irrespective of the date of the statute changed), concluding with the most recent full year. More current developments can be checked using the *Current Law Monthly Digest*. The *Current Law Legislation Citator* volumes feature both a "Statute Citator" section and a "Statutory Instrument Citator" section. The exception is the first volume in the series, which was published as the *Current Law Statute Citator*. 4.19

Acts are listed by year and in chronological (i.e. chapter number) order in each of the volumes. A helpful alphabetical list of statutes at the start of each bound volume can be used to check the chapter number if this is not already known. If changes have occurred to an Act, these are listed section by section in the volume covering the years in which the changes were made. The year and chapter numbers are given of amending Acts, and commencement orders are referred to by statutory instrument number. As a result, the information contained in each volume can take time to decode, as the relevant Act or statutory instrument needs to be found in order to check the details of an amendment, or the date legislation came into force. Citations are also given for cases which have interpreted a particular section of an Act.

It is important to remember that it may be necessary to use more than one volume of the *Citator* to gain a complete picture of legislative change or relevant case law. Details of the changes made to the Dangerous Dogs Act 1991, for example, need to be traced in the *Current Law Legislation Citator* volumes covering 1989 to 1995 and 1996 to the present. The changes made by the Dangerous Dogs (Amendment) Act 1997 can only be found in the volume covering 1996 to 1999. For the most recent case law interpreting the Act you need to use the current volume.

Chronological Table of the Statutes

The *Chronological Table of the Statutes* is an official publication which lists every statute which has been passed since 1235, and shows, for each one, whether it is still law. This is done by the use of different type faces—an entry in italic type indicates that the statute in question is no longer law, whilst entries in bold type represent Acts which are still wholly or partly in force. 4.20

Entries for Acts are arranged in date order in three print volumes. Part 1 currently covers 1235–1968; Part 2 covers 1969–1992; Part 3 covers 1993–2013. If a complete section of an Act, or an entire Act, has been repealed, the abbreviation "r" is used, followed by a note of the repealing legislation. Other abbreviations used are explained at the front of Pt 1.

Unfortunately, the *Chronological Table* is usually two or three years out of date. It has been updated by an annual publication, entitled *The Public General Acts and General Synod Measures: 20 . . . : Tables and Index*. This may not be published separately in future. The last volume, for 2012, was published in 2013.

The Public General Acts: Tables and Index is also printed at the end of the annual volumes of the *Public General Acts and Measures*. Recent amendments to statutes can be checked using the "Changes to Legislation" search on the legislation.gov.uk website, as noted in para.4.17.

OLDER STATUTES

4.21 Acts, or sections of Acts, which are in force, whatever their date, can be found in the online and print sources introduced in para.4.12. However, it will sometimes be necessary to look at an Act of Parliament which is no longer in force and dates back beyond 1831 when the Public General Acts series (para.4.6) was first published. These can be found in the collections described below and in the Justis UK Statutes database (para.4.9).

The earliest statute which is still part of the law of the land was passed in 1267. The first parliamentary statute dates from 1235 (the Statute of Merton), although some collections of the statutes commence in 1225. Collections of the legislation prior to 1225 do exist (e.g. A.J. Robertson, *The Laws of the Kings of England from Edmund to Henry I*) but they are not regarded as forming part of the statutes of the realm.

Statutes of the Realm

4.22 Produced by the Record Commission, *Statutes of the Realm* is generally regarded as the most authoritative collection of the early statutes. It covers statutes from 1235 to 1713, including those no longer in force, and prints the text of all Private Acts before 1539. There are alphabetical and chronological indexes to all the Acts and there is a subject index to each volume, as well as an index to the complete work. An online version of the *Statutes of the Realm* volumes covering the period from 1628 onwards can be found on the British History Online website (at *http://www.british-history.ac.uk*). This is a non-subscription website and the volumes form part of the "Parliamentary history" and the "Sources" pages. If your university subscribes to the *English Reports* from HeinOnline, all 11 volumes of the Statutes are available as part of the English Reports Library.

Statutes at Large

4.23 The title of *Statutes at Large* was given to various editions of the statutes, most of which were published during the 18th century. They normally cover statutes published between the 13th and the 18th or 19th centuries. The text used in the Justis UK Statutes database (para.4.9) is taken from Ruffhead's editions of *Statutes at Large* for the period pre-dating the *Public General Acts* series. Scanned online versions of Ruffhead's editions can be found in Eighteenth Century Collections Online (ECCO), available to all UK universities, though the screen images of the original volumes can be difficult to use.

Acts and Ordinances of the Interregnum

4.24 Acts passed during the Commonwealth are excluded from the collections of the statutes mentioned above. They can be found in C.H. Firth and R.S. Rait, *Acts and Ordinances of the Interregnum 1642–1660*. The Firth and Rait edition of the *Acts and Ordinances* can be found online from the British History Online website (at *http://www.british-history.ac.uk*) in the "Parliamentary history" section, along with the Statutes of the Realm.

LOCAL AND PERSONAL ACTS

In addition to *Public General Acts*, which apply to the whole population or a substantial part of it, there are also a few Local and Personal Acts passed each year. These Acts affect only a particular area of the country or a particular individual or body, e.g. City of London (Various Powers) Act 2014; Humber Bridge Act 2014. 4.25

The chapter number of a Local Act is printed in roman numerals, to distinguish it from the Public General Act of the same number. Thus the Humber Bridge Act may be cited as 2014, c. vi (i.e. the 6th Local Act passed in 2014), whilst 2014, c. 6 is the citation for a Public General Act, the Children and Families Act 2014.

Personal Acts are cited in the same way as Public General Acts, but with the chapter number printed in italics, e.g. *c. 3*. The citation of Local and Personal Acts was amended in 1963. Prior to that date, they are cited by regnal years, in the same way as Public General Acts, e.g. 12 & 13 Geo. 5, c. xiv relates to a Local Act, whilst 12 & 13 Geo. 5, c. 14 is a Public General Act (para.4.3).

Local and Personal Acts are listed in alphabetical order in the annual *Local and Personal Acts 20 . . . : Tables and Index*, which can also be found in the bound volumes of the *Public General Acts and Measures*. From 1991 onwards, Local Acts are available on the legislation.gov.uk website (at *http://www.legislation.gov.uk*). In addition, HMSO published two cumulative indexes: the *Index to Local and Personal Acts 1801–1947* and the *Supplementary Index to the Local and Personal Acts 1948–1966*.

Although most libraries will possess copies of the Public General Acts in some form, printed copies of the Local and Personal Acts are not so widely available. Those which are published are listed in the TSO Daily Lists, which are cumulated in the TSO Catalogues. Local Acts since 1992 are printed in the final volume of *Current Law Statutes Annotated* each year. To obtain a copy of the text of an older Local Act or a Personal Act, you may need to contact the local library or the organisation affected by the legislation.

STATUTORY INSTRUMENTS

In order to reduce the length and complexity of statutes and increase flexibility in the light of changing circumstances, Parliament may include in an Act an "enabling" section, which grants to some other authority (usually a Minister of the Crown) power to make detailed rules and regulations on a principle laid down in general terms by the Act. The various Road Traffic Acts, for example, give the Secretary of State for Transport power, amongst other things, to impose speed limits on particular stretches of road, to vary these limits at any time, to create experimental traffic schemes, to introduce new road signs, to control the construction and use of vehicles and to impose regulations concerning parking, pedestrian crossings, vehicle licences, insurance and numerous other aspects of the law relating to motor vehicles. An advantage of this power is that the rules can be readily changed, without the necessity for Parliamentary debate and approval of every amendment. 4.26

Statutory instruments, together with statutory codes of practice and byelaws, form what is called *secondary* or *subordinate* legislation, often also called *delegated* legislation, since Parliament has delegated the power to make this legislation to another authority.

The term *statutory instruments* is a generic one, and includes rules, regulations and orders. Commencement orders are a particularly important type of statutory instrument, since they set the date for the commencement of an Act or bring certain provisions of an Act into force (see point 7 of para.4.2). Like statutes, statutory instruments may be of general or of purely local interest. Local instruments are not always printed and published in the normal way. An Order of Council, made by the Queen and her Privy Council, is also a form of statutory instrument. These are printed as an appendix to the annual volumes of statutory instruments, together with Royal Proclamations and Letters Patent.

Citation of statutory instruments

4.27 Each statutory instrument published during the year is given its own number. The official citation is: SI year/number. For example, the Films (Definition of "British Film") Order was the 86th statutory instrument to be passed in 2015 and its citation is therefore SI 2015/86.

Statutory instruments typically have a title which includes the word "Rules", "Regulations" or "Order", e.g. Rules of the Supreme Court, the Safety of Sports Grounds (Designation) Order, the Registration of Births and Deaths Regulations. If you are undecided whether the document you are seeking is a statutory instrument, check in the Alphabetical List of Statutory Instruments in *Halsbury's Statutory Instruments* (if available).

Tracing statutory instruments

4.28 Statutory instruments are listed by year and number on the "Browse Legislation" page of the legislation.gov.uk website (at *http://www.legislation.gov.uk*). The full text is available and complete coverage begins in 1987. A limited selection of statutory instruments is available for the period 1948 to 1986. Details of new statutory instruments are published in the TSO Daily Lists (para.6.15) and paper copies of single statutory instruments can also be purchased from TSO. Bound volumes are available for previous years and may be held by your library. The instruments have been printed in numerical order since 1962; before that date, they were arranged by subject. The last volume of each yearly set contains a subject index to all the instruments published during the year.

All the statutory instruments that were still in force at the end of 1948 were reprinted in a series of volumes entitled *Statutory Rules and Orders and Statutory Instruments Revised*. This was arranged in subject order, showing all the instruments which were then in force.

The full, unrevised, text of statutory instruments from 1987 onwards is also available online from the BAILII website (para.2.15) and the Justis UK Statutory Instruments database (para.2.6). The Justis UK Statutory Instruments Archive provides online access to the full, unrevised, text of all statutory instruments published between 1671 and 1986. Both Justis databases are subscription databases, so you will need to check if your library can provide access.

The databases of law in force noted in para.4.12 contain both statutes and statutory instruments in their legislation searches. Use the full title (including year and statutory instrument number if known) when searching these databases. Database results are presented as described in para.4.12. The print volumes of *Halsbury's Statutory Instruments* (para.4.29) provide an alternative approach to tracing statutory instruments in force.

Halsbury's Statutory Instruments

Halsbury's Statutory Instruments provides up-to-date information on every statutory instrument of general application in force in England and Wales. It does not reproduce the text of all statutory instruments in force. Instead it reproduces the text of a selected number and provides summaries of others. The work consists of 22 volumes, in which the statutory instruments are arranged in broad subject categories. The service is kept up to date by a *Service* binder containing notes of changes in the law and the text of selected new instruments. 4.29

If you know the year and number of a statutory instrument, the easiest way to locate it in *Halsbury's Statutory Instruments* is through the Chronological List of Instruments in the *Service* binder. Alternatively, if you know the name of the statutory instrument, look in the Alphabetical List in the back of the annual paperback volume of the *Consolidated Index*. You may, for example, be looking for information on the Flexible Working Regulations 2014. The relevant page from the Alphabetical List is shown in fig.4.6. The list tells us that the number of the statutory instrument is 1398 and that it has been allocated the subject title "Employment" in *Halsbury's Statutory Instruments*. (Entries in the chronological list in the *Service* binder are displayed in the same way.)

On the inside front cover of each of the main volumes, there is a list of subject titles, indicating in which volume they are printed. "Employment" is located in Vol.7(1). Turn to the Chronological List of Instruments at the beginning of the section headed "Employment" in Vol.7(1). A page reference is given for the entry in the volume for the statutory instrument itself. The text of the Flexible Working Regulations 2014 is printed in full.

Subsequent changes are recorded in the Monthly Survey Section of the *Service* binder. The Monthly Survey is arranged by subject titles as in the main volumes. Look for the number of the instrument in the "Amendments and Revocations" section.

Checking whether a statutory instrument is in force or has been amended

If you have searched for and found a statutory instrument using one of the online sources of legislation in force (para.4.12), you do not need any further confirmation that it remains in force. The same applies if you are using the print volumes of *Halsbury's Statutory Instruments* (para.4.29). However, for some important statutory instruments, you may wish to track whether the statutory instrument has been amended, and if so, the dates at which different provisions came into force. This might be the case, for example, if you were tracking the way EU directives have been implemented in the UK, since implementation generally makes use of statutory instruments rather than statutes. The Westlaw UK "Legislation" search provides the best way of tracking such changes. Suppose you wish to track changes to the Working Time Regulations which implement EU legislation on working time. You might begin by searching for the Working Time Regulations 1998/1833 using the Legislation title search. Commencement information and amending legislation can then be checked for the separate parts of the Regulations using the entries under "Legislation analysis", just as it can for the sections of an Act (para.4.18). The Working Time Regulations 1998/1833 have been amended a number of times, for example, by the Working Time (Amendment) Regulations 2003/1684 and the Working Time (Amendment) (No.2) Regulations 2009/2766 as changes concerning different categories of workers have been made to the original regulations. Case law citing the different parts of the 1998 Regulations can also be found. 4.30

Fig 4.6 Example page from the Consolidated Index of *Halsbury's Statutory Instruments*

Flexible *Alphabetical List of Instruments*

Serial No	*Description*	*Title*
3236	Flexible Working (Eligibility, Complaints and Remedies) Regulations 2002	Employment
3207	Flexible Working (Procedural Requirements) Regulations 2002	Employment
1398	Flexible Working Regulations 2014	Employment
865	Flood and Coastal Erosion Risk Management Information Appeal (Wales) Regulations 2011 (W 127)	Water
1770	Flood and Water Management Act 2010 (Commencement No 1 and Transitional Provisions) (England) Order 2011	Water
2169	Flood and Water Management Act 2010 (Commencement No 1 and Transitional Provisions) Order 2010	Water
95	Flood and Water Management Act 2010 (Commencement No 2) Order 2011	Water
1590	Flood and Water Management Act 2010 (Commencement No 2, Transitional and Savings Provisions) (England) Order 2013	Water
694	Flood and Water Management Act 2010 (Commencement No 3 and Transitional Provisions) Order 2011	Water
2204	Flood and Water Management Act 2010 (Commencement No 4 and Transitional Provisions) Order 2011	Water
2856	Flood and Water Management Act 2010 (Commencement No 5 and Transitional Provisions) Order 2011	Water
879	Flood and Water Management Act 2010 (Commencement No 6 and Transitional Provisions) Order 2012	Water
2000	Flood and Water Management Act 2010 (Commencement No 7) Order 2012	Water
2048	Flood and Water Management Act 2010 (Commencement No 8 and Transitional Provisions) Order 2012	Water
2880	Flood Risk (Amendment) (Wales) Regulations 2011 (W 308)	Water
1102	Flood Risk (Cross Border Areas) Regulations 2010	Water
2232	Flood Risk Management Functions Order 2010	Water
697	Flood Risk Management Overview and Scrutiny Committee (England) Regulations 2011	Water
3042	Flood Risk Regulations 2009	Water
261	Fluorinated Greenhouse Gases Regulations 2009	Environment
3238	Food Additives (England) Regulations 2009	Agriculture
2210	Food Additives, Flavourings, Enzymes and Extraction Solvents (England) Regulations 2013	Agriculture
2591	Food Additives, Flavourings, Enzymes and Extraction Solvents (Wales) Regulations 2013 (W 255)	Agriculture
3378	Food Additives (Wales) Regulations 2009 (W 300)	Agriculture
1798	Food and Animal Feedingstuffs (Products of Animal Origin from China) (Emergency Control) (Wales) Regulations 2002 (W 173)	Agriculture
1770	Food and Environment Protection Act 1985 (Guernsey) (Amendment) Order 1997	Water
665	Food and Environment Protection Act 1985 (Guernsey) Order 1987	Water
3205	Food and Environment Protection Act 1985 (Isle of Man) (Revocation) Order 1994	Water
1771	Food and Environment Protection Act 1985 (Jersey) (Amendment) Order 1997	Water
667	Food and Environment Protection Act 1985 (Jersey) Order 1987	Water
1232	Food (Animal Products from Belgium) (Emergency Control) (Revocation) (England and Wales) Order 2000	Agriculture
2289	Food (Emergency Control) (Revocation) (England) Regulations 2006	Agriculture
2830	Food (Emergency Control) (Revocation) (Wales) Regulations 2006 (W 251)	Agriculture
3235	Food Enzymes Regulations 2009	Agriculture
3377	Food Enzymes (Wales) Regulations 2009 (W 299)	Agriculture
3051	Food for Particular Nutritional Uses (Addition of Substances for Specific Nutritional Purposes) (England) Regulations 2009	Agriculture
3254	Food for Particular Nutritional Uses (Addition of Substances for Specific Nutritional Purposes) (Wales) Regulations 2009 (W 283)	Agriculture
2591	Food for Particular Nutritional Uses (Miscellaneous Amendments) (England) Regulations 2007	Agriculture
295	Food for Particular Nutritional Uses (Miscellaneous Amendments) (England) Regulations 2010	Agriculture
2753	Food for Particular Nutritional Uses (Miscellaneous Amendments) (Wales) Regulations 2007 (W 232)	Agriculture

460 **Enquiry Bureau hsieb@lexisnexis.co.uk**

The Statutory Instrument Citator section of the *Current Law Legislation Citator* provides a print alternative to the Westlaw UK "Legislation" search. Search for statutory instruments by year and number.

Tracing statutory instruments made under a particular Act

The Westlaw UK "Legislation" search (para.4.18) provides an effective way of searching for statutory instruments made under a particular Act. Search for an Act by title and check the entries for individual sections to find a list of statutory instruments made under powers granted in that section. Links are available to the full text of the relevant statutory instrument. In the entry for section 1 of the Dangerous Dogs Act 1991, for example, an entry can be found for the Dangerous Dogs (Designated Types) Order 1991/1743 and the Dangerous Dogs Exemption Schemes (England and Wales) Order 2015/138. A similar approach can be used with the Lexis Library legislation search (para.4.13). 4.31

Lawtel (para.2.5) provides an alternative online approach to tracing statutory instruments made under an Act. For statutes passed since 1984, Lawtel provides links to all statutory instruments which are enabled by the Act. Again, search by the title of the Act. The "Statutory Status Table" provides links to the relevant statutory instruments. *Halsbury's Statutes* (para.4.16) provides a print alternative for tracing statutory instruments made under an Act.

5 Journals

TYPES OF JOURNALS

5.1 It is essential that you are aware of what has been written in journals (or periodicals). Understanding how to make use of articles published in journals is a vital element in your preparation for seminars, assignments and moots. Law journals do not just keep lawyers up to date with developments in the law, they also publish extensive legal research articles, running to many pages, that aim to provide an in-depth analysis of the nature of law and legal developments taking place in the UK and across the world. It is these articles that take you beyond what is written in textbooks, which are always to some degree out of date and limited in their coverage.

For convenience, a distinction can be made between journals aimed at the legal profession, and academic journals that publish more extensive research articles, although there is some overlap between the two. They are, however, treated in much the same way by libraries. The journals aimed at the legal profession are often published weekly. Examples would be the *New Law Journal*, *Justice of the Peace*, the *Solicitors Journal* and the *Law Society Gazette*. They provide reports and comments on recent cases, statutes, statutory instruments and the latest trends and developments in the law, together with some longer articles, usually on topical or practical subjects. They focus on UK law, taking into account EU law and the case law of the European Court of Human Rights. The articles are often written by legal practitioners. Other journals in this category are more specialist, and are effectively newsletters designed as current awareness bulletins for practitioners. Examples would be the *Property Law Bulletin*, and *Simon's Tax Intelligence*. They are only a few pages in length and summarise and briefly comment on the latest legal developments.

Academic journals, in contrast, are published less frequently. Along with lengthy articles, they are likely to contain book reviews and sometimes comments on recent cases and statutes. Some examples are the *Law Quarterly Review*, the *Modern Law Review* (six issues a year) and the *Journal of Law and Society* (four issues a year). Many of the academic journals are devoted to specific subject areas. Examples would by the *Criminal Law Review* (monthly), the *Journal of Environmental Law* (three issues a year) and the *Journal of Immigration, Asylum and Nationality Law* (four issues a year). Articles in these journals are likely to be written by university academics and are not necessarily confined to UK law. They are often comparative and international, taking into account international law and the law of other jurisdictions, as well as European law. The comparative and international aspect of academic legal research, also means that academic journals published outside the UK can be as important to legal research as those published by UK publishers. Examples are the *Yale Law Journal* (eight issues a year), the *Harvard Law Review* (eight issues a year), the *Canadian Bar Review* (four issues a year) and the *Australian Law Journal* (monthly).

An important aspect of articles published in academic journals is the 'peer review' process that will have taken place before an article is published. When an article is submitted to a journal for publication, the advice of experts in the relevant subject area is sought to ensure that the article meets the quality standards expected of an academic publication. They will consider the accuracy, originality and significance of the article, for example, and ensure that it fully takes into account other academic research in the subject area. They may also make recommendations and suggestions for changes. This means you can place some reliance on the content of the articles. Only those articles which reach the quality standards of the journal are published.

Online access to journals

Almost all law journals are available online. Some are directly available from the publishers own website, others from an intermediary archive site such as HeinOnline or JSTOR. Almost all universities subscribe to HeinOnline, an American archive of online journal articles, which has also added archives of some UK and European journals. Non-US titles include the *Modern Law Review* and the *European Journal of International Law*. The JSTOR journals archive contains some law journals, along with a significant number of politics and social science journals of potential value for legal research. Many journals can, in addition, be found in the full-text journal content available from the Lexis Library (para.2.3) and Westlaw UK (para.2.4). This means there is no single route to online versions of journal articles, complicating access. ▶ 5.2

Your library website is the best place to start if you wish to discover whether you have access to a particular journal online. Entries made for a journal in the library catalogue, for example, will feature links to website or database sources that provide full-text access to a journal. A separate journal finder, or A–Z list of journals by title, is often also present. These resources enable you to discover whether a particular journal is available, and provide links to the appropriate website or database for access. Current issues of a particular journal may, for example, be available for you from the publisher's website, archive issues might be available from HeinOnline or JSTOR.

It is important to remember that a subscription must be paid by your library before you can be provided with access to the full-text content of a journal. This means that though your library will be able to provide access to a very large number of journals, it cannot give you full-text access to all journals currently being published. There are simply too many. Often library subscriptions will include all the journals published by the major UK academic journal publishers, such as the Oxford University Press, the Cambridge University Press, and Taylor and Francis, but you cannot rely on this being the case. Even then, library subscriptions may not cover access to all issues. Access to older, "archive" issues of a journal, published before the mid-1990s, is often sold separately, so you may find that the earliest issues of a journal are not available, even when current or recent issues are. There are, in any case, many journals potentially relevant to your research not published by the major UK academic publishers. Your library is likely to subscribe to some of these on a title by title basis.

As many of the law journals available online can be found in the Lexis Library or Westlaw UK, it is also worth familiarising yourself with the journal titles available from these two sources

Fig 5.1 Example page from an article in the *Oxford Journal of Legal Studies*

Oxford Journal of Legal Studies, Vol. 31, No. 3 (2011), pp. 437–453
doi:10.1093/ojls/gqr012

Rights, Laws and Language

AMARTYA SEN*

Abstract—Words have meanings, often more than one. Many words also have evocative power and communicative reach. It is important to look beyond the legal route in making human rights more effective, and to endorse but proceed beyond human rights being seen as motivation only for legislation (the particular connection on which Herbert Hart commented). Within the legal route itself there is the important issue of interpretation of law that can stretch beyond the domain of fresh legislation. In assessing the 'originalist' disciplines of legal interpretation, the article discusses the distinction between interpreting the original text in terms of changing linguistic conventions (on which some commentators have focused) and taking note of public reasoning today in the light of the original 'constitutional motivation'.

Keywords: human rights, rules of language, words and meanings, originalism, constitutional motivation

1. *Introduction*

I feel very fortunate in having this opportunity of talking today in memory of Herbert Hart. I have drawn on Hart's ideas for many years and have also valued the encouragement and affection I always received from him. Hart was a far-reaching social thinker in addition to being one of the outstanding legal and political philosophers of our time, and he taught us a great deal about how these distinct disciplines interrelate. As will be clear from what I will try to say in this talk, I have been much influenced by the broad perspective on legal and political philosophy that Herbert Hart presented to us.

* Lamont University Professor, and Professor of Economics and Philosophy, at Harvard University. Email: asen@fas.harvard.edu. I have greatly benefitted from discussions with, and suggestions from, Bernard Bailyn, Stephen Breyer, Charles Fried, Joseph Raz, Emma Rothschild, Stephen Sedley and Leon Wieseltier. I am also most grateful for wonderful editorial assistance from Aditya Balasubramanian and Laura Bennett. This is an extended version of my HLA Hart Memorial Lecture given on 17 May 2010.

© The Author 2011. Published by Oxford University Press. All rights reserved. For permissions, please e-mail: journals.permissions@oup.com in particular, assuming both are available. This can be done by selecting the "Browse" option from the "Journals" search page present in both the Lexis Library and Westlaw UK. The Lexis Library, as might be expected, holds the full text of LexisNexis Butterworths journals, along with journals from some other publishers (over 60 titles in all). Westlaw UK provides access to approximately 80 titles, including those from Sweet & Maxwell. There is no overlap in the journal coverage provided by the two services. However, some of the journals available from the Lexis Library and Westlaw UK are also available from the websites of the relevant journal publishers. This is true of the *Oxford Journal of Legal Studies*, for example, which can be found in the Lexis Library and also accessed from the Oxford University Press website.

Subscriptions to the full range of titles from particular publishers also means that quick and effective searches can be made from the websites of the journal publishers. Archives such as HeinOnline and JSTOR can also be searched directly in a similar way. As noted though in para.2.8, you need to use library links to these websites if you are off campus, in order to confirm that you have access rights to the full text of articles from these sources. The library web pages are again the key. Search the library catalogue by the name of the publisher or archive, or look for any A–Z or other list of databases available.

An important recent trend in recent years has been the move towards "open access" for journal articles. Though a relatively small number of subscription-free open access law journals have been published on the internet for many years, journal articles from subscription journal publishers are now becoming available in free-to-access versions. A small and slowly growing number of these articles are available directly from the journal publisher websites themselves. Though the great majority of articles published in a journal will require a subscription before the full text can be accessed, a few articles might be available even where your library has no subscription to the journal. This is the result of UK funding which has allowed universities to pay publishers to make particular articles available to everyone. A more significant trend is the creation by universities of web repositories or archives of articles published by their academic staff. These repositories include articles accepted by journal publishers, usually available in their final draft form, incorporating any changes made as a result of the peer review process noted in para.5.1, but lacking publisher pagination. Unfortunately, agreements entered into with academic journal publishers when an article is accepted for publication, mean that the full text of these open access articles can only be made available one to two years after journal publication. Open access articles can be found using the keyword searches described in para.5.5.

FINDING A JOURNAL ARTICLE ONLINE IF YOU ALREADY HAVE A REFERENCE

Journal references, or citations, found in the bibliographies and footnotes of books, or on course reading lists, need to be understood before you can find the article online. You might, for example, find something like the following in a course reading list: 5.3

Sen, Amartya, "Rights, Laws and Language" (2011) 31 O.J.L.S. 437

The simplest approach to finding this article online, is to use a keyword search as described in para.5.5 and search using the full title of the article, "Rights, Laws and Language", adding quotation marks to ensure that articles matching the exact phrase are likely to appear at or near the top of the search results page. Author names could also be added if, as here, the title uses very common words. This approach will be successful much of the time. However, web search engines and online indexes do not encompass all possible sources for a journal article. The source found may also not be the correct subscription source for your library. If a title keyword search fails, the remaining publication details found in the journal citation provide the information needed to continue your search.

To search further, any abbreviations used for the title of the journal publishing the article, must first be deciphered. A journal citation, like those for law reports, is likely to use standard abbreviations for the journal name, whereas library catalogues and databases use the full spelled-out version. The Cardiff Index to Legal Abbreviations (at *http://www.legalabbrevs.cardiff.ac.uk*) provides the best online source for interpreting abbreviations and additional print sources are noted in para.3.5. In the example given above, O.J.L.S. stands for the *Oxford Journal of Legal Studies*.

When you have the full title of the journal, check library A–Z journal lists or the library catalogue for access as noted in para.5.2. If library subscriptions allow full-text access from the publisher's website or an intermediary database, an entry will be found. In this case, the entry for the *Oxford Journal of Legal Studies* will provide links to the appropriate source.

Once connected to the appropriate source, search the publisher's site or the intermediary database in order to find the relevant year and volume number of the journal article you wish to find, browsing the journal archive and selecting the relevant year, 2011 (Vol.31) in the example given above. Journal websites usually group articles for a year or volume using issue numbers which are not given in standard legal journal citations. As a result the first page of the article is often a useful means of locating the appropriate issue, in this case p.437.

If the journal article you wish to find is available from either the Lexis Library (para.2.3) or Westlaw UK (para.2.4), an approach similar to that used for a publisher archive can be adopted. If the journal is available from the Lexis Library, select the "Journals" tab from the Lexis Library home page. Title, author and citation searches are available, but be sure to enter the details you have accurately. A small error in title or citation, for example, means that an article will be missed.

The process is much the same for the "Journals" search on Westlaw UK. Select the search from the home page, then enter the title of the journal article in the "Article Title" search box. As the journals search in Westlaw UK includes article details drawn from the wide-ranging entries of the *Legal Journals Index* (para.5.5), you may also find it necessary to add an author surname in the "Author" search box in order to narrow down the number of potential title matches.

Both the Lexis Library and Westlaw UK also include a browse facility on their "Journals" pages. Selecting "Full Text Articles" in the browse section of the Westlaw UK journals page, for example, displays an alphabetical list of the journals available in full text versions on Westlaw UK. Particular publication years can then be selected and the contents list for individual issues displayed with full-text links to the articles themselves.

FINDING A JOURNAL ARTICLE IN PRINT

Very few current journals are now held in print by university libraries. A small number of current awareness or newsletter publications aimed at the legal profession might be held in a separate current journals or periodicals area, along with a selection of academic journals, usually retained in print because online versions are unavailable or prohibitively expensive. However, a much larger archive of bound print volumes is likely to have been retained of titles which have ceased publication, or for which recent print issues are no longer held. Although most of the articles contained in these bound volumes are available online, there are exceptions. If you have failed to find a journal article online, it is worth checking for the possibility that the article you are looking for is held by your library in print. 5.4

A full journal citation is needed to find an article in print. Any abbreviations used for the journal title will also need to be deciphered as noted in para.5.3. Once you have the full title of the journal which published the article, the library catalogue can then be searched to find the location of the bound volumes of the journal on the library shelves.

If a journal is held in print by your library, the library location is displayed in the catalogue entry for the journal. In most cases there are separate entries for print and online versions of a journal. The last copy received is also noted if there is still a current print subscription to the journal. Law journals are usually arranged alphabetically by title in a single sequence in an area set aside for bound journal volumes.

FINDING ARTICLES ONLINE USING KEYWORDS

You could rely on footnotes in recent books or journal articles to provide references to articles on a particular topic. If an article is well researched, it may give numerous citations to journal articles worth reading. You are likely, however, only to get coverage of those articles which support the view of the author. Using footnotes from textbooks and citations from key articles is a good way to widen your search for documents on a subject, but a comprehensive approach to finding journal articles requires the identification of relevant subject keywords and the use of online search engines and indexes. Using subject keywords ensures that you are able to find references to journal articles covering all aspects of the subject which interests you, from a variety of different points of view. The basic principles identifying and combining subject keywords are covered in para.2.11. Paragraph 5.8 below provides a detailed example of keyword searching using the *Legal Journals Index* available from the "Journals" section in Westlaw UK. 5.5

A systematic approach to finding articles on a subject would involve the identification of a single set of keywords which are then used to search as many of the search engines and indexes listed in the remainder of this chapter as are available and likely to find relevant results. A search for articles held in university repositories of open access articles could also be undertaken as described in para.5.23. Key articles would of course be found many times over and a systematic search approach would also involve the elimination of duplication and the creation of a single set of relevant articles.

However, for most purposes, the use of quick general searches using library searches (para.5.6), supplemented perhaps by the use of Google Scholar (para.5.7) will provide a means of searching much of the available journal literature. An in-depth search for articles published in UK law journals requires, however, the use of the *Legal Journals Index* (para.5.8). The Index of Legal Periodicals & Books (para.5.10) and Lawtel (para.5.11) can also be helpful, if available, if you want to be sure that you have not missed potentially relevant articles published in law journals.

The HeinOnline archive (para.5.9) provides a means of searching for articles published in North American journals by keyword. The Index to Foreign Legal Periodicals (para.5.12) provides a means of widening the search to include articles on the law of countries other than the US and the UK. This index is only available from a minority of university libraries however. If the subject of your search involves the need to search more widely for articles published beyond the content of law journals, be sure to include at least some of the indexes introduced in para.5.13.

Library Keyword Searches

5.6 Many university libraries now provide a single library search which supplements the traditional library catalogue by presenting details of potentially relevant journal articles matching the keywords entered (para.2.10). If a single search box is used, details of journal articles are mixed in with details of books held by the library. Other books of potential interest are also usually included in the results. Sometimes more than one search box is presented, enabling a choice between the wider general search option, mixing library holdings with journal articles and other books of interest, and a library-only search for books and journal subscriptions. In either case, search results can be filtered using options on the search results page, so that results from a wider combined search are only displayed, for example, for peer-reviewed or academic journal articles. This is likely to be a good first step, excluding book details which may not be wanted at this stage, along with less useful articles.

More particularly, an option will be available to limit your search results to ensure that the only article details displayed are those of articles which are available in full text from the library. This option may be pre-set. An advantage of library single search options is that the general indexes used can be linked to a "knowledge base" of library subscriptions, allowing a general search for articles to be combined with options that relate to local library availability.

It is also worth noting, that though library single search options are designed to look much like Google Scholar (para.5.7), the search method used is quite different. In library searches, the indexes used are derived from content data supplied by journal publishers, sometimes supplemented by other subject indexes. The library search matches keywords against this index or indexing. It is not a web search engine. This means that the relevance ranking of search results does not match that of Google Scholar, providing a useful contrast in the results obtained. This is the case, whichever search product your library has chosen to support its single search capability. There are in fact three such search products currently available: the Summon search from ProQuest, the EBSCO Discovery Service (EDS) and Primo from Ex-Libris.

Google Scholar

5.7 The Google Scholar search (at *https://www.scholar.google.co.uk*) is based on an index of the web pages of most academic publishers and article repositories. Book reviews and editorials are largely excluded. The index is created from a trawl of websites, as is the index for the main Google search, but Google Scholar indexing is entirely separate. Like Google itself, Google

Scholar does not search websites directly. This has a consequence for the currency of the links and references found. New pages are added quickly, but updates to existing records are slower, as the source website needs to be trawled again for information to be updated. Contents of databases such as Westlaw UK and the Lexis Library are also not included in Google Scholar searches, as database services such as these do not present static web pages for indexing. Any website content that can only be accessed using a subscription login is also excluded unless the website owner allows access for indexing.

A typical Google Scholar search results page includes title links to articles on the main publisher, repository, or archive source for an article. Links to alternative sources can also be found under an "all versions" link. However, these often include sites which record the publication of an article rather than provide full text access. Links to books on the results page are to books scanned for Google Books (at *https://books.google.com*), or added from publisher content. These book links can be useful, but it is important to remember that though Google book scanning has been extensive, and a great deal of publisher content has been added, the range of titles included is not comprehensive and new titles may be missing. The full text of books found is rarely available for copyright reasons.

A Google Scholar results page also includes many unlinked citation references derived from the full text of articles and books indexed by Google Scholar. These entries are useful in themselves as a means of checking references. The indexing of citation information is also the key to one of the most valuable aspects of Google Scholar, as it enables the creation of a "Cited by" link for the articles and books included in Google Scholar results. This means that a particularly effective way of using Google Scholar is to search for an article you already know to be a key article, and then use the "Cited by" link to find later articles or books which have cited that article. In this way, it is possible to gain a quick sense of the academic discussion generated by the article.

Citation data is also a significant element in the relevance ranking used by the Google Scholar. This is both a strength and a weakness. It means that the most cited articles matching your search words are likely to appear near the top of results lists, leading you fairly directly to the articles which have been most referred to in academic discussion. However, it also means that you may miss a particularly relevant article which has been published very recently or has been overlooked by others. A simple way to deal with this aspect of Google Scholar, is to select the "Sort by Date" link to the left of the results display.

Search results from Google Scholar can often also be improved by using a number of "Advanced Search" options. These are found by selecting the drop down arrow placed at the end of the Google Scholar search box. The search can then be changed, for example, so that the search words used must be found in article titles. Words can also be entered that exclude articles from results pages. One search feature missing from Google Scholar, however, and present in standard index searches, is the ability to truncate search words. It is not possible, for example, to use "feminis*" to search for both "feminist" and "feminism".

Details of articles found in traditional index databases can also often be linked by libraries to the appropriate full text source. For Google Scholar the position is different. If you are using Google Scholar on a university network, links to articles allow the full text of an article to be downloaded from publisher websites if the university library pays a subscription to the journal publisher. This is also the case for subscription archive websites such as HeinOnline and JSTOR. The university website is recognised as a full-text access site by the publisher or archive. As a consequence, links to articles will find full text much of time. If you are not able to access the full text of an article directly, it is advisable also to check the library catalogue as described in para.5.3. Your university library may only have access to the text of the article through a database source which is not indexed by Google Scholar, such as Westlaw UK or the Lexis Library.

If you are using Google Scholar off campus, outside the university network, links to full text sources do not recognise library subscriptions and full text access will not be directly available. A solution to this problem is possible using the "Settings" link from the Google Scholar homepage. A "Library Links" section within the settings options provides a search box designed to "show library access links". Search here using your university name. If a match is found to the name of the library link used by your university, the library access link can be saved, enabling the display of library access links against Google Scholar search results where full text should be available from your university. Select the library link against any search result to open a login screen requesting your normal access ID and password to find a link to the publisher website or other relevant article source.

Legal Journals Index

5.8 The *Legal Journals Index* began publication in 1986 and is the most useful source for tracing law articles in journals published in the UK. It is available online as part of the Westlaw UK service (para.2.4) and has been fully integrated into the Westlaw UK "Journals" search. All *Legal Journals Index* coverage is included in Westlaw UK from 1986 onwards, along with entries from the print *European Legal Index*, which carried references to articles on EU law from 1993 onwards. The index covers articles from close to 500 legal journals and provides the most comprehensive coverage of articles on UK law. Some libraries may continue to keep the print volumes of both the *Legal Journals Index* and the *European Legal Index*, though online access has made them largely redundant.

Each entry in the *Legal Journals Index* database includes details of the title and the author (or authors) of the journal article, along with details of the journal in which the article is published. The volume, issue and page numbers of the article are also included. An abstract, or summary, of the content of each journal article is provided, though some of the earlier summaries contained in the database may only consist of a single sentence. In addition to the summary, subject terms and keywords are added, to aid searching. The subject entries correspond to the subject headings used in the subject index of the printed volumes and use a standard vocabulary. The keywords are additional identifying subject words taken from each journal article.

To use the *Legal Journals Index*, enter your keywords in the "Subject/Keyword" search box on the Westlaw UK "Journals" search page. This is the entry point for *Legal Journals Index* searches. Any words you enter in the "Subject/Keyword" search box are matched against the subject terms and keywords added by the *Legal Journals Index*. Possible keywords are suggested as you enter your words and a match must be present before any search results can be found.

This might seem an extremely restrictive way of searching for journal articles which match a subject which interests you. You will soon discover though, that an enormous number of legal journal articles are published in the UK during the course of a single year, with the result that the problem facing the researcher is usually that of sifting out the articles most directly relevant to the research being undertaken. Matching your search words to the subject keywords used by the *Legal Journals Index* greatly improves the relevance and focus of your search results.

Though prompts are provided by Westlaw UK, using the "Subject/Keyword" search requires that you first consider the range of keywords which might be added to the articles which you would like to find. The most effective searches often involve combining these keywords using "and" to focus and refine your search (see para.2.11). If you select the "Advanced Search" from the journals page, a "List of Terms" link below the "Subject/Keyword" search box displays the subject terms used by the *Index* arranged in a subject hierarchy. This can help choose relevant keywords. However, it is usually sufficient to try searching using the keywords which seem most likely at the outset and then noting the subject terms and keywords used in any index entries you find. These can then be combined in further searches.

Suppose that you are interested in finding articles which discuss privacy issues in the context of the Human Rights Act. You might start by searching for index entries that contain both "privacy" and "human rights". To do this, enter "privacy and human rights" in the "Subject/Keyword" search. Your search then retrieves all index entries for articles that contain both "privacy" and "human rights" in either the subject or keyword entries. This initial search will find well over 3,000 index entries—far too many to begin looking at the index entries and deciding which articles might be useful. Further search words will need to be added to reduce the number of matching index entries. At this point it becomes important to think more precisely about your research topic. Perhaps media intrusion is the focus of your interest, in which case simply add "media" and search for "privacy and human rights and media".

Once you have begun to narrow the range of articles found in this way, take a look at the index entries made for some of the most relevant articles found and pay particular attention to the subject keywords which have been used in the index entries. There are still around 600 matching index entries. Search again using the keywords which now seem to offer the closest match to your interests, or use the "Search within results" feature to achieve the same end. You might note that "celebrities" has been used as a keyword, or that articles discussing the various *Douglas v Hello*! cases have been found, and that these are indexed under "breach of confidence". If your interest in privacy issues had been sparked by the *Douglas v Hello*! cases, you could narrow your search using "breach of confidence and privacy and human rights".

As noted in para.2.11, there are no right answers, and it is advisable to try out different searches, saving references of particular interest as you examine the results of each search. Individual entries can be marked (ticked) on the results screen and details of those articles later emailed or saved to a file. There is no need to write down or copy and paste the references you find to useful articles.

Select the "Legal Journals Abstract" link against any of the article details displayed to read the summary provided by the *Legal Journals Index*. A "Full Text Article" link is also displayed if the article text is available directly from Westlaw UK. Bear in mind though, that Westlaw UK contains only some of the journal articles available online. Once references to articles have been found using the "Subject/Keyword" search, all of the potential online and print sources of the articles need to be pursued as described in para.5.2 and para.5.3. It would

Fig 5.2
Westlaw UK
Journals search

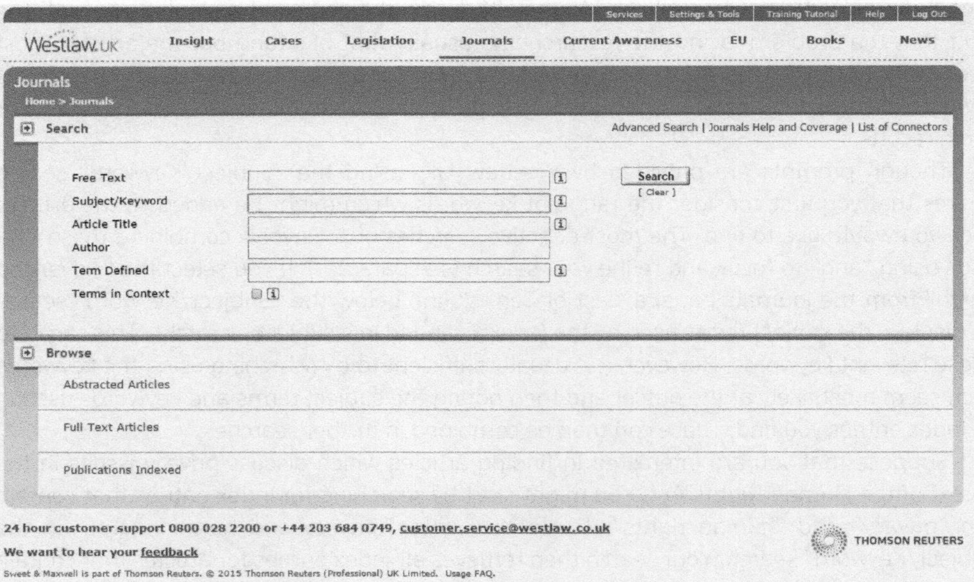

be unduly restrictive to narrow your interest to articles available in full text on Westlaw UK (effectively to articles published by Sweet & Maxwell).

Note also that the results achieved using this index-based approach to searching differ greatly from those achieved using a "Free Text" search. The "Free Text" search on the Westlaw UK "Journals" page includes not just the full text of the *Legal Journals Index* summaries, but also the entire text of all journals held in full text versions in the Westlaw UK journals database. One consequence is that many articles are found in which your subject terms are only mentioned in passing. More importantly, articles available in full text dominate the results screens. An important article which happens not to be available in Westlaw UK may be easily missed. Other articles which may only have a tangential relation to your research may be displayed first.

TIPS • *Make an initial search for articles using the "Journals" "Subject/Keyword" search in Westlaw UK. Then look at the keywords added to the entries for the articles found. They can give you ideas for new searches.*

HeinOnline

5.9 The HeinOnline archive includes the full text of just over 2,000 law and law-related journals in its "Law Journal Library", most of them North American. The full range of academic law publishing is included for the US and Canada, both current journals, and journals which have ceased publication. All journals included are archived from issue one onwards. However, publisher agreements mean that the most recent issue or issues of a journal are not usually included.

The full text available in the archive makes HeinOnline a particularly useful source for finding North American law articles by keyword. The best results can be obtained using the "Advanced Search", selected from a link just below the main search box. Searches can then be restricted using the advanced search, for example, to titles and article descriptions only. Searches can also combine a search for keywords in titles with, perhaps, an additional search for keywords or phrases appearing in full text of articles.

Your library's HeinOnline subscriptions may also include access to the *Index to Foreign Legal Periodicals* (para.5.12), which can be searched directly from the HeinOnline search pages.

Index to Legal Periodicals & Books

The *Index to Legal Periodicals & Books*, which commenced in 1908, is published in the US. Most of its coverage is of American journals, but it includes some journals from the UK, Canada, Ireland, Australia and New Zealand. The online version is available from EBSCO and a multi-volume print version continues to be published. 5.10

If you are using the online version, select the "Subjects" field from the "Select a field" dropdown menu choice in the EBSCO advanced search to use the subject keywords (or descriptors) added by the *Index*. If you are interested in the concept of "inherent jurisdiction" for example, a search might use the keywords "inherent jurisdiction AND Great Britain".

Subject keywords present in the results might then lead you to search using the more general terms "Jurisdiction and Great Britain". As with any index search it makes sense to take full note of any subject or descriptor terms you find, as they provide a means of improving the accuracy and relevance of your search results. Subject keywords use American terminology and spelling which may occasionally cause difficulties.

If you wish to search for articles indexed before 1981, you must use the print volumes of the *Index*. Check if these are available in your library. If you are using the print volumes, brief article details are listed in each volume under the relevant subject descriptor.

Lawtel

The Lawtel service includes an articles index which contains references to the contents of 60 UK publications. The emphasis is on publications that are likely to be of interest to legal practitioners. *Corporate Briefing*, *Counsel and Pensions World* are included, for example, along with academic law journals such as the *New Law Journal* and *Modern Law Review*. References to the legal sections of *The Times*, *The Guardian* and *The Independent* are included in a separate "News and Press" search. Most of the publications are indexed from 1998 onwards, a few from 1995. 5.11

Each entry for the article index has a paragraph summarising the contents of the article along with references to any case law or legislation cited in the article. As with other indexes it is possible to search for articles using a case name or the name and section of a statute. Searches using subject headings can be undertaken in much the same way as that outlined for the Subject/Keyword search in Westlaw UK (para.5.8) .

Index to Foreign Legal Periodicals

The *Index to Foreign Legal Periodicals* commenced in 1960. It indexes articles on international and comparative law and the municipal law of countries other than the US, the UK and the common law of Commonwealth countries. Close to 500 legal journals are indexed. The Index is available online from 1985 onwards from HeinOnline. 5.12

FINDING ARTICLES USING NON-LAW INDEXES

5.13 The effective study of law will, of necessity, take you into other disciplines. Your research might lead you to articles published in social science journals if you are studying criminal justice or family law for example. Articles in economics journals will be relevant to corporate governance. Politics journals are likely to have articles relevant to constitutional and human rights law. Research on environment and regulation could take you further still.

A number of online indexes are available that can help you to widen your search. All of the indexes listed below add keywords and standard subject terms to details of articles published in a selected range of journals. As a result, the approaches to searching described in para.2.11 and for the *Legal Journals Index* (para.5.8) remain valid. One advantage of almost all these databases is that library access or link resolving software integrated into results pages means that you have direct access to the full text of articles available from library subscriptions. You will also discover that you do not need to become familiar with a wide range of online database services when using non-law indexes. Many of the indexes listed below are available from ProQuest. Access to the Philosopher's Index and Econlit is provided by EBSCO,

The indexes listed are by no means the only indexes available. Library web pages are likely to list available indexes by subject, and library staff will help you find out which indexing services might be most useful to your research.

Index to Periodical Articles Related to Law

5.14 This index commenced in 1958. It contains a selective coverage of English-language articles not included in the *Legal Journals Index*, or the *Index to Legal Periodicals & Books*. The index is available online from HeinOnline.

Applied Social Sciences Index and Abstracts (ASSIA)

5.15 ASSIA is aimed at those in practice in social services, prison services, employment, race relations, etc. and includes articles on many aspects of the law. Articles from approximately 650 journals are indexed. Although produced in Britain, the index covers English-language journals from 16 countries.

International Bibliography of the Social Sciences (IBSS)

5.16 Produced in the London School of Economics, the International Bibliography of Social Sciences has the most wide-ranging coverage of the social science indexes. It is particularly strong in its coverage of European journals. Coverage goes back to 1961.

Sociological Abstracts

5.17 *Sociological Abstracts* includes coverage of law, penology and the police and is available from a variety of online sources. Online coverage is from 1963 and abstracts are added to records from 1974 onwards.

British Humanities Index

This covers a broad range of subjects and includes articles from British newspapers and popular weekly journals, as well as more scholarly periodicals. Online coverage is from 1985 onwards. 5.18

The Philosopher's Index

This index contains references (with abstracts) to articles found in almost 500 philosophy journals from a wide range of countries. Records of books and contributions to anthologies are included. Online coverage is from 1940 onwards. Philpapers (at *http://www.philpapers.org*) provides a more limited alternative if the *Philosopher's Index* is not available. 5.19

Psychological Abstracts (PsycINFO)

The scope of this is far wider than the title suggests, covering abortion, drug use, alcoholism, etc. Over 1,300 journals are indexed and dissertations, books and book chapters are included. Online coverage begins as early as 1887. 5.20

Econlit

Econlit covers a wide range of areas related to economics and articles are indexed from 1886 to the present. Econlit searches can also be supplemented searching two full text business databases, Business Source Premier and ABI/INFORM. 5.21

Web of Science

Web of Science indexes journals from a wide range of subjects, drawing its indexing from the *Social Sciences Index*, the *Arts and Humanities Citation Index* and the *Science Citation Index*. These citation indexes include a list of all the articles referred to (or "cited") by articles included in the database. The number of articles indexed citing an article is also presented as a link, enabling you to explore later articles citing the article in question. A similar approach to research using later citing articles was noted for Google Scholar (para.5.7). Scopus is another general index database containing citation data for articles. 5.22

FINDING OPEN ACCESS ARTICLES

Open access sources are included in the websites indexed by Google Scholar (para.5.7). However, a number of websites offer more direct access to open access articles. The CORE (COnnecting REpositories) website (at *http://www.core.ac.uk*) is a particularly useful starting point, as it aims to bring together open access articles, along with conference and working papers, from repositories and open access journals from around the world. Following an initial search on the Core website, results can be filtered by source. An "Advanced Search" link is also displayed on the results page, which allows searches to be restricted, e.g. to words in the title, or words in the title and abstract. 5.23

Core aims to include the open access repositories of individual universities along with various subject repositories. Another approach is to search key subject repositories directly. These include the Social Science Open Access Repository (SSOAR) (at *http://www.ssoar.info*), the Archive of European Integration (at *aei.pitt.edu*) and Research Papers in Economics (at *http://www.*repec.org). A full list of open access repository sites can be found on the OpenDOAR (Directory of Open Access Repositories) site (at *http://www.opendoar.org*). It is important to bear in mind, as explained in para.5.2, that these repositories cannot provide immediate access to articles published in academic journals. Agreements with publishers mean that open access versions of these articles can only be made available after the elapse of an agreed time limit, usually one to two years after publication.

Open access journals place no restrictions on access. These are listed in the Directory of Open Access Journals (at *https://www.doaj.org*).

NEWSPAPER ARTICLES

5.24 In addition to factual reporting, newspapers often contain commentary, analysis and background information on recent legal developments and controversial topics. If your law library has a subscription to Nexis, the full text of UK national (and many regional) newspapers is available from the mid-1980s onwards.

The Nexis home page allows news sources to be chosen from a wide range of English language sources. Use the "All English Language News" dropdown selection to restrict the source used, for example, to "UK Broadsheets". Once a particular source is chosen, an information icon can be used to display a list of newspapers contained in the source. Search results can be filtered later to display articles from particular newspapers, *The Guardian*, *The Times*, *The Independent*, etc.

The news coverage of even a single newspaper over a number of years is, however, considerable, so it is advisable to make full use of the options which restrict the way in which your search is carried out. To continue with the example used in para.5.8, you might wish to find newspaper articles which discuss privacy as a human rights issue, so the keywords "privacy" and "human rights" would need to be included in your search. It would not be especially helpful, though, to find all articles which happen to include these words. Once you have entered your search terms, menu choices can be used to improve your search by specifying, for example, that the search terms must occur in the lead paragraphs and indexing, or that there must be at least three occurrences of a search term in the text.

> **TIPS** • *Use the options available in the Nexis news databases to limit your search words e.g. in the lead paragraphs or indexing. If using multiple search words ensure that they must be found close to each other in the text of newspaper articles.*

As a search for articles including "privacy" and "human rights" combines two search terms, the proximity of the two terms can also be specified by clicking to add another search term, and then specifying that the two words or phrases must occur within five words of each other, or in the same sentence. Finally, date limits can be set, to restrict the search to a particular period of time. Limiting searches in this way can mean that a search for "privacy" and "human rights" can be restricted to produce a long but manageable results list of perhaps a hundred or so articles over a number of years, some of which will provide useful leads to important legal issues. These might be pursued using the academic coverage provided by legal journals.

The current awareness features of both the Lexis Library and Westlaw UK can also be used to find newspaper articles on recent legal developments. The Lexis Library "Current

Awareness" search includes brief summaries of articles of legal interest drawn from UK national newspapers. Legal news can also be found using the Westlaw UK "Current Awareness" search.

OBTAINING ARTICLES NOT AVAILABLE FROM LIBRARY SUBSCRIPTIONS

If you find that you are unable to find an article from your library subscriptions, check with library staff on the procedure for obtaining articles using the library's "inter-library loan" or document delivery service. Libraries are able to obtain articles for you from a variety of sources, often delivered in scanned emailed versions. There may, however, be restrictions on the use you can make of the service. It is also necessary to allow up to a week for article delivery. 5.25

If you find that there are a significant number of journals not available to you from library subscriptions, it may also be worth considering visiting another library to use the resources available there. If you are a current UK student, or staff member, check the SCONUL access web page (at *http://www.sconul.ac.uk/sconul-access*). Once you have specified your home institution and level of study or status, you will be able to discover which academic libraries you can use, along with the associated access rights you would have. An application for access can then be initiated from the SCONUL page. It is also advisable to check the possibility of network access with any library you are visiting. If you are able to access the library network, most of the online resources of the library will be open to you, as subscription licences usually allow access for "walk in users".

6
UK official publications

INTRODUCTION

6.1 Almost all official publishing now takes place on the internet. This includes parliamentary publications and the publications of government departments and other official bodies. As a result, official publications have become much more accessible than they once were. However, tracing official publications is not always straightforward. This is a field in which you should not hesitate to seek the advice of library staff whenever you have a difficulty. Most libraries which have a collection of official publications have at least one person who is responsible for helping readers find this material, whether online or in print.

The Stationery Office (TSO) has published a high proportion of UK official publications in print since the privatisation of UK official publishing in 1996, which means that the TSO bookshop catalogue is a significant source for tracing official publications (para.6.15) whether in print or online. TSO has not, however, been the only source of UK official publications since privatisation. Some of the publications you may wish to consult will have been published elsewhere, often on the websites of government departments and other official bodies. Databases are available to help trace these publications (para.6.16).

The merging of the Office of Public Sector Information (OPSI) and the National Archives in 2005, also means that the National Archives now has a significant role in UK official publishing online, hosting UK legislation on National Archives web pages (at *http://www.legislation.gov.uk*) and the UK Government Web Archive (at *http://www.nationalarchives.gov.uk/webarchive*).

Another significant development has been the progressive merging of UK official publishing into the GOV.UK website (at *http://www.gov.uk*) (para.6.13). This has been accompanied by an increasing tendency to publish official publications as online-only documents. Libraries are likely to hold only a limited range of recent official publications in print, acquiring key documents where these are available from TSO.

Before privatisation in 1996, UK official publishing was undertaken by Her Majesty's Stationery Office (HMSO), which acted as the government printer. This means that HMSO catalogues are a key source for locating earlier official publications in print.

Parliamentary publications are the most important category of UK official publications for the law student. These include papers brought before Parliament (Command Papers), Bills, House of Commons Papers and *Hansard* reports of parliamentary debates. Most of this chapter is concerned with these sources. Acts of Parliament, which are also official publications, are covered in Ch.4. Parliamentary papers are published by TSO.

Documents other than parliamentary publications published by, or on behalf of, government departments or other official bodies, are often referred to as non-parliamentary publications. These items vary considerably and include, for example, public information pamphlets such as the *Highway Code* and guidance documents for schools published by the Department for Education.

PARLIAMENTARY PUBLICATIONS

There are four main categories of Parliamentary Papers: 6.2

- House of Commons Papers;
- House of Commons Bills;
- House of Lords Papers and Bills; and
- Command Papers.

All Command Papers and House of Commons Papers from the 2005/2006 parliamentary session onwards are available online from the UK.GOV website (at *https://www.gov.uk/government/publications*). Selected papers are also available for the period 1993–2005. Command Papers are covered in more detail in para.6.3. Access to the text of Bills before Parliament is explained in para.6.9 and *Hansard* debates (both online and in print) in para.6.11. If print versions of recent parliamentary papers are available, they are usually gathered into boxes corresponding to some or all of the categories noted above. Every parliamentary paper has its own number and the papers are usually arranged in number order. TSO ceased printing the full range of Parliamentary Papers in 2014. Annual reports and accounts presented to Parliament as Parliamentary Papers no longer appear in print.

Bound collections of printed parliamentary publications, may be held in your library as *sessional papers* or *sessional sets* containing all the material produced during a particular session of Parliament. Alternatively, bound collections of Command Papers and House of Commons Papers may be kept as separate sequences. A Sessional Index provides a subject approach to papers held in sessional sets. Other index approaches are covered in para.6.16.

Libraries with large collections of official publications do not usually enter parliamentary publications in the library catalogue, relying instead on the indexes described in paras 6.14—6.16 to trace relevant material. You will probably also find that the print volumes of the parliamentary publications have been housed in an official publications collection in a separate area of the library (which may not form part of the law library). Therefore, you should ask the librarians whether there is a collection of official publications available and seek help in exploring where they are located and how they are arranged. If, however, your library has only a small collection of parliamentary publications, they may be catalogued and shelved individually.

Older parliamentary papers are available from the House of Commons Parliamentary Papers database from ProQuest, which can be accessed from any UK university library. The database contains scanned versions of papers available in sessional sets and includes papers from 1688 to 2003/2004. Even large libraries are relatively unlikely to have original print volumes pre-dating 1801. Parliamentary papers may also be available on microfiche or microfilm, or in the form of reprints published by bodies such as the Irish University Press. (These reprints are arranged in subject order.)

Official publications in print may be purchased from the tso shop website (at *https://www.tsoshop.co.uk*). A print on demand service from TSO means that older material can often be purchased also. Print publications may also be available on loan through the inter-library loan service.

Command Papers

6.3 This is a very important category of parliamentary papers and one to which you may frequently be referred. It includes many significant government papers, e.g. *Impact of Changes to Civil Legal Aid under Part 1 of the Legal Aid, Sentencing and Punishment of Offenders Act 2012* (2015). Some, though not all, of the reports of the Law Commission are also included, along with the reports of all Royal Commissions. A Command Paper is, as it states on the front cover, presented to Parliament "By Command of Her Majesty". In practice, this means that it is presented to Parliament by a Minister of the Crown on his or her own initiative; its preparation has not been requested by Parliament. Command Papers are often statements of government policy, which are likely to be the subject of future legislation, or they are presented for the information of the Members of Parliament. Command Papers include:

- statements of government policy (often referred to as *White Papers*);
- some annual statistics and annual reports (many more are issued as non-parliamentary publications);
- reports of Royal Commissions;
- reports of some committees (other committee reports may be issued as non-parliamentary publications);
- reports of tribunals of inquiry; and
- state papers (including the Treaty Series).

Citation and location of Command Papers

6.4 Command Papers are each given an individual number, prefaced by an abbreviation for the word "command". This abbreviation and the number are printed at the bottom left-hand corner of the cover of the report. The numbers run on continuously from one session of Parliament to another. The present abbreviation "Cm." has been used for publications issued since 1986. Prior to 1986, different abbreviations of the word "command" were used. They are:

- 1st series 1833–1869 — [1]–[4222] (the abbreviation for "Command" was omitted in the first series);
- 2nd series 1870–1899 — [C. 1]–[C. 9550];
- 3rd series 1900–1918 — [Cd. 1]–[Cd. 9239];
- 4th series 1919–1956 — [Cmd. 1]–Cmd. 9889;
- 5th series 1956–1986 — Cmnd. 1–Cmnd. 9927; and
- 6th series 1986— — Cm. 1—.

(The use of square brackets was abandoned in 1922.) It is important to note exactly the form of the abbreviation so that you have some idea of the date of the report. For instance, Cmd. 6404, which relates to social insurance and allied services (the Beveridge Report), is a different item from Cmnd. 6404, which is an international agreement relating to pensions. One was published in 1942 and the other in 1976.

Listings of Command Papers published from 2004 onwards can be obtained using the GOV.UK website (at *https://www.gov.uk*). The "Official document status" menu choice on the GOV.UK official publications page (at *https://www.gov.uk/government/publications*) allows the document type to be restricted to "Command papers only" and additional menu choices can be used to set date limits. A keyword search can also be combined with the "Command papers only" limiter.

The browse facility within the ProQuest House of Commons Parliamentary Papers database can be used to display Command Papers pre-dating 2004/2005 by year. Keyword searches can be limited to Command Papers from the main search page.

If your library keeps print versions of Command Papers in boxes arranged by command number, you will have no difficulty in tracing the report you want (assuming your reference is correct). However, if the publications are arranged by sessions or are bound into sessional sets (see para.6.2), it will be necessary to have some idea of the date of the Command Paper. An online approach using the sources noted above would be the easiest way to proceed. However there are print sources which can help. You might, for example, find the Concordance of Command Papers 1833–1972, which is in J.E. Pemberton, *British Official Publications* (2nd edn), pp.65–66, useful for older papers. Some further difficulties that can be encountered when locating print Command Papers located in sessional sets are noted in the following paragraph.

Occasionally, a report is published later than the Command Papers with adjoining numbers, with the result that it appears in a different session of Parliament (and is therefore in a different sessional set (para.6.2)). If you know the Command Paper number of a publication issued before 1979–80 and wish to locate it in the bound sessional sets, first ascertain the correct session by consulting Pemberton's list or the *HMSO Annual Catalogues* (see para.6.14). Until the 1979–80 session, Command Papers were not arranged in number order in the sessional sets. They were arranged alphabetically by subject in a sequence with all reports, accounts and papers. To find a Command Paper in the sessional sets before 1979–80 therefore, you need to consult the Sessional Index at the back of the last volume of the session. There you will find a list of Command Paper numbers indicating, for each one, the volume and page within the sessional set where it can be found. Command Papers bound in the sessional sets since 1979–80 can be readily traced under the Command Paper number.

Some Command Papers also form part of another series. For instance, some of the reports of the Law Commission (but not all) are Command Papers: but each Law Commission report also bears its own running number. For convenience, law libraries may keep all Law Commission reports together, regardless of whether they are issued as Command Papers, House of Commons Papers, or non-parliamentary papers (and some of the series have been issued in all these categories). Another major series within the Command Papers are the state papers known as the Treaty Series. These are Command Papers and each has a number, but, in addition, each has its own Treaty Series number. If they are not bound into the sessional sets, the library may keep all the Treaty Series together. There are separate annual and three- or four-yearly consolidated indexes to the series; in addition, they also appeared in annual *HMSO* or *TSO Catalogues*. Both the Treaty Series number and the Command Paper numbers are given. In 1970, HMSO published an *Index of British Treaties 1101–1968* (compiled by Clive Parry and Charity Hopkins). There are entries under subjects (Vol.1) and by the date of the treaties (Vols 2 and 3).

Papers of the House of Lords and House of Commons

6.5 Until 1988, the House of Lords Papers and Bills were issued in a common numerical sequence, so the Papers and Bills were integrated. Since then, they have been issued in separate numerical sequences in the same way as the House of Commons Papers.

The number of each House of Lords Paper is printed in round brackets at the foot of the front cover. The citation is: H.L. session (paper number), e.g. H.L. 1993–94 (7) 1st Report [Session 1993–94]: *Enforcement of Community Competition Rules: Report with Evidence—Select Committee on the European Communities*.

The Papers of the House of Commons include reports of some committees, together with accounts, statistics and some annual reports which are required by Parliament for its work. The citation of a House of Commons Paper contains the initials H.C., the session and the paper number. e.g. H.C. 2014–15 23 is the *Ministry of Justice Annual Report and Accounts 2013–14*.

House of Commons Papers, like Command Papers, can be found online using the GOV.UK official publications page (at *https://www.gov.uk/government/publications*) and the ProQuest database of House of Commons Parliamentary Papers. The approach is much the same. However the "Official document status" choice on the GOV.UK official publications page includes House of Commons Papers in the wider category of "Act papers", which includes e.g. Codes of Practice.

As House of Commons and House of Lords Papers are numbered by session, they are usually straightforward to find in print if you have the correct session and number. Note, that though complete print collections of House of Commons Papers are not unusual, few libraries have collections of House of Lords Papers.

Bills

6.6 Bills are the draft versions of Acts, laid before Parliament for its consideration and approval. If your library has a print collection of parliamentary papers, the Bills will be shelved with this collection. Where parliamentary papers are bound in sessional sets, Bills form the first volumes of each set. Libraries are unlikely to hold collections of current Bills in print.

A Bill may be introduced into Parliament by a Member of Parliament (or by a peer) as an independent action (called a Private Member's Bill), or it may be introduced by a Minister as a Government Bill. Ultimately, however, if it is passed, it becomes a Public General Act whoever introduces it. Private Members' Bills are not always published by TSO: if not otherwise available, they can usually be obtained by contacting the Member of Parliament concerned directly.

Stages in the passage of a Bill

6.7 Before a Bill can become law, it passes through a number of stages. The exact stage which any Bill has reached on its passage through Parliament can be discovered by consulting the "Bills before Parliament" page of the Parliament website (at *http://www.parliament.uk*), using the "Bills & Legislation" section of the website.

A Bill may be introduced into the House of Lords or the Commons. If they commence in the House of Commons, Bills progress through the following stages. Bills fail if they do not pass through all these stages before the end of the parliamentary session.

(i) First Reading—a purely formal reading of the Bill's title by the Clerk of the House; after this, the Bill is published, a day is fixed for its Second Reading and it becomes available to the public;
(ii) Second Reading—the principles of the Bill are debated. If the Bill fails to gain the approval of the House at this stage, it cannot proceed. The debate is reported in *Hansard* (see para.6.11);
(iii) Committee stage—the whole House may sit in committee to examine the clauses of a Bill. More usually, the Bill is discussed in a Public Bill Committee (previously a "Standing Committee") consisting of approximately 20 Members of Parliament. The Public Bill Committee debates are found on the Parliament website (at *http://www.parliament.uk*), on the "Hansard" pages. The link to the debates is under the "Commons Hansard" heading, where they can be found under the name of the Bill under discussion. Links are also available from the "Bills before Parliament" entry for a Bill;
(iv) Report stage—if the Bill has been amended by the Public Bill Committee, this stage gives the House an opportunity to consider the changes. If necessary, the Bill may be referred back to the committee. (If the Bill was debated and approved without amendment in a Committee of the Whole House, then this stage is a formality.);
(v) Third Reading—a general discussion of the Bill as amended, after which it is passed to the House of Lords for its approval; and
(vi) Lords' stages—the Bill is published again when it is passed to the Lords for their consideration and approval. If the Lords make any amendments, these are referred back to the Commons for their approval. Normally, both Houses must be in agreement on the text before the Bill can receive the Royal Assent. The Parliament Acts 1911 and 1949 provide for certain exceptions to this rule. Finance Bills are the standard exception.

Changes to the text of a Bill

Bills before Parliament are found on the Parliament website (at *http://www.parliament.uk*). Public Bills are arranged in an alphabetical sequence on the "Bills before Parliament" page, found under "Parliamentary business" and "Bills and legislation". Bills which originated in the House of Lords have [H.L.] after the title. Selecting any of the Bills listed for the current session displays a "Last Events" entry which confirms the point the Bill has reached in its progress through Parliament e.g. "2nd reading: House of Commons" with the relevant date. Below that, the "Read debates on all stages" link is particularly useful, as entries for each stage link directly to the Hansard debates for the various readings and committee stages the Bill has already passed through. An "All Bill documents" link under "Latest Bill" links to the full text of the Bill as introduced. Further links display the Bill as it was reprinted to incorporate amendments made during its passage through Parliament. 6.8

Perhaps confusingly, the number of a Bill changes with each new version (there is a

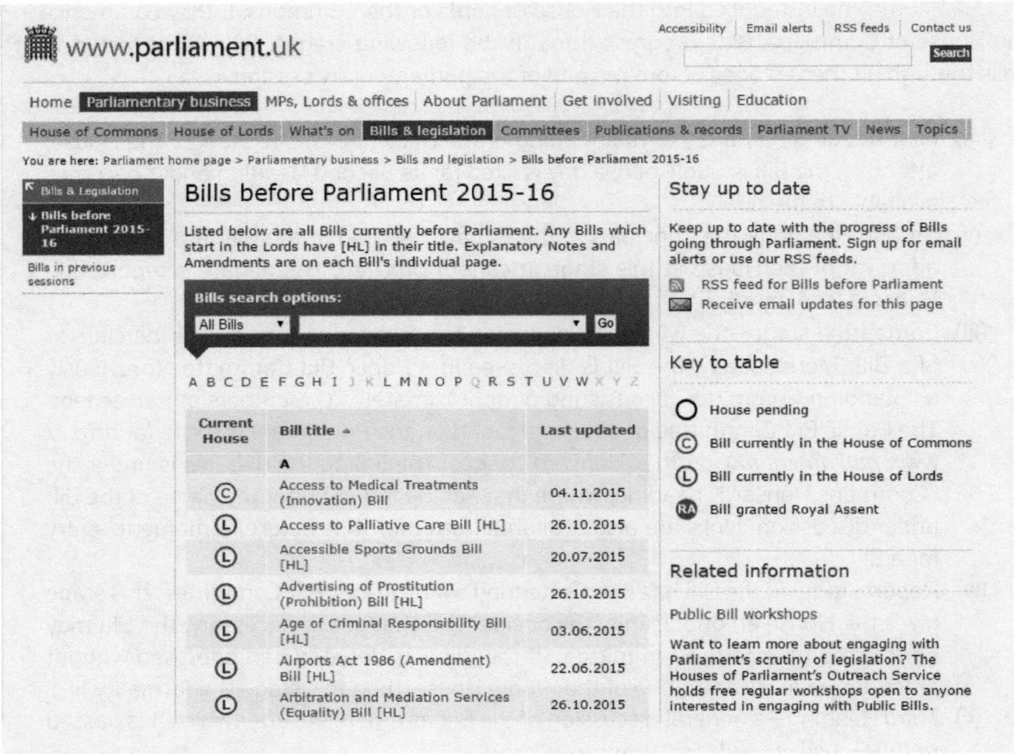

Fig 6.1 Bills before Parliament page on the Parliament website

running sequence for the session). The Criminal Justice and Courts Bill, for example, was introduced to the House of Commons in the 2014–15 session as Bill 169, and would be fully cited as the Criminal Justice and Courts Bill [H.C.] [2014–15] 169. Following amendments made at the Public Bill Committee stage it was then republished as Bill 192, cited as Criminal Justice and Courts Bill [H.C.] [2014–15] 192. After its first reading in the House of Lords it was again renumbered as House of Lords Bill 30, cited as Criminal Justice and Courts Bill [H.L.] [2014–15] 30.

The different versions of the Bill can be viewed as PDF files, and these correspond to the versions of the Bill published by TSO. If you wish to refer to a Bill, and significant amendments have been made, it is clearly important to state which version of a Bill you are using. If a significant number of amendments have been moved, e.g. at the committee stage of a Bill, marshalled lists of amendments are also published by TSO. These bear the same number as the original Bill, but add a roman number, e.g. Criminal Justice and Courts Bill: fifth marshalled list of amendments to be moved in committee [H.L.] [2014–15] 30-V.

Tracing recent Bills

6.9 Finding the full text of a Bill as currently before Parliament is relatively straightforward using the "Bills before Parliament" page in the "Bills & legislation" section of the Parliament website (at *http://www.parliament.uk*).

If you wish to trace the development of legislation, the numbers of the various versions of a Bill can be used to establish the correct sequence. The "Bills before Parliament" web page is the most obvious source for confirming the sequence as noted above (para.6.8). The Bills themselves are also available in PDF versions for printing. The various versions of a Bill can also be traced using the TSO catalogue (para.6.15), or the UKOP catalogue (para.6.16). Both catalogues list individual versions of Bills.

Tracing older Bills

It is not often that you will need to refer to Bills from earlier sessions, for either they will have become law (in which case you should consult the resultant Act) or they will have lapsed. However, Bills from relatively recent sessions of Parliament can be traced using the approaches noted in the previous section. The various printed versions of a Bill are all available online from the Parliament website for the 2005–06 session onwards and are organised in much the same way as Bills for the current session. Select the "Bills in previous Sessions" link from the "Bills before Parliament" page to see a full listing of the Bills. First printings of Bills can be found for the 2002–03 and 2003–04 sessions. 6.10

Earlier Bills can be found online using the ProQuest House of Commons Parliamentary Papers database. This is a subscription service available to all UK universities. Bills can be found from the main search page using both title and subject searches. The "Browse" section of the database can also be used to find a complete listing of House of Commons Bills printed by session year.

If your library has the bound sessional sets available, the text of all the versions of the Bill printed in a session, together with all amendments, will be found in alphabetical order in the volumes entitled *Bills* at the beginning of the sessional set. If the bound sets are not available, details of all the published versions of a Bill will be found at the beginning of the *TSO* or *HMSO Annual Catalogue* and in the *House of Commons Weekly Information Bulletins* during that session. As noted in para.6.9, it becomes important to consider which version of a Bill you wish to find, in order to find the relevant numbered version. Publication details for Bills from the 1970s onwards can also be found using TSO's website (para.6.15) or the UKOP catalogue (para.6.16).

Parliamentary debates (Hansard)

The first semi-official reports of Parliament's debates were published in 1803 by William Cobbett. The man whose name is so closely linked with the publication, Hansard, was a subsequent printer of the reports. There have been six series of *Parliamentary Debates*. The first series covered 1803–20, with subsequent series for 1820–30, 1830–91, 1892–1908 and 1909–1981. The sixth series covers 1981 to the present. Since 1909, the *Official Reports of Parliamentary Debates* have been published by the House of Commons itself. The House of Lords Debates have been published separately since 1909; previously, Lords and Commons Debates were published together. 6.11

House of Commons debates are available online from the 1988–89 sessions onwards on the Parliament website (at *http://www.parliament.uk*) by session. An "Archived Commons Hansard" link can be found under "House of Commons debates by date" displaying pre-current sessions. House of Lords debates can be found in full text on the same site from 1995–96. A project to digitise the volumes of *Hansard* covering the entire period from 1803 to 2005 has also been completed, and debates for the period can be accessed from the "Historic Hansard" link on the "Hansard" page.

The text of current debates can be viewed on the "debates by date" pages for either the House of Commons or House of Lords. Ministerial statements and oral and written answers are also included, along with an index. A PDF file version of the printed daily edition is also available from the relevant "debates by date" page. This corresponds to the daily editions of *Hansard* published by TSO. After a few months, the debates are organised, both online and in print, into numbered volumes. It is these volumes which constitute the "record copy". Each volume covers debates taking place over a two- or three-week period. One peculiarity of these volumes worth noting is that both print and online versions use column rather than page numbering. All *Hansard* references to the record copy are to column numbers.

Indexes to the *Hansard* volumes can help trace a debate if you do not have an exact date. The indexes are bound with the volumes in print, and appear online alongside the volume entry in the *Hansard* listing for the session in the "Archived Commons Hansard" section of the Hansard by date page. The indexes contain an alphabetical listing of debates by subject matter and by name of speaker. The subject of written questions and the names of those asking them are also included. References are to the column number of the printed *Hansard*, rather than page numbers. Index references ending in "w" indicate written questions.

The search engine for the Parliament website provides an alternative approach to tracing debates. A basic search is available at the top of each page and search results can be filtered to results relating to parliamentary business. More complex searches can be undertaken using a "Search parliamentary material" page (at *search-material.parliament.uk*). Searches can be restricted to "Parliamentary proceedings" and particular types of debates specified under the "Parliamentary proceedings" heading, e.g. "Committee debates" or "Queen's speech debates". Particular sessions of Parliament can also be specified. The search has been launched as a test site, so changes may be made to the way the search engine can be used.

Using online sources to trace debates on a Bill

6.12 For the period from 2005/2006 onwards, the most effective way to find debates on a particular Bill is to use the "Bills before Parliament" web page on the Parliament site, described in para.6.8. The "All previous stages of a Bill" section for a particular Bill can be used to find the *Hansard* debates relating to each stage of the Bill's passage through Parliament.

Your library may also provide access to subscription services which can help trace debates on a Bill. The Public Information Online service, for example, features a "Bill Tracker" section which lists Bills by Parliamentary session for the period from 2005–06 onwards. For each Bill, PDF files are provided of each Daily Hansard issue which printed debates on the Bill, along with PDFs of the various printed versions of the Bill itself. Justis Parliament, another subscription service, indexes proceedings of both Houses of Parliament from 1979 onwards. Notes of debates are provided for each Bill indexed, along with references to oral and written questions. Though the database itself provides only index entries for debates, noting *Hansard* references, links are provided to the full text of *Hansard* debates available from the Parliament website. It is possible to find, for example, the oral statement that introduced a Bill to one of the Houses of Parliament, and follow the link to the *Hansard* full text.

Vol. 594]

INDEX—SESSION 2014–15
9th March, 2015—26th March, 2015

Closure of NatWest Branch in Eccleshall
34-5p

Closure of the Seven Stars Public House in Sedgley
12p

Clwyd, Ann
Questions
Female Genital Mutilation/Early Forced Marriage 745

Co-operative Schools
116wh

Coaker, Vernon
Chamber Debates
Falkland Islands Defence Review 1303-4

Code of Conduct and Guide to the Rules Relating to the Conduct of Members
706

Coffey, Ann
Chamber Debates
Troubled Families Programme 162
Questions
Youth Justice and Criminal Evidence Act (Section 28 Pilots) 633-4

Collins, Damian
Chamber Debates
Amendment of the Law 805, 811-4
Fishing Discards and Quotas 869-71, 873
Questions
Inshore Fishing Fleet (Discard Ban) 384

Colvile, Oliver
Questions
Devolution, South-west 1276

Commission Work Programme 2015
76

Committee on Standards (Reports)
695

Commonwealth Day
(24.03.2015) 411wh

Communications Data
1099

Communities and Local Government
519, 6ws, 11ws, 55ws, 77ws, 102ws, 130ws, 148ws, 7p, 11p, 29p

Companies House
Public Targets 111ws

Compulsory CPR and Public Access Defibrillator education
267, 30p

Condition Improvement Fund
173ws

Confiscation Orders (Sentencing and Offence) Bill
932

Conflict, Stability and Security Fund
19ws

Connarty, Michael
Chamber Debates
Amendment of the Law 786, 842-4
Modern Slavery Bill 649, 651-2, 663, 666-9, 679, 690-1
Penrose Inquiry 1596
Valedictory Debate 1681-2
Questions
Engagements 760, 1429
Tax Devolution 145

Constitutional and Political Reform
1277

Consumer Rights Bill
55

Contingencies Fund
130ws

Convergence Programme
102ws

Cooper, Rosie
Chamber Debates
Burial and cremation services in West Lancashire 730-1
VAT, refunds to certain charities 1536
Questions
Engagements 293
Firefighters Pensions 528-9
Flags and Parades 283-4
Police Forces, Finance 1109-10
Topical Questions 536, 640, 753, 1279
Uncollected Tax 135

Cooper, Yvette
Chamber Debates
Undercover Policing 1590-1
Questions
Topical Questions 1113

Corbyn, Jeremy
Chamber Debates
Business of the House 412
Falkland Islands Defence Review 1308
Nuclear Non-Proliferation Treaty Review Conference 105-9, 124
Shaker Aamer 718-20, 722, 728
Transport for London Bill [Lords] (16.03.2015) 568, 575, 577, 579, 583, 587, 589-92, 594, 596-604, 608
Undercover Policing 1586, 1591
Westminster Hall
Democratic Republic of the Congo (Human Rights) 502-6wh
Local Newspapers (19.03.2015) 335wh, 372wh
Questions
Human Rights, Domestic and International Obligations 1287
Topical Questions 642
Visas, Income Threshold 1108

Cost of Living
284

Council Tax
531

Counter-terrorism
1375

Counter-Terrorism (Statutory Instruments)
226, 545

Cox, Mr Geoffrey
Chamber Debates
Committee on Standards (Reports) 703-5
Defence Spending 471-2
Westminster Hall
Tourism Industry and VAT 226-7wh

Creagh, Mary
Chamber Debates
Changes to Budgets for GPs 1544-5
Ebola 420-2
Questions
Working Conditions 750

Creasy, Stella
Chamber Debates
Barts Health NHS Trust 899-900
Westminster Hall
Women Entrepreneurs (18.03.2015) 268-74wh, 278-80wh, 282-3wh
Questions
Engagements 286
Small Businesses 1563

Crime (Northamptonshire)
1111

Crime Rates
1105

Crockart, Mike
Questions
Post-study Work Visas 1108-9
Tax Devolution 146

Cross-border Crime
336

Cross-boundary Local Authority Co-ordination
519

Crossrail 2 Safeguarding Consultation Response
123ws

Crouch, Tracey
Chamber Debates
Asbestos in Schools 737-8
Westminster Hall
First Aid Techniques, National Curriculum 36-9wh

Cryer, John
Questions
Topical Questions 154
Visas, Income Threshold 1108
Zero-hours Contracts 1573

Culture, Media and Sport
21ws, 114ws, 169ws

Cunningham, Alex
Chamber Debates
Budget Resolutions and Economic Situation 946, 970-3, 1001
Fiscal Responsibility and Fairness 915
Questions
Basic Maths and English Skills 1568-9
Cost of Living 284-5
Migration 1097
Topical Questions 1575

Cunningham, Mr Jim
Chamber Debates
Budget Resolutions and Economic Situation 1153, 1166, 1182-3, 1206-7
Consumer Rights Bill 63
Fiscal Responsibility and Fairness 917
Modern Slavery Bill 672-3
School Funding Formula (10.03.2015) 256, 261
Shaker Aamer 711
Small Business, Enterprise and Employment Bill (24.03.2015) 1342
Westminster Hall
The Shrewsbury 24 466-7wh
Questions
Anti-radicalisation Programmes 1100
Local Government Funding 522
Topical Questions 20

Cunningham, Sir Tony
Westminster Hall
Vaccine Damage Payments Act 443wh

Cyber-security
1314

Cycling Delivery Plan
178ws

Dairy Farmers
383

Dakin, Nic
Chamber Debates
Procedure of the House 1627
School Funding Formula (10.03.2015) 255-6
Questions
Business Rates 527

Fig 6.2
Example page from the Volume Indexes to *Hansard*

Fig 6.3 Example page from *Hansard Debates*

24 Mar 2015 : Column 1314

Cyber-security

1.43 pm

The Minister for the Cabinet Office and Paymaster General (Mr Francis Maude): With permission, Mr Speaker, I will make a statement on the Government's national cyber-security programme.

Every day, the cyber threat is growing and we face ever more sophisticated attacks. According to one survey, 81% of large businesses and 60% of small businesses suffered a breach last year. Back in 2010 the coalition Government identified cyber as one of four tier 1 national security threats, and Britain has been among the fastest adopters of the digital economy. We are a world leader in digital services, which are a key part of our long-term economic plan. We cannot let our economic progress be undermined by those who would do us harm. No national Government can tackle the cyber threat alone, and international collaboration is central to our strategy, as is the closest partnership with the business community.

In 2011 we published our cyber-security strategy and have committed £860 million of funding over five years to the national cyber-security programme. That is to ensure that Britain remains one of the safest places to do business online. Cyber-security skills are scarce, and collaboration between Government, industry and academia is essential to build the skills and expertise we need.

Despite the huge budget deficit that we inherited, we have invested in our intelligence agencies and the National Crime Agency to build our capabilities to understand cyber threats and tackle cybercrime. GCHQ—often the object of poorly informed criticism—is home to a hugely impressive and patriotic collection of public servants, and I put on record my appreciation for the dedicated and highly skilled work they do to keep Britain safe.

We have worked with business to establish the cyber essentials scheme to raise awareness of five basic measures to keep companies safe. That scheme is now mandatory for certain types of Government procurement, and today 88% of FTSE 350 companies have cyber-security firmly on their risk registers. We created the national computer emergency response team—CERT-UK—to respond to major cyber incidents, and it played a significant role in protecting the Commonwealth games and the NATO summit in Wales. Following the Prime Minister's successful visit to the US, CERT-UK will be leading joint exercising with its American counterpart later this year. The cyber-security information sharing partnership, based within CERT-UK, provides a safe space for businesses and Government to exchange information and develop responses in real time. CiSP now has 914 members and reports on 215,000 abused IP addresses daily.

Technology moves at an astonishing pace and we cannot stand still. Today I will set out further steps to keep us safe. Our new Cyber First scheme will be an elite development programme for the next generation of UK cyber-security talent. It draws heavily on Israel's hugely successful Talpiot programme, which I saw first-hand on a visit to Israel in November. Talpiot provides the state of Israel with formidable cyber-security skills, and is also the seedbed for a fertile array of new businesses. Partly as a result, Israel now has more start-ups per capita than any other country.

24 Mar 2015 : Column 1315

Initially we will pilot Cyber First with a few tens of students. Each will receive £4,000 funding per year to study relevant undergraduate courses in science, technology, engineering and maths. They will be required to work during summer vacations or years out, either within government or in leading UK cyber-security companies. Participation in this elite programme will carry a commitment to work for the Government for at least three years before members start to see their financial support written down. This programme will be a vital pipeline of top-end cyber talent in the service of Britain's national security.

NON-PARLIAMENTARY PUBLICATIONS

The term "non-parliamentary publications" is used to cover the vast range of government publications which are not presented to Parliament. As might be expected, finding recent non-parliamentary papers is largely a question of finding documents on official websites. However, changes to UK government websites, combined with the scale of UK official publishing, mean that this is not always a straightforward task. Since 2014, TSO has only published high demand reports from government departments and agencies in print. 6.13

As noted in para.6.1, UK official publishing online is now being consolidated into the GOV.UK website (at *https://www.gov.uk*), making the site the key starting point for recent official publications. One approach to finding non-parliamentary publications is to use the "Departments, agencies and public bodies" section of the website (at *https://www.gov.uk/government/organisations*). Departments are listed alphabetically with an additional link provided to view associated agencies. A "Documents" section for each department or agency then filters publications on the GOV.UK site to the relevant body. An alternative approach is to go to the "Publications" section of the GOV.UK site (at *https://www.gov.uk/government/publications*) and use the search filters available on the page to filter keyword search results by department or document type. This approach can be helpful if you are not sure of the department likely to have published a document, or are interested in searching for documents on a particular subject across all departments and agencies. There are limitations with this approach at present however. The current keyword search is not particularly effective and relevant official publications may not be available from the GOV.UK website.

If a non-parliamentary paper was published on a government website but cannot be found on the GOV.UK site, it may have been archived on the UK Government Web Archive (at *http://www.nationalarchives.gov.uk/webarchive*). The archive can be browsed by theme and government departments and agencies selected within each theme. Government websites can then be viewed as they appeared at various points in time. The earliest available sites date from 1998. The nature of website archiving means, however, that links on the archived sites may no longer connect to other website pages or retrieve documents. The "Advanced Search" available from the website search page enables search results to be restricted by format to PDF, which can be useful when searching for papers by keyword.

Another keyword subject approach is to use a standard Google search and to limit the search to all websites that use the .gov.uk domain, i.e. all UK government websites. This is achieved by adding "site: gov.uk" to any keyword search. A search for UK official publications relating to vulnerable witnesses would then be:

"vulnerable witnesses" site:.gov.uk

The range of official publishing can still present a challenge, though, when using search engines for subject searching. The more traditional approaches to tracing official publications using catalogues and databases remains helpful, even for recent publications (para.6.14). They can help identify particular documents from keyword searches, which can then be more easily found online.

Libraries have also continued to collect print copies of important UK official publications, and the use of the library catalogue to find non-parliamentary publications should not be overlooked. Bear in mind that the library may not keep all its print copies of non-parliamentary publications in one location. Checking the catalogue is particularly important in those libraries where non-parliamentary publications are scattered among the book collections according to the subject matter of their content, rather than being kept in a single central location. In some cases, your library catalogue may also contain records linking to online versions of key non-parliamentary publications.

If you are searching for older non-parliamentary publications, then the TSO catalogues and HMSO catalogues which pre-dated them are an important resource (para.6.15). The UKOP catalogue (para.6.16) can also play a useful role in tracing non-parliamentary publications as its database includes official publications not published by TSO. Copies of some documents have also been archived from 2000 onwards.

TIPS • *Use site:.gov.uk to limit Google searches to UK government websites.*

TRACING OFFICIAL PUBLICATIONS

6.14 A number of sources are available for tracing both parliamentary and non-parliamentary papers. These include TSO Daily Lists and catalogues (para.6.15), and the UKOP catalogue (covered in para.6.16). It often may not be clear whether a document—an annual report perhaps—is a parliamentary, or a non-parliamentary paper, so the ability to search for all kinds of official publications is helpful.

TIPS • *Use the "Boolean Search" (under "Advanced Search") when searching the UKOP database. Combine search keywords using "AND".*

Stationery Office catalogues, indexes and website

6.15 The *TSO Daily Lists* are useful for tracing very recent legislation and other recent government publications. The lists appear both in print and on the tso shop website. The current list can be found on the website under "Parliamentary & Legal" (at *https://www.tsoshop.co.uk/parliament*). The site also features links to previous lists by month and year. Using the *Daily List* parliamentary section, you can find publication details of House of Lords and Commons Papers and Bills, Command Papers, Acts and Debates. Non-parliamentary publications appear in the official publications section. Other sections are devoted to Scottish Parliament publications, Northern Ireland Assembly publications and Northern Ireland official publications. The final section is devoted to agency publications. These are publications, by bodies such as the Council of Europe, the UN and the WHO, that are sold, but not published, by TSO.

If your required publication is more than a few days old, it is easier to search using TSO Parliamentary & Legal Bookshop search (at *https://www.tsoshop.co.uk/parliament*). Other sources for keyword searching are covered in para.6.16. The TSO shop site includes details of all publications sold by TSO and it is possible to keyword search for any TSO publication, along with HMSO publications, including some "print on demand" titles from as early as 1930. Use search page options to limit your search to Bills, Acts, House of Commons Papers, etc. The author search allows searches by the names of chairmen of committees and date limits can

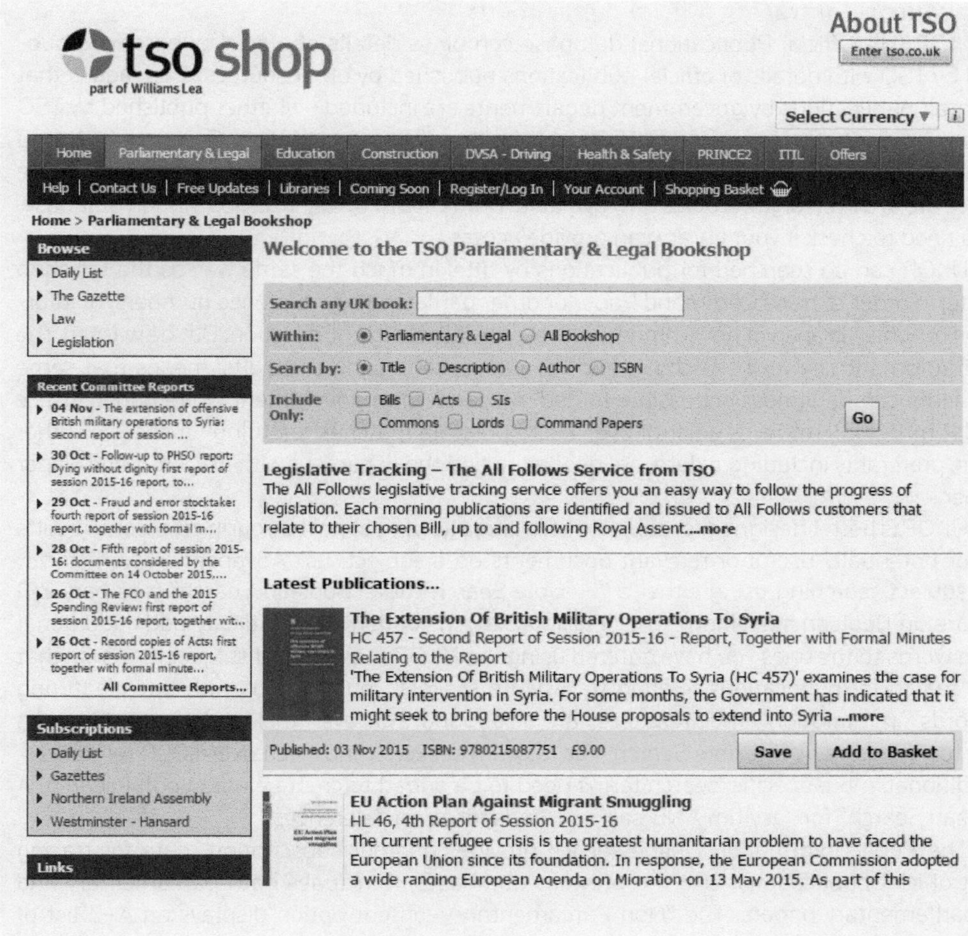

Fig 6.4 TSO Parliamentary & Legal Bookshop page

also be set. The tso shop website is an internet bookshop, which means that pricing information is provided and documents can be ordered from TSO. If the item you are interested in is out of print, a price is given for TSO's print on demand service.

If you are looking for earlier material, which may not appear on the TSO website, you should use the annual catalogues which appeared as either the *HMSO Annual Catalogue 19 . . .*, or before that, *Government Publications 19 . . .* As you go back through the catalogues you see that where the name of the Ministry began with the word "Ministry" or "Department", the entry was inverted, as, for example, Environment, Department of. Otherwise the structure and layout of the catalogues is much like the structure of the current Daily List.

Every five years a *Consolidated Index* was produced for the older catalogues, e.g. for 1961–65, 1966–70, 1971–75, 1976–80 and in many libraries, the catalogues for these years are bound together. To allow for this, the pagination of the catalogues was continuous over the five-year period.

Other sources for tracing official publications

6.16 The UKOP (UK Official Publications) database combines details of official publications published by TSO with details of official publications published by other sources. This means that almost all publications by government departments are included—whether published by TSO or not—along with the full range of TSO published parliamentary papers. Coverage begins in 1980 and since 2000 links have been added to the full text source of many publications. Some of these are archived digital copies only available from UKOP. UKOP is a subscription database, so you need to check if your library can provide access.

UKOP can be searched for publications by title, in much the same way as the tso shop website, in order to trace Command Paper or other parliamentary reference numbers, or information on which branch of government was responsible for the publication. But be warned, the use of automatic keyword searching, and the relevance ranking of results, means that some documents can be almost impossible to find. A search for a government white paper *Justice for All* (Cm. 5563), retrieves a list of over 1,000 possible matches featuring "Justice". Further details, preferably including a date, are needed to find the document with its Command Paper number.

UKOP is better designed for subject searching, allowing a trawl through often long results lists for potentially useful or relevant documents on a subject. Its "Advanced Search" facilitates subject searching using either a "Flexible Search" or a "Boolean Search" (see para.2.11 for more on Boolean searching). The "Flexible Search" option automatically adds additional search words to the ones you have entered using the UKOP thesaurus of subject terms, so that if you search for publications relating to "asylum seekers", publications with titles featuring the words "immigration" and "refugees" are also found. However, this kind of searching can be all too inclusive. A "Flexible Search" for "asylum seekers" finds well over 1,000 references, so additional, more specific, search terms need to be added to create a meaningful search. A "Boolean Search" for "asylum AND seekers" finds far fewer references.

The Public Information Online service provides another subscription route for tracing recent official publications. Like the previous databases, it includes both parliamentary and non-parliamentary papers. The "Non Parliamentary" content option displays an A–Z list of public bodies and a selection of full text documents is held on the website for each department. Keyword searches can also be restricted to find publications from particular public bodies. A similar subscription service, Official Publications Online, is available from TSO (at *http://www.officialpublicationsonline.co.uk*).

If you wish to trace older official publications, selective coverage for the period 1833 to 1974 is provided by the print indexes of the Ford lists and breviates. Abstracts are provided for all the papers included. An online database based on the indexes and records was created by the BOPCRIS project co-ordinated by the University of Southampton and records for the extended period 1801 to 1995 can be searched from the University of Southampton library catalogue. Searches can be restricted by material type to "British Official Publications" to find the BOPCRIS records. Links to PDF versions of the document full text are also available for some entries.

If you already know that the publication which interests you is a parliamentary paper, the ProQuest database of House of Commons Parliamentary Papers can be used both to trace and access papers prior to the 2004–05 parliamentary session. Keyword searches can be restricted to document titles, which can be preferable to searching the full text of the entire database, as large papers of documents are often found using full text searching, even if date limits are set. A more structured approach to searching the papers by subject is possible using the subject search box. Subject terms can be chosen from a searchable list, and range from the relatively general ("asylum"), to the very specific ("asylum and immigration bill 1995/96"). The "hierarchical 19th century subject list" is derived from the *Subject Catalogue of the House of Commons Parliamentary Papers, 1901–1900*, by Peter Cockton. Using the subject list, detailed subject entries can be found within broad categories.

A comprehensive approach to finding older material requires the use of printed indexes. Along with the indexes published by HMSO (para.6.15), the general indexes printed for the House of Commons covering the 19th century should be examined. These provide a detailed alphabetical approach to finding parliamentary papers and were published as the *General Index to the Accounts and papers . . . Printed by Order of the House of Commons or Presented by Command for 1801–1852, 1852/53 to 1868/69 and 1879–1878/79*. The Ford lists and breviates, already mentioned, were published as *Select list of British Parliamentary Papers for 1833–99; A Breviate of Parliamentary Papers*, with volumes covering the period from 1900 to 1954; *Select List of British Parliamentary Papers, 1955–1964*; and *Ford List of British Parliamentary Papers*, with volumes covering 1965 to 1983. Your library may also retain the *Index to the House of Commons Parliamentary Papers* on CD-ROM, which contains references to Bills, Command Papers and House of Commons Papers. Coverage begins in 1801.

Tracing Law Commission reports and working papers

Some of the Law Commission reports are published as Command Papers and others are House of Commons Papers, whilst many more are non-parliamentary papers. As a result you may find that print copies in your library are not all shelved as one collection. Every report and working paper has its own individual number. 6.17

The Law Commission website (at *http://www.lawcom.gov.uk*) has a "Find a Publication" section which allows searches to be limited by document type and area of law. Publications included date from the 1990s. Law Commission papers can also be traced using the tso shop's website for recent publications and the HMSO catalogues for older reports and publications (para.6.15).

Tracing news and press releases from government departments

Recent news and press releases from government departments are relatively easy to trace using the GOV.UK website (para.6.13). Older news from government websites can be found using the UK Government Web Archive (at *http://www.nationalarchives.gov.uk/webarchive*), described in para.6.13. 6.18

Updates on press releases with brief summaries can also be found in the "Current Awareness" section of Westlaw UK. Press releases can be browsed "by document type" or searched as part of the current awareness database. Press releases of legal interest are included from UK government departments, the Commission of the European Communities and the European Court of Human Rights.

Tracing official statistics

6.19 UK official statistics from all government departments and agencies can be found on the statistics page of the GOV.UK website (at *https://www.gov.uk/government/statistics*).

The website of the Office for National Statistics (at *http://www.ons.gov.uk*) provides a more structured approach to finding official statistics by theme, e.g. "Crime and Justice". More specific areas can then be selected within each theme, e.g. "Criminal Justice".

7 How to find information on a subject

INTRODUCTION

7.1 Preparation for your essays, tutorials and seminars will often require you to know not simply the present state of the law but also to be aware of its development and any criticisms and suggestions for reform that have been made.

To find information on a subject you will need to consult some or all of the following sources:

- Acts of Parliament;
- Delegated legislation;
- EU law, and International Treaties and Conventions;
- Cases;
- Textbooks;
- Journal articles;
- Relevant government publications, including Law Commission Reports (especially those which have made suggestions for reform of the law);
- Reports and comments in newspapers; and
- Bills and Parliamentary Debates.

In order to tackle a legal problem, you may need to ask yourself the following questions:

QUESTION: Where can I find a general statement of the law on this subject?
ANSWER: In encyclopedias, such as *Halsbury's Laws* (para.7.3) and in textbooks (para.7.29).

QUESTION: What books are there on this subject?
ANSWER: Consult library catalogues (para.7.29) and bibliographies (para.7.30).

QUESTION: What journal articles have been written on this subject?
ANSWER: Use keyword searches to find articles (para.5.5).

QUESTION: What cases have there been on this topic?
ANSWER: Use online databases or print indexes (para.7.8).

QUESTION: What judicial interpretation has been placed on particular words?
ANSWER: Look in *Words and Phrases Legally Defined* and similar works (para.7.19).

QUESTION: Which Acts of Parliament deal with this subject and are in force?
ANSWER: Use online databases (para.7.21) and catalogues (para.7.22) or *Halsbury's Statutes* (para.7.24).

QUESTION: Are there any relevant statutory instruments?
ANSWER: Use online databases (para.7.26) or *Halsbury's Statutory Instruments* (para.7.27).

QUESTION: Have there been any government reports or Law Commission reports on this topic?
ANSWER: Use the TSO or UKOP databases (para.6.15 and para.6.16) and Law Commission website (para.6.17).

QUESTION: Are there any Bills before Parliament which would change the law on this subject? Has the issue been discussed in Parliament?
ANSWER: Consult the "Bills before Parliament" web page (para.6.8) and *Parliamentary Debates* (para.6.11 and para.6.12).

Having mapped out the ground, you can now proceed to tackle these questions. Your first task will be to clarify the key words or concepts to be used when searching for cases and journal articles or using encyclopedias. Textbooks can provide useful starting points for this (para.7.29) along with lecture notes and handouts. If you are using the wider book collection of the library, work well within the time limits set, otherwise you may discover that the material is unavailable because of high demand. If you encounter any difficulties with your research, do not hesitate to ask library staff or your lecturer for help.

LEGAL ENCYCLOPEDIAS

7.2 These contain detailed up-to-date statements of the law on a particular subject. The major general legal encyclopedia is *Halsbury's Laws of England*, which is now in its fifth edition (para.7.3). It is a most useful source of information on a wide variety of topics. In addition, there are a number of more specialised encyclopedias, many of them available online, or issued in looseleaf form so that the information can be kept up to date.

The "Insight" section of Westlaw UK also provides a useful starting point for research across a range of subject areas, as it consists of brief, up-to-date statements on the law, written by legal academics or practitioners.

To use Insight, search from the "Insight" page of Westlaw UK using key phrases, e.g. "Right to Silence", "Passing Off", "Offer and Acceptance". By no means are all areas of law covered, but where a match is found an overview of the topic is provided, along with links to key cases in Westlaw UK. Further reading suggestions are sometimes also added.

Halsbury's Laws of England

7.3 *Halsbury's Laws* covers all areas of English law and is a useful starting point for research on any legal topic. Because it is kept up to date, it has the advantage over textbooks of including recent information.

The encyclopedia is available either online from the Lexis Library (para.2.3), or as just over 100 print volumes. The fifth edition was completed in 2014 and its volumes are periodically updated and reissued. The volume arrangement of the printed encyclopedia also forms the basis of the online version, which features separate on-screen updating sections. Recent updates to the printed encyclopedia are handled by a *Cumulative Supplement* and a "*Noter-Up*" binder. The print volumes selected for reissue are those which have been most affected by changes in the law.

Whether online or in print, *Halsbury's Laws* provides an effective statement of the whole of the law of England and Wales. The print volumes are arranged alphabetically by subject, from "Agency" to "Wills and Intestancy" and these divisions are also present in *Halsbury's Laws* online. Each print volume covers between one and seven subjects. The subjects are in turn divided into numbered paragraphs and each paragraph gives a description of the law relating to a particular topic, together with copious footnote references to relevant statutes and cases. Remember that *Halsbury's Laws* gives a useful summary of the law: you will need to go to other works to find the actual text of an Act of Parliament or law report.

How to use Halsbury's Laws online

Select the "Commentary" page from the Lexis Library home page (para.2.3), to check if your 7.4
library has a subscription to *Halsbury's Laws of England*. *Halsbury's Laws* can be found using the "Sources" drop-down menu. If your library has subscriptions to other LexisNexis Butterworths works providing commentary on the law, their titles are displayed on the same menu. These might include *Clarke Hall and Morrison on Children*, for example, or *Tolley's Employment Law Service*.

If you are sure of the area of law you wish to research, one approach is to use the "Browse" link available under the commentary heading. The subject headings found in the print volumes of *Halsbury's Laws* are then displayed alphabetically. Within each heading, contents listings can be used to work through the hierarchy of sub-headings used in the encyclopedia, until the full text of a particular section is reached. The "Juries" heading (Vol.61) might be selected, for example, followed by "Constitution and duties of juries" then a further subheading, in order to reach a section on the meaning of "jury".

However, the subject heading to choose may not be obvious. In this case, a more effective way of using *Halsbury's Laws* is to search the full text of the entire encyclopedia using the "Search Terms" section displayed on the commentary search page. As this is a full text source it is important to consider the different ways in which the subject you are interested in might be described, in order to be sure that you have adequately explored the database (see para.2.11 for more on database searching).

Suppose, for example, you wish to discover the current law on bomb hoaxes. How should you phrase your search? Fortunately, the Lexis Library commentary sources can be searched using the same proximity limiters that operate in the Lexis Library generally. This means that you can specify how close you wish terms to be found in the text of the encyclopedia in order to ensure that all potentially relevant results are found. Searching for "bomb w/6 hoax", for example, specifies that the two words should be between six words of each other. This means that text including the phrase "bomb hoax" is found, but also text including the phrase "hoax bomb call", or "hoax call suggesting that a bomb", etc. A further refinement of the search

Fig 7.1
Example results page from *Halsbury's Laws* online

Halsbury's Laws of England/NUISANCE (VOLUME 78 (2010))/1. SCOPE OF NUISANCE/(1) DESCRIPTION AND CLASSIFICATION/(i) Public, Private and Statutory Nuisances/106. Criminal liability for public nuisance.

106. Criminal liability for public nuisance.

There are statutory provisions[1] which impose penalties for nuisances affecting public health and comfort. However, the common law liability remains, and any person who by any act unwarranted by law or by any omission to carry out a legal duty endangers the life, health, property, morals or comfort of the public commits an offence known as public nuisance[2]. A landowner may be criminally liable for public nuisance if he should have known of the likely consequences of activities taking place on his land, even if he had no actual knowledge[3].

1 See the Environmental Protection Act 1990 ss 79-82; and PARAS 115, 155-172, 199-212, 225-226.

2 The common law offence is compatible with the legal certainty requirements of the common law and the Convention for the Protection of Human Rights and Fundamental Freedoms (Rome, 4 November 1950; TS 71 (1953); Cmd 8969), but the circumstances in which there should be resort to the common law offence are now rare in view of the existing statutory provisions: *R v Goldstein; R v Rimmington* [2005] UKHL 63, [2006] 1 AC 459, [2006] 2 All ER 257. Examples are the keeping of a corpse unburied (*R v Vann* (1851) 2 Den 325 at 331, CCR), provided the person charged has the means for paying for its burial (see CREMATION AND BURIAL vol 24 (2010) PARA 1104); the exposure in a public place of a person infected with smallpox (*R v Vantandillo* (1815) 4 M & S 73), although it would be a defence to an indictment if it could be shown that there was lawful and sufficient excuse for so doing (*R v Burnett* (1815) 4 M & S 272; and see *Metropolitan Asylum District Managers v Hill* (1881) 6 App Cas 193 at 204, HL, per Lord Blackburn; *A-G v Nottingham Corpn* [1904] 1 Ch 673); the keeping of explosives or highly inflammable matter in a manner calculated to terrify the neighbourhood or to do damage to neighbouring property (*R v Lister and Biggs* (1857) Dears & B 209, CCR; *R v Taylor* (1742) 2 Stra 1167; *R v Bennett* (1858) Bell CC 1; and see EXPLOSIVES vol 47 (2014) PARA 451 et seq; for statutes now regulating the keeping of explosives see EXPLOSIVES); going about a public street armed so as to terrify the public (*R v Meade* (1903) 19 TLR 540); making obscene telephone calls on many occasions to numerous women (*R v Johnson* [1997] 1 WLR 367, CA; cf *R v Ireland* [1998] AC 147, [1997] 4 All ER 225, HL, where there was a series of silent telephone calls to three women, this was held to constitute assault). The actual, not potential, danger to the public must be considered, so that a hoax telephone call about the planting of a bomb was held not to be a public nuisance: *R v Madden* [1975] 3 All ER 155, [1975] 1 WLR 1379, CA; cf *R v Soul* (1980) 70 Cr App Rep 295, CA. As to criminal liability for bomb hoaxes see CRIMINAL LAW vol 26 (2010) PARA 791. As to the common law and statutory liability for selling unwholesome food see FOOD AND DRINK vol 51 (2013) PARAS 626-627.

3 *R v Shorrock* [1994] QB 279, [1993] 3 All ER 917, CA. As to where an injunction restraining public or private nuisance may exceptionally be granted in aid of the criminal law see *City of London Corpn v Bovis Construction Ltd* [1992] 3 All ER 697, 49 BLR 1, CA; and PARAS 188 note 2, 231 note 3. See also CIVIL PROCEDURE vol 11 (2009) PARA 331 et seq.

UPDATE

106 Criminal liability for public nuisance

NOTE 2--A single act by a male on foot soliciting a woman for prostitution within a recognised vice area does not amount to the common law offence of public nuisance: *DPP v Fearon* [2010] EWHC 340 (Admin), (2010) 174 JP 145, DC.

would be to use "hoax!", where the exclamation mark ensures that all words beginning "hoax" are found, e.g. "hoax" and "hoaxes". Using proximity searches in this way ensures that you are not defeated by the variety of natural language.

In this particular case, searching *Halsbury's Laws* for matches to "bomb w/6 hoax!" finds six relevant sections in the encyclopedia. Three can be found under the "Criminal Law" heading, on "Bomb hoaxes", "Threats to destroy or damage property" and "Improper use of a public electronic communications network", another, on "Criminal liability for public nuisance", can be found under the "Nuisance" heading.

Once you have found the encyclopedia's description of the law on a subject, it is important to check if there is an update section at the end of the main text. The section on criminal liability for public nuisance, for example, includes an update section referring to the relatively recent case, *DPP v Fearon* [2010] EWHC 340 (Admin), (2010) 174 J.P. 145.

> **TIPS** • *Be as specific as you can when searching Halsbury's Laws using keywords. Use single words and short phrases and combine them with "AND".*

How to use Halsbury's Laws in print

To use *Halsbury's Laws* in print, start by looking up the subject that interests you in the *Consolidated Index* volumes. The entry refers you to the appropriate volume number (in bold type) and paragraph number (not page number). The presence of "n" followed by a small number indicates that you are being referred to one of the footnotes at the end of the appropriate paragraph number. For information on the law related to bomb hoaxes, you would turn to Vol.26, para.791. Paragraph 791 gives a statement of the law relating to bomb hoaxes, together with footnotes which refer you to relevant statutes. *Halsbury's Laws* also refers you to cases and other sources of information, as appropriate. ▶ 7.5

Remember that it is possible that the information in the volumes is out of date. New legislation, or other changes in the law, could have made the information incomplete or inaccurate. To find out if there have been any changes in the law since the volumes were published, make a note of the relevant volume and paragraph numbers, and turn to the *Cumulative Supplement*. For example, the information on bomb hoaxes was contained in Vol.26, para.791. If you turn to the latest *Cumulative Supplement* (only the latest Supplement should be used) and look up the entry for Vol.26, para.791, you can check to see if there have been changes in the law since Vol.26 was written. It is therefore important to read the information in the *Cumulative Supplement* in conjunction with that found in the main volume.

These two volumes bring the information up to date to the end of last year. But have there been changes in the law since then? To find out, turn to the looseleaf *Noter-Up* in Binder 2. The *Noter-Up* is arranged in the same way as the *Cumulative Supplement*, in volume and paragraph number.

SUMMARY: HOW TO USE HALSBURY'S LAWS IN PRINT

1. Look up the subject in the *Consolidated Index*. This tells you the number of the volume and paragraph which contains the information.
2. Find the relevant volume and paragraph number in the main work.
3. To make sure the information is up to date, consult:
   (a) the *Cumulative Supplement*, and
   (b) the *Noter-Up* in Binder 2, under the relevant volume and paragraph number.

Remember there are four steps in using *Halsbury's Laws*:

- *Consolidated Index*;
- main volume;

- *Cumulative Supplement*; and
- *Noter-Up* service.

At the back of each volume of the main work, there are separate indexes to each of the subject areas dealt with in the volume.

The *Monthly Reviews* (published as booklets and filed in Binder 1) can be used as a general means of keeping up with new developments in subjects you are studying since they give, under subject headings, recent changes in the law with summaries of cases, statutes, statutory instruments and other materials. The *Monthly Reviews* are not arranged in the same volume and paragraph order as the main volumes, so in order to find relevant information you will need to look up the subject again in the *Cumulative Index* to the *Reviews* at the back of the Binder. The *Monthly Reviews* are replaced by an *Annual Abridgment*, which summarises all the changes in the law during a particular year. At the beginning of the volume, a section headed "In brief" summarises the major development in the law of each subject during the year. At the beginning of each subject, there is a reference to the main volume of *Halsbury's Laws* which deals with that subject and there is a highly selective list of journal articles written on the subject during the year.

Specialised encyclopedias

7.6 There are a number of specialised encyclopedias which can provide you with an up-to-date statement of the law in particular subject areas. They are particularly useful in subjects such as taxation, where the law changes very rapidly. Many are issued in looseleaf format, so that the information can be updated by the insertion of replacement pages whenever there is a change in the law. Most are also available online. *Woodfall: Landlord and Tenant*, for example, can be searched or browsed from the "Books" section of Westlaw UK. Other specialised encyclopedias available from Westlaw UK cover topics such as copyright, tort, and sale of goods. The titles you will be able to use will depend on library subscriptions. Specialised encyclopedias from the Lexis Library cover, among other subject areas, education law, family law and landlord and tenant. As with Westlaw UK, the titles available online from the Lexis Library will depend on library subscriptions. Check the "Commentary" section of the service to discover the titles available.

When using the looseleaf version of a specialised encyclopedia, you should check the pages near the beginning of the volume which tell you how recent the information is. This will enable you to be certain that the latest supplementary pages have all been inserted. Specialised encyclopedias usually contain an explanation of the law, together with the up-to-date versions of the relevant statutes, statutory instruments and government circulars, and notes of relevant cases. Publishers have also issued some books for practitioners in looseleaf format, so that the text can be kept up to date. This is a development of the long-established practice of issuing cumulative supplements in between editions, to update the last edition.

Precedent books and rule books

7.7 These are principally intended for the practitioner. The basic object of precedent books is to provide specimens of wills, conveyances, tenancy agreements or other forms of legal documents which solicitors are called upon to draw up. In addition, there are some precedent books which provide specimens of the types of forms that will be required whenever a case is taken to court. Rule books contain the rules that govern procedure in court, and specimen copies of the various orders and forms used by the courts and by the parties to litigation.

The multi-volume *Encyclopaedia of Forms and Precedents* aims to provide a form for every transaction likely to be encountered by practitioners, except for court forms. The *Encyclopaedia* is also available from the Lexis Library (para.2.3). The entries are arranged by subject, e.g. "Animals", "Mortgages". Some idea of the wide scope of the work can be obtained by glancing through the subject headings. For instance, the section on animals covers such diverse topics as the sale and leasing of animals, applications for a licence to keep mink or to keep an animals' boarding establishment; a veterinary surgeon's certificate for the destruction of an animal, and the relevant documents prohibiting movement of animals during an outbreak of disease. If you are using the print version, the looseleaf service volume keeps the information up to date. The *Cumulative Index* refers you to the volume (in bold type) and paragraph number that you require. Each individual volume also has its own index. References in the index to paragraph numbers in square brackets refer to precedents: paragraph numbers not enclosed in brackets refer to the preliminary notes. Checklists of procedures to be followed are provided under some subject headings.

Atkins Court Forms is a complementary publication, covering the procedure in civil courts and tribunals. Again, the volume is available from the Lexis Library. The print volume on divorce, for instance, contains all the necessary documents needed during the court action, together with a detailed list of the steps to be taken and the forms required at each stage. The volumes are reissued from time to time to incorporate new material. An annual supplement keeps the information up to date. The *Consolidated Index* is also published yearly.

There are many precedent books dealing with specific areas of the law, e.g. the looseleaf *Jackson & Powell: Professional Liability Precedents*. In addition, some textbooks designed for practitioners will include precedents.

The rules and procedures governing various courts are set out in a number of places. Sweet & Maxwell's *White Book* service and *Bullen & Leek & Jacob's Precedents of Pleading* are available online from Westlaw UK (para.2.4) and can be searched or browsed from the "Commentary" page. *Archbold: Criminal Pleading, Evidence and Practice* is used by those engaged in criminal work. It is also available from the Westlaw UK "Books" page.

The *Law Society Gazette* is also of particular interest to practitioners. It often includes specimen forms and precedents, and details of Home Office circulars and practice directions. Practice directions are also published in the major series of law reports, e.g. the *All England Law Reports* and the *Weekly Law Reports*.

TRACING CASES ON A SUBJECT

Cases on a particular subject can be traced by consulting the following sources: 7.8

- The Westlaw UK Subject/Keyword search (para.7.9);
- Full-text case law databases (para.7.10);
- Databases of recent judgments (para.7.11);
- *Current Law* (para.7.12 and para.7.13);

- *The Digest* (para.7.14 and para.7.15);
- *Halsbury's Laws of England* (para.7.4);
- Indexes to individual series of law reports (para.7.16);
- Updates on recent cases (para.7.17);
- Indexes to articles in legal journals (para.5.5); and
- Relevant textbooks (para.7.29).

How to use the Westlaw UK Subject/Keyword search

7.9 To find cases on a subject using the Westlaw UK "Cases" search, it can help greatly to restrict your search, so that only keywords or subject terms are searched. The database used in the cases search contains abstracts of almost all England and Wales cases reported since 1947, whether present in full text or not. These are the abstracts which appear in print in the *Current Law Year Books* (para.7.13). Standard subject terms and keywords are added to the abstracts, and your search can be restricted to search only those terms. Abstracts are available for an extremely wide range of cases and it is likely that the cases found using keywords contained in the abstract will be highly relevant to your subject search.

Suppose, for example, that you wish to find cases that might concern privacy and human rights (you might already have found some relevant journal articles using Westlaw UK "Journals" search as suggested in para.5.8). If you were to use keyword search terms such as "privacy" and "human rights" in a standard "Free Text" search, your results list would contain numerous minor and incidental mentions of the search words, making it difficult to find relevant cases. The inclusion of both "human rights" and "privacy" in the added keywords for a case, on the other hand, means that the case is much more likely to be of interest.

To restrict the cases search to keywords, enter your search words using the "Subject/Keyword" search box on the "Cases" page. To continue with the privacy and human rights example, a "Subject/Keyword" search finds just over 100 cases. Well over 1,500 cases are found using a "Free text" search. However, the cases found are still quite wide ranging, and you might then decide to narrow the search using another standard keyword phrase, such as "right to respect for private and family life". If you are unsure which keywords to use, try a "Free text" keyword search first and note the keywords and keyword phrases which appear in "Case Analysis" entries of some of the cases that seem relevant. If you were interested in cases related to the *Douglas v Hello* cases mentioned in para.3.15, for example, keywords such as "breach of confidence", "celebrities" or "media" will prove relevant, along with "privacy".

> **TIPS** • *Only search using the Westlaw UK "Subject/Keyword" search when you have already identified standard subject and keyword terms for a subject.*

Using the Cases search in this way allows you to explore subject areas and find relevant cases, many of which can then be found in full text.

How to use full-text databases to find case law by subject

7.10 The full text databases of case law found in the Lexis Library (para.2.3) and Westlaw UK (para.2.4) provide the largest archives of law reports and judgments available for subject searching. Your library may also have particular series of law reports available from Justis Publishing (para.2.6) in particular, constituting additional potential sources of case law. If you wish to include the widest possible range of relatively recent judgments, the judgments on the

BAILII website (para.2.13) should also not be ignored. The nature of law reporting means that a particular judgment is likely to appear in more than one of these databases. However, there remain specialist law reports whose judgments only appear online in one of these sources. As a result, a comprehensive approach to subject searching using full text sources of case law, requires that you repeat your search on all of the databases to which you have access.

For all of these databases, the process of searching is straightforward. They all have some form of free text search box in which you can enter your search words and they accept the search syntax described in para.2.11, in particular the use of "AND", "OR", etc. to combine search words. Some form of proximity searching will also be available, ensuring that your search words must occur close together in the text being searched.

If you are using a full text database of case law, the most important thing to remember is that you must be as specific as possible in your choice of search words. As noted in para.2.11, if you enter general terms such as "copyright" or even "copyright AND software", you will obtain as a search result, either a list of the many thousands of cases in which the word "copyright" appears on its own, or the many hundreds of cases in which both the word "copyright" and the word "software" appear, but not necessarily in any proximity to each other. A corollary is that you need a good understanding of what it is you are researching in order to be able to hone in on the important keywords. It makes sense to use full text databases as the last stage in your subject searching. Try looking at likely textbooks, before you make your search, in order to select key terms to use. *Halsbury's Laws of England* (para.7.3), either online or in print, can also help you in the initial stages of a subject search, clarifying terminology and listing key cases.

You should think of different ways your topic is likely to be discussed in a judgment. For the most part you are only searching the text of the words used in the judgment and you will need to think about the different ways the same basic issue can be expressed. Ensure also that you use the symbol or "search operator" for the database that specifies that your keywords must be found close to each other in the long text of a judgment. Many databases allow "NEAR" to specify a standard proximity, the Lexis Library uses "w/" so that "w/6" specifies within six words. For Westlaw UK, use "/number", so that "/6", for example, specifies within six words. Once you have considered various possibilities and tried different searches, the time will come to read the law reports you have found and see which cases they have cited.

> **TIPS** • *Use textbooks or Halsbury's Laws to clarify the keywords you should use when searching full text databases of case law.*

How to use databases of recent judgments

The sources of recent judgments described in para.3.20 provide a means of searching for judgments from a range of UK courts. BAILII, Casetrack and Lawtel all allow the full text of judgments to be searched using keywords. The need to decide your key search words and think of alternative ways in which the same idea can be expressed applies to these databases just as much as it does to the databases noted in para.7.10. Keywords and phrases can be combined and "proximity" searches are possible. Check the search and help screens of the databases you are using for further information on how to combine search words. 7.11

How to use the Current Law Monthly Digest

7.12 *Current Law* is published monthly under the title *Current Law Monthly Digest*. The main part is arranged by subject and under each subject heading is given a summary of recent cases on the subject, new statutes and statutory instruments, government reports and recent books and journal articles on that subject. Full details are given to enable you to trace the cases and other materials mentioned in your own library. A page from the Monthly Digest is shown in fig.7.2. On this page alone, an article is mentioned (item 161), a case is summarised (item 163) and a statutory instrument is outlined (item 162).

At the back of each issue is a Table of Cases which contains a list of all the cases which have been reported during the current year. It is therefore only necessary to look at the Table of Cases in the latest issue of the *Current Law Monthly Digest* to trace a case reported at any time during the year. (This list of cases brings the information in the *Current Law Case Citators* up to date (para.3.16)).

The *Current Law Monthly Digest* also contains a subject index. Again it is cumulative, so it is only necessary to consult the "Cumulative Index" section at the end of the latest month's issue. This enables you to trace any development in the law during the current year. The reference given, e.g. Feb 80, is to the appropriate monthly issue (in this example, the February issue) and the item number in the issue, i.e. item 80. If the reference is followed by an S (e.g. Jan 821S), the item contains Scottish material.

The Subject Index can also help if you are unsure of the names of the parties in a case or have an incomplete reference.

How to use the Current Law Year Books

7.13 The issues of the *Current Law Monthly Digest* are replaced by an annual volume, the *Current Law Year Book*.

The *Year Book* is arranged by subject, in the same way as the *Monthly Digest*, and contains a summary of all the cases, legislation and other developments in that subject during the year. Lists of journal articles and books written on a subject during the year are printed at the back of the volume. (The 1956 *Year Book* contains a list of journal articles published between 1947 and 1956.)

Since 1991, the *Current Law Year Book* contains Scottish material as well as that from England. Before then, there was a separate Scottish version, called the *Scottish Current Law Year Book*. Despite the name, this included all the English material, plus a separate section at the back of the volume containing Scottish developments during the year. The Scottish section remains separate from the English material in the *Current Law Year Book* and there are separate indexes to the two sections.

At the back of the 1976 *Year Book*, there is a Subject Index to all the entries in all the *Year Books* from 1947 to 1976. Entries give the last two digits of the year, and a reference to the individual item number within that year's volume, e.g. 69/3260 is a reference to item 3260 in the 1969 *Year Book*. Entries which have no year in front of them will be found in the *Current Law Consolidation 1947–1951*. Cumulative indexes were also published in the 1986 and 1989 *Year Books*. These indexes, together with the *Year Books* since 1989 and the latest *Current Law Monthly Digest*, provide complete coverage of any developments in the law of that subject since 1947.

Fig 7.2 Example page from the *Current Law Monthly Digest*

INTERNATIONAL LAW

INTERNATIONAL LAW

161 Articles

Legacy of war (*Reyes, Eduardo*): L.S.G. 2015, 112(26). Reports on the International Criminal Tribunal for the former Yugoslavia, the challenges it faced and what it has achieved. Considers the challenges presented: by the judges and counsel having being drawn from disparate legal cultures; in conceiving, investigating and presenting the vast complexity of the events involved; and in supporting victims and witnesses.

INTERNATIONAL TRADE

162 Export controls–Sanctions–Yemen

THE EXPORT CONTROL (YEMEN SANCTIONS) REGULATIONS 2015, SI 2015/1586; made under the European Communities Act 1972 s.2(2). In force: 27 August 2015.

These Regulations make provision for the enforcement of certain trade restrictions in view of the situation in Yemen as specified in Regulation 1352/2014. The Regulations set out offences in relation to these restrictions and those offences can be committed by any person in the United Kingdom and, around the world, by any United Kingdom person, as defined in the Export Control Act 2002 s.11.

LANDLORD AND TENANT

163 Repair covenants–Dampness–Flat damaged by rising damp–Landlord's duty to repair

[Landlord and Tenant Act 1985 (c.70) s.11; CPR PD 32 (Evidence) 1999 para.27; Civil Procedure Rules 1998 r.52.11(3)(b)]

The appellant local authority appealed against a decision awarding the respondent tenants damages for breach of the local authority's repairing obligations. The respondents were weekly tenants of a maisonette in the basement and ground floor of a Victorian house. The letting was subject under the Landlord and Tenant Act 1985 s.11 to an implied covenant obliging the local authority to keep in repair the structure and exterior of the property, including drains, gutters and external pipes. Soon after moving into the property the tenants complained about rising damp, and most of the judge's award related to that issue. The local authority submitted that (1) the judge had been wrong to rely on two 2004 surveyors' reports included in the trial bundle; (2) there was not sufficient evidence to support the judge's finding that there had been a defective damp-proof course; (3) the claim had been insufficiently pleaded; (4) the judge had wrongly changed the date in his draft judgment from which damages were to run.

Held: Appeal dismissed. (1) The reports both indicated that there had been previous attempts to install a damp-proof course and to deal with rising damp by re-plastering or rendering the lower part of the internal walls. The local authority argued that the judge admitted the reports not as evidence of the truth of their contents but only as showing that the property had been inspected and reports had been made. The tenants argued that there would have been no point admitting them for that purpose and they were admissible as evidence of what the surveyors had seen on their inspections. The appeal court could not resolve that dispute but in any event the reports were admissible under CPR PD 32 para.27 to prove the truth of their contents since they had been included in the trial bundles without objection. (2) Where rising

114

Master Volumes were published in the 1956, 1961, 1966 and 1971 *Year Books*. These volumes contain, under the usual subject headings, detailed entries for all developments during the year in which they were published, together with a summary of the developments during the previous four years. References are given to enable you to trace the full details in the appropriate *Current Law Year Book*. Thus it is possible, by using the *Master Volumes* and the *Current Law Consolidation 1947–1951*, to see at a glance a summary of every entry that has appeared in *Current Law* on a particular subject over a five-year period.

SUMMARY: HOW TO USE CURRENT LAW IN PRINT

(1) If you know the name of a case and want to find out where it has been reported and whether the case has subsequently been judicially considered, consult:
 the *Current Law Case Citator* volumes (see para.3.16); and
 the Table of Cases in the latest *Current Law Monthly Digest*.

(2) To trace any developments (cases, statutes, etc.) on a particular subject, consult:
 the Cumulative Index covering 1947–1976 at the back of the 1976 *Current Law Year Book*;
 the Cumulative Index at the back of the 1986 *Year Book* covering the years 1972–1986;
 the Cumulative Index at the back of the 1989 *Year Book* covering the years 1987–1989;
 the Indexes in the back of the *Year Books* since 1989; and
 the Subject Index in the latest issue of the *Current Law Monthly Digest*.

(3) To obtain a general view of developments in a topic over a number of years, consult:
 the *Current Law Consolidation 1947–1951*;
 the *Master Volumes* (1956, 1961, 1966, 1971 *Year Books*);
 all the *Year Books* published since the last *Master Volume* was issued; and
 all the issues of the *Current Law Monthly Digest* for this year.

(4) To trace books and journal articles on a subject, look in the back of the 1956 *Year Book* and each subsequent Year Book and in the *Current Law Monthly Digests* under the appropriate subject heading. There are, however, quicker and more comprehensive sources for tracing journals (para.5.5) and books (para.7.29 et seq.).

Remember that *Current Law* only contains information on cases reported or mentioned in court since 1947 and other developments in the law since 1947. To trace earlier cases, use *The Digest*.

The Digest

7.14 *The Digest* (formerly known as the *English and Empire Digest*) contains summaries of cases that have appeared in law reports from the 13th century to the present day, arranged in subject order. It enables you to trace cases of any date that deal with your particular subject. In addition to English cases, reports of Irish, Scottish and many Commonwealth cases are included, together with cases on EU law. These are printed in smaller type to enable them to be easily distinguishable from English cases.

For each case, a summary of the decision is given, followed by the name of the case, and a list of places where the case is reported. The subsequent judicial history of the case is also shown, in the annotations section. A list of the abbreviations used for law reports will be found in the front of Vol.1 and also in the front of the *Cumulative Supplement*.

How to use The Digest to trace cases on a subject

To find cases on a particular subject using *The Digest*, start by looking at the multi-volume *Index*. This is reissued every year. The *Index* includes both broad subject categories and highly specific entries for particular subjects. These can take you directly to a summary of the judgment in a particular case. Suppose you are interested in finding human rights cases related to the European Convention right to manifest religion or belief. You will first need to try likely subject entries in the *Index*. A number of relevant cases will be found, for example, under the main "Freedom of Conscience" heading, grouped under a European Convention on Human Rights sub-heading (see fig.7.3). Of these, you might be particularly interested in the case noted under "religious and philosophical convictions". The reference for "religious and philosophical convictions" gives a volume number, and notes the relevant subject heading within the volume: 7.15

26(3) H Rghts [i.e. Human Rights] 560.

In the main volumes, cases are listed in number order for the volume under appropriate subject headings. Turn to case number 560 to see a summary of *R. (on the application of K) v Newham LBC* (2002) *Times*, 28 February (see fig.7.4). Scots, Irish and Commonwealth cases are grouped together at the end of each section within the volume.

After finding the relevant case in the main volumes, you should now check to see if there have been more recent cases on the subject since the volume was written. To do this, consult the *Cumulative Supplement*. Make a note of the volume number, subject heading and case number(s) in the main volumes which contain relevant information. Now turn to the *Cumulative Supplement* and look to see if there is an entry for that volume, subject heading and case number. If there is an entry, this will provide information on any later cases relevant to the subject area. A number of cases are, in fact, noted against Vol.26(3) 560 and these are noted as 560a, 560b, etc. (see fig.7.5). All these cases are more significant than the case summarised in the main volume. 560b, for example, is the case, *R. (on the application of Begum) v Head Teacher and Governors of Denbigh High School* [2006] UKHL 15; [2006] 2 W.L.R. 719 on the right to wear particular clothing (a jilbab) in a school for religious reasons. A further line notes cases which applied the ruling in the *Begum* case:

Apld *Miss Behavin' Ltd v Belfast City Council* [2007] 3 All ER 1007; *R. (on the application of X) v Head Teacher and Governors of Y School* [2008] 1 All E.R. 249.

The *Cumulative Supplement* is revised annually; the front cover tells you how recent the information is. If you are looking for new cases on a particular subject, within the last few months, then *The Digest* is not sufficiently up to date and you should use online sources (para.7.8) or print publications, such as *Current Law*, the latest *index* to the *Law Reports* or the *Monthly Reviews* in *Halsbury's Laws of England*.

One consequence of putting the cases in number order is that case numbers change

Fig 7.3 Example page from *The Digest* Index

FREE OF TAX 192

FREE MOVEMENT OF PERSONS, SERVICES AND CAPITAL (EU)—*cont*
workers—*cont*
dependant of—*cont*
rights of—*cont*
spouse to obtain leave to remain indefinitely in UK **20**(4) *EU Law* 934, 937, 938
deportation **21**(1) *EU Law* 971
discrimination
criminal proceedings **20**(4) *EU Law* 924
vocational training **20**(4) *EU Law* 923
entry of EC national **21**(1) *EU Law* 969
equality of treatment **21**(1) *EU Law* 940–953
exceptions to the right
public health **21**(1) *EU Law* 1056
public policy **21**(1) *EU Law* 1046–1054, 1057, 1058
public security **21**(1) *EU Law* 1055
public service **21**(1) *EU Law* 1059–1063
failure to find employment in host state **20**(4) *EU Law* 926
"freedom of movement", meaning of **20**(4) *EU Law* 896–901
hospital workers **21**(1) *EU Law* 1060
implementation of right **21**(1) *EU Law* 970
non-discrimination **21**(1) *EU Law* 954
personal scope **20**(4) *EU Law* 907–939
prohibition of discrimination on grounds of nationality **20**(4) *EU Law* 916–921
remuneration **21**(1) *EU Law* 972
researchers **21**(1) *EU Law* 1063
residence, right of **21**(1) *EU Law* 1044, 1045
retraining and rehabilitation activities **20**(4) *EU Law* 925
social security benefits
aggregation of insurance periods **21**(1) *EU Law* 984
appeal **21**(1) *EU Law* 1016
applicability of national rules against overlapping of benefits **21**(1) *EU Law* 996–998, 1000
claim made in EC member state **21**(1) *EU Law* 1014
combined sickness/invalidity insurance **21**(1) *EU Law* 1012
disability benefit **21**(1) *EU Law* 1025
double payment of contributions prohibited **21**(1) *EU Law* 1013
early retirement benefit **21**(1) *EU Law* 1026
effect of change of residence to another EC member state **21**(1) *EU Law* 975
employment in EC states only **21**(1) *EU Law* 1002–1007
entitlement **21**(1) *EU Law* 985–994
equality of treatment regarding **21**(1) *EU Law* 1029
family allowance **21**(1) *EU Law* 1028
for families of frontier workers **21**(1) *EU Law* 1030
income support **21**(1) *EU Law* 982
invalidity benefit **21**(1) *EU Law* 1020, 1021
language of claim **21**(1) *EU Law* 1027
migrant worker **21**(1) *EU Law* 1031–1043
national provisions **21**(1) *EU Law* 1024
national residence requirement **21**(1) *EU Law* 981
nationality and residence conditions **21**(1) *EU Law* 980
notice of refusal **21**(1) *EU Law* 1017
orphans' pensions and family allowances **21**(1) *EU Law* 1001
overlapping benefits **21**(1) *EU Law* 999–1009
qualifying insurance periods **21**(1) *EU Law* 1018
reimbursement of medical expenses incurred in another member state **21**(1) *EU Law* 1015

FREE MOVEMENT OF PERSONS, SERVICES AND CAPITAL (EU)—*cont*
workers—*cont*
social security benefits—*cont*
residence conditions **21**(1) *EU Law* 976–979
right to have periods of employment aggregated **21**(1) *EU Law* 983
sickness benefit **21**(1) *EU Law* 1010
sickness insurance **21**(1) *EU Law* 1011
unemployment benefit **21**(1) *EU Law* 1022–1024
voluntary or optional insurance **21**(1) *EU Law* 1749
widow's pension **21**(1) *EU Law* 995
worker resident in one EC member state occasionally employed in another **21**(1) *EU Law* 1019
spouse of, rights of **21**(1) *EU Law* 961–963
supra-national rights **21**(1) *EU Law* 955–960
tax benefits **21**(1) *EU Law* 973
taxation **21**(1) *EU Law* 964–966
teachers **21**(1) *EU Law* 1061, 1062
transitional provisions **20**(4) *EU Law* 904
travel **21**(1) *EU Law* 968
visiting worker **21**(1) *EU Law* 967
within member state **20**(4) *EU Law* 905
"workers", meaning of **20**(4) *EU Law* 907–912

FREE OF TAX
See TAX FREE PAYMENT

FREE PARDON
meaning of **30** *Juries* 4331

FREE WARREN
alienation reserving franchise **11**(1) *Comns* 708
beasts and fowl of warren **11**(1) *Comns* 695–699
demise **11**(1) *Comns* 703–707
extent of right
lands
charter, by, **11**(1) *Comns* 687–691
prescription, by, **11**(1) *Comns* 692–694
persons other than owner **11**(1) *Comns* 700–702
extinguishment **11**(1) *Comns* 709–712
prescription, by **11**(1) *Comns* 681, 684, 685
Queen's forest, in **11**(1) *Comns* 681
rabbits, liability for damage by **11**(1) *Comns* 686
royal grant, by **11**(1) *Comns* 682, 683

FREEBENCH
widow's, payment of debt out of **23**(2) *Exors* 5094

FREEDOM OF CONSCIENCE
European Convention on Human Rights
generally **26**(3) *H Rghts* 561–563
recognition of religious bodies **26**(3) *H Rghts* 559
religious and philosophical convictions **26**(3) *H Rghts* 560
right to own clothes **26**(3) *H Rghts* 547
right to practice religion **26**(3) *H Rghts* 548–558
under Commonwealth constitutions
Jehovah's Witnesses **26**(3) *H Rghts* 898
Rastafarianism **26**(3) *H Rghts* 901
requirement for Government to protect freedom of religion **26**(3) *H Rghts* 903
right of religious schools to administer corporal punishment **26**(3) *H Rghts* 899
right to freedom of religion **26**(3) *H Rghts* 900
right to wear hijab (Muslim dress) **26**(3) *H Rghts* 902

FREEDOM OF ESTABLISHMENT
authorisation to deal in securities **9**(1) *Coys* 39
movement of company within EEC **9**(1) *Coys* 37

Fig 7.4 Example page from *The Digest* Vol 26(3)

Case **559** HUMAN RIGHTS

R (on the appln of Ullah) v Special Adjudicator (2002) Times, 5 September

559 Recognition of religious bodies — Refusal by state to recognise church divided from recognised church — State's duty to remain impartial

Under Moldovan law, religions practised in Moldovan territory had to be recognised by the government and, accordingly, the applicant church sought official recognition. Recognition was refused on the basis that the church was a schismatic part of a recognised Moldovan church rather than a distinct religious body, and that the state authorities should not intervene in the dispute. The applicant church complained that this refusal violated its members' freedom of religion guaranteed by the European Convention on Human Rights art 9. *Held*, the freedom of religion implied the freedom to manifest one's religion, but it did not protect every act motivated or inspired by a religion. Where several religions co-existed in a population, it may be necessary to impose restrictions on this freedom in order to reconcile the different interests of different groups. However, the state had a duty to remain neutral and impartial in the exercise of its regulatory power, and should not seek to remove tensions in a divided society by doing away with pluralism. The Moldovan government had failed in this duty by considering that the applicant church was not a new religious body and making its recognition dependent on the will of a recognised ecclesiastical authority. In a democratic society, the state did not need to take steps to ensure that religious communities were subject to a single governing body. Similarly, where the exercise of the right to freedom of religion was made subject to a system of prior approval, intervention by a recognised ecclesiastical authority in the approval procedure could not be reconciled with art 9. Judgment would be given accordingly.

Metropolitan Church of Bessarabia v Moldova (Application 45701/99) (2002) 35 EHRR 306, European Court of Human Rights

560 Religious and philosophical convictions — Right to education — Allocation of places in schools — Parental preference

The respondent local education authority provided a pamphlet to parents setting out its admissions policy. One criteria for selection was the preference of parents for a single-sex school. The applicant, a devout Muslim, indicated that he wished to send his daughter to a local single-sex school, but his application was rejected on the basis that it would be against the efficient use of resources. The applicant sought judicial review of that decision on the ground that the respondent ought to have taken into account his religious convictions. *Held*, it was accepted that the applicant's religious convictions were genuine and fell within the European Convention on Human Rights First Protocol art 2, which provided that member states had to respect the right of parents to ensure education in conformity with their own religious convictions. Since the coming into force of the Human Rights Act 1998, religious convictions were to be taken into account and there was no doubt that the applicant's religious convictions were an important consideration in the instant case. Further, it had to be borne in mind that under the School Standards and Framework Act 1998 s 86(1)(*b*), parents had to be enabled to supply reasons for their preferences. In order to comply with the Convention First Protocol art 2, the state was obliged to take some positive action. First, the respondent had to recognise religious convictions and take them into account in formulating its admissions policy. It followed that there ought to be a means of recognising religious convictions. In that respect, all that was needed was space to include reasons on the relevant application form. In the instant case, the respondent had failed to fulfil the requirements of the Convention First Protocol art 2. Accordingly, the decision would be quashed and remitted for reconsideration.

R (on the appln of K) v Newham London Borough Council (2002) Times, 28 February

561 Right to freedom of thought, conscience and religion — Application to company

A profit-making corporation can neither enjoy nor rely on the right to freedom of thought, conscience and religion guaranteed by the European Convention on Human Rights art 9(1).

Company X v Switzerland (Application 7865/17) (1981) 16 DR 85; (1981) 16 Decisions and Reports 85, European Commission of Human Rights

562 Right to freedom of conscience — Pacifism — Objection to payment of taxes directed towards military purposes

The applicant, a pacifist, did not wish any part of her income tax to be used for military purposes. She alleged that the fact that this was not allowed in the UK amounted to a violation of the European Convention on Human Rights art 9 (right to freedom of conscience): *Held* in declaring the complaint inadmissible, art 9 primarily protected the sphere of personal beliefs and religious creeds together with acts which were intimately linked to these attitudes such as acts of worship or devotion which were aspects of the practise of a religion or a belief in a generally recognisable form. However, in protecting this personal sphere art 9 did not necessarily guarantee the right to behave in the public sphere in a way which was dictated by such a belief, as, for

Fig 7.5 Example page from *The Digest* Cumulative Supplement

Vol 26(3) — HUMAN RIGHTS 774

ance with her beliefs — Whether author's right to freedom of thought, conscience and religion violated

The author was a student at the Tashkent State Institute. As a practising Muslim, she dressed appropriately, in accordance with the tenets of her religion, and in her second year of studies started to wear a headscarf. The institute adopted new regulations, under which students had no right to wear religious dress. The author was requested to sign the new regulations, which she did although she refused to remove her headscarf. Subsequently the deputy dean called her to his office during a lecture and showed her the new regulations again and asked her to take off her headscarf. She refused to do so and was excluded from the institute because of her negative attitude towards the professors and because she had infringed the internal regulations of the institute. She wrote to, inter alia, the Minister of Education and was advised by the deputy minister to comply with the regulations of the institute. Thereafter a new law on the liberty of conscience and religious organisations entered into force. According to the new law, nationals could not wear religious dress in public places. The author filed a complaint with the district court requesting to acknowledge the illegality of her dismissal from the institute and to have her student rights restored but the court dismissed her claim. The city court upheld that decision and the Supreme Court informed the author that it could find no reasons to challenge the decisions in her case. The author complained, inter alia, that her right to freedom of thought, conscience and religion under art 18 of the International Covenant on Civil and Political Rights 1966 (the covenant) had been violated as she had been excluded from university because she wore a headscarf for religious reasons and refused to remove it. *Held* (by a majority), the freedom to manifest one's religion encompassed the right to wear attire in public which was in conformity with the individual's faith or religion. Furthermore, to prevent a person from wearing religious clothing in public or private might constitute a violation of art 18(2) of the covenant, which prohibited any coercion that would impair the individual's freedom to have or adopt a religion. However, the freedom to manifest one's religion or beliefs was not absolute and might be subject to limitations which were prescribed by law and were necessary to protect public safety, order, health, or morals, or the fundamental rights and freedoms of others. In the instant case, the author's exclusion was based on the provisions of the institute's new regulations, which did not permit the wearing of religious clothing on its premises, and her refusal to comply with the ban. However, no specific ground had been invoked to justify the restriction imposed on the author. In the particular circumstances of the instant case and in the absence of any justification there was a violation of art 18(2).

Hudoyberganova v Uzbekistan (Communication 931/2000) (2005) 19 BHRC 581

560e Freedom to manifest religion or belief — Ban on wearing Islamic headscarf in institutions of higher education — University Vice-Chancellor issuing circular providing that students wearing Islamic headscarf not to be admitted to lectures, courses or tutorials — Applicant student excluded from examinations and lecture pursuant to circular — Whether ban constituting unjustified interference with applicant's right to freedom of religion

The applicant came from a traditional family of practising Muslims and considered it her religious duty to wear the Islamic headscarf. She enrolled at the medical faculty of Istanbul University. In February 1998 the Vice-Chancellor of the university issued a circular which provided, inter alia, that students wearing the Islamic headscarf would not be admitted to lectures, courses or tutorials. In accordance with the circular, the applicant was refused access to written examinations and a lecture and was not permitted to enrol with the university's administrative department because she was wearing the Islamic headscarf. She lodged an application for an order setting aside the circular submitting that its implementation had infringed her rights guaranteed by the Convention for the Protection of Human Rights and Fundamental Freedoms 1950 (the convention). The Administrative Court dismissed the application holding that a university Vice-Chancellor, as the executive organ of the university, had power to regulate students' dress for the purposes of maintaining order and that neither the regulations in issue, nor the measures taken against the applicant could be considered illegal. The Supreme Administrative Court dismissed the applicant's subsequent appeal. The applicant complained to the European Court of Human Rights that the ban imposed by the public authorities on wearing the Islamic headscarf in institutions of higher education constituted an unjustified interference with (i) her right to freedom of religion, in particular, her right to manifest her religion, contrary to art 9 of the convention and (ii) her right to education contrary to art 2 of the First Protocol to the Convention for the Protection of Human Rights and Fundamental Freedoms (the first protocol), because it had resulted in her being refused access to examinations and a lecture and prevented from enrolling with the university's when a volume is reissued. This is because additional cases have been inserted into the sequence. In the back of each volume of *The Digest* is a Reference Adaptor. Wherever you find a cross-reference to a volume which has been reissued very recently, you need to look in the volume's Reference Adaptor to convert the reference. The Reference Adaptor consists of a long list of all the case numbers in the old volume, alongside the number which replaces it in the reissued volume.

SUMMARY: TRACING CASES ON A SUBJECT IN THE DIGEST

1. Look up the subject in the *Index*. This will refer you to the volume, subject heading and case numbers where cases on that subject can be found.
2. To see if there have been any more recent cases on the same subject, look in the *Cumulative Supplement* under the relevant volume, subject heading and case number. This will provide you with up-to-date information.

How to use individual indexes to series of Law Reports to trace cases on a subject

If the facilities in your library are limited, you may need to use the indexes to individual series of law reports to trace relevant cases on a subject. The most useful is the *Law Reports Index* (para.3.18) because it covers a number of other important series in addition to the *Law Reports*. Indexes are available covering each 10-year period since 1951 and supplementary annual indexes bring the information up to date. The *Law Reports Index* is easier to use than *The Digest*, but remember that it covers far fewer law reports. 7.16

In addition to the *Law Reports Index* (and the series of *Digests*, which preceded it, going back to 1865) there are indexes to other series, such as the *All England Law Reports*, which has a *Consolidated Tables and Index* in three volumes, covering 1937–2014. This is kept up to date by supplements (para.3.18). In addition, there is an *Index* volume to the *All England Law Reports Reprint*, which includes a subject index to selected cases from 1558–1935.

Finding updates on recent cases by subject

The "Current Awareness" section of the Lexis Library provides summaries of a wide range of recent judgments. These can be found by entering keywords in the "Search terms" box on the current awareness search page, or by clicking the "Add topics to search" link. The Add topics option allows subject headings to be selected from a hierarchy, e.g. first "Banking", and then more specifically, "Regulation of Banks", within the Banking heading. Selected search terms are then entered into a "Topics You Added" search box. Searches can also be limited by period, to find results for the previous month, six months, etc. The resulting search returns results from case digests, along with summaries of legislation and journal articles. To view case summaries only, click the "Cases" link on the left margin of the search page. 7.17

A similar approach can be used with the Westlaw UK "Current Awareness" search. Keywords can be entered in the "Free text" search box, or "Subject/Keyword" search box, which prompts for standard terms. The standard search is for current awareness items added in the last 90 days; alternative date ranges can be selected using "Advanced Search". To limit searches so that only case summaries are found, click the "By Document Type" entry under "Browse" and select "Cases". Searches using the "Free Text" and "Subject/Keyword" boxes are then restricted to cases only.

The summaries of journal and newspaper articles available from the current awareness sections of both the Lexis Library and Westlaw UK should not themselves be overlooked as a route to the identification of recent cases. To read the text of the articles, you need to turn to a source such as the Nexis service for newspapers (para.5.24), or the various online and print sources of journal articles (para.5.2 and para.5.3). However the citation for the case included in the summary of the journal or newspaper articles may be all you need. The case itself can then be located directly.

TRACING THE SUBSEQUENT JUDICIAL HISTORY OF A CASE

7.18 Judges often rely on earlier cases to support the reasons they have given for a decision, and from time to time a judge will review the case law in an attempt to explain the principles stated in earlier cases, or to use them as a springboard to create a new application of the principles. Occasionally a case will be "distinguished" in order that the judge will not feel obliged to follow it. Less frequently, a superior court will state that an earlier case was wrongly decided, and will overrule it, so that the principles laid down in the case will not be followed thereafter.

The treatment a case receives when it is subsequently judicially considered has a direct bearing on its importance and reliability. For example, if in an essay you cited as an authority the common law rules laid down in a particular case, you would be embarrassed to discover that the rules were later abolished by statute. Similarly, you should check that a particular case you have referred to, e.g. *Gillick v West Norfolk and Wisbech AHA* [1984] 1 All E.R. 365, was not later reversed on appeal to the House of Lords, as happened in *Gillick v West Norfolk and Wisbech AHA* [1985] 1 All E.R. 533. Consequently, you must be alert to the need to trace the full judicial history of a particular case.

The simplest way to do this is to use the "Case Analysis" information available from the Westlaw UK "Cases" search (para.3.15). The well-known old case *Carlill v Carbolic Smoke Ball Co*, for example, can be found using the "Party Names" search because it has been considered several times since 1947 (the case itself dates from 1893). The "Cases citing this Case" section of the case analysis page for *Carlill v Carbolic Smoke Ball Co* shows that the decision in the case has been most recently applied by *Bowerman v Association of British Travel Agents Ltd* [1996] C.L.C. 451. It was also distinguished in *Pharmaceutical Society of Great Britain v Boots Cash Chemist (Southern) Ltd* [1952] 2 Q.B. 795. The most recent case noted as applying the ruling was *Azevedo v IMCOPA* [2013] EWCA Civ 364. The case analysis suggests, in other words, that the case is still of relevance. The case analysis page also gives a citation for a 2008 journal article in the "Journal Articles" section, which discusses the case in the context of contracts of indemnity, gambling and insurance contracts, [2008] J.B.L. 432.

If you were using the print volumes of the *Current Law Case Citator* the same information could be traced by checking first the volume covering 1947 to 1976. This gives page and volume numbers to entries in the *Current Law Year Book* after the case citations. These enable you to check the *Year Book* summaries for cases which have applied, approved, distinguished or considered the *Carlill* case between 1947 and 1976. Subsequent volumes of the *Current Law Case Citator* then need to be checked in order to discover *Year Book* summaries of the 1996 and a 2003 case, *Bardissy v D'Souza* [2003] W.T.L.R. 929.

HOW TO FIND WORDS AND PHRASES JUDICIALLY CONSIDERED

The meaning of words is of great importance to lawyers. The interpretation of statutes and documents may hinge upon the meaning of a single word. For example, does "day" in banking terms mean 24 hours, or does it end at the close of working hours? How should the words "on a road" be interpreted in the Road Traffic Act 1988? 7.19

Two specialised dictionaries record the courts' decisions on problems such as these. *Stroud's Judicial Dictionary* provides the meaning of words as defined in the case law and in statutes. *Words and Phrases Legally Defined* is a similar publication; both are kept up to date by supplements.

The *Law Reports Index* includes a heading "Words and Phrases", in which full details of cases defining a particular word or phrase are given (see fig.7.6).

The *Current Law Monthly Digests* and *Year Books* also include an entry "Words and Phrases" and the *Index* to the *All England Law Reports* and the *Consolidated Index* to *Halsbury's Laws* have a similar heading.

HOW TO TRACE STATUTES ON A SUBJECT

- Full-text databases (para.7.21); 7.20
- Other online sources (para.7.22);
- *Halsbury's Statutes of England* (para.7.23); and
- *Current Law* (para.7.24).

How to use full-text databases of legislation

The Lexis Library "Legislation" search (para.4.13) and the Westlaw UK "Legislation" search (para.4.14) can both be used to trace statutes in force by subject. The Justis UK Statutes database (para.4.9) adds the ability to search for statutes no longer in force. 7.21

Effective subject searching using the Lexis Library and Westlaw UK is possible using the subject indexing provided by both databases. Differences in the indexing terms used by the databases also mean that it is advisable, where possible, to explore the subject terms used in each of them. The search results obtained may differ.

Suppose, for example, you wanted to find legislation relevant to criminal evidence and the right to silence. Using the "Legislation" search in the Lexis Library, select the "Add topics to search" link below the "Search terms" box to open the "Add topics" hierarchy. This is the hierarchy of subject terms that can be used to guide your search. From the separate "Add topics" page or tab, select "Criminal Evidence" and then "Silence and Non production of Evidence". Once selected, the subject terms are added to an additional search box. The search itself finds relevant sections of four different Acts, including the Criminal Justice and Public Order Act 1994, the Criminal Justice Act 2003 and the Counter-Terrorism Act 2008.

Using the Westlaw UK "Legislation" search, the "Subject/Keyword" search box can be used to search for sections of legislation indexed under "Right to Silence". If the search term you wish to use does not match the terms prompted by the "Subject/Keyword" search, use the "Advanced Search" to check the subject terms used by Westlaw UK from the "List of terms" link. A Westlaw UK search finds two different Acts: the Criminal Justice and Public Order Act

Fig 7.6
Example "Words and Phrases" entries in the *Law Reports* Index

Subject Matter 553

WORDS AND PHRASES—*continued*

"*Consent*"—Council Directive 85/337/EEC, art 1(1)
Pro-Braine ASBL v Commune de Braine-le-Château (Veolia es treatment SA intervening) (Case C-121/11), ECJ [2012] PTSR D29

"*Consent*"—Council Directive 89/104/EEC, art 7 **Martin Y Paz Diffusion SA v Depuydt** (Case C-661/11), ECJ [2014] Bus LR 329

"*Consideration*"—Local Government Act 1972, s 123(2)
R (London Jewish Girls High Ltd) v Barnet London Borough Council, Mitting J [2013] PTSR 1357

"*Consideration*"—Council Directive 77/388/EEC, art 11A(1)(a); Council Directive 2006/112/EC, art 73 **Dixons Retail plc v Revenue and Customs Comrs (Case C-494/12),** ECJ [2014] Ch 326; [2014] 2 WLR 893

"*Consideration payable . . . for the right to carry out the works*"—Telecommunications Act 1984, Sch 2, para 13(2)(e)(ii) **The Bridgewater Canal Co Ltd v Geo Networks Ltd,** Lewison J [2010] 1 WLR 2576
CA [2011] 1 WLR 1487

"*Constabulary maintained by virtue of an enactment*"—Employment Rights Act 1996, s 200(2)
Redbridge London Borough Council v Dhinsa, CA [2014] ICR 834

"*Construction*"—Council Directive 85/337/EEC, arts 1(2), 5(1) (as amended)
Brussels Hoofstedwlijk Gewest v Vlaams Gewest (The Brussels Airport Co NV intervening) (Case C-275/09), ECJ [2011] PTSR D37

"*Consumer*"—Parliament and Council Regulation (EC) No 805/2004, art 6(1)(d)
Vapenik v Thurner (Case C-508/12), ECJ [2014] 1 WLR 2486

"*Consumer*"—Unfair Terms in Consumer Contract Regulations 1999, reg 3(1)
Overy v Paypal (Europe) Ltd, Judge Hegarty QC [2013] Bus LR D1

"*Consumer contracts*"—Council Regulation (EC) No 44/2001, art 15
Pammer v Reederei Karl Schlüter GmbH & Co KG, ECJ [2012] Bus LR 972

"*Contained in . . . any document*"—Freedom of Information Act 2000, s 32(2)
Kennedy v Information Comr (Secretary of State for Justice intervening) (Secretary of State for Justice intervening), Calvert-Smith J [2010] 1 WLR 1489
CA [2012] 1 WLR 3524

"*Continuity of residence*"—Parliament and Council Directive 2004/38/EC, art 16(3)
Onuekwere v Secretary of State for the Home Department (Case C-378/12), ECJ [2014] 1 WLR 2420

"*Contract of carriage*"—Carriage of Goods by Road Act 1965, Sch, art 31.1(a)
British American Tobacco Switzerland SA v Exel Europe Ltd, Cooke J [2013] 1 WLR 397

"*Contract of employment*"—Employment Rights Act 1996, s 230(2) **Welton v Deluxe Retail Ltd (trading as Madhouse),** EAT [2013] ICR 428

"*Contracted*"—Employers' Liability (Compulsory Insurance) Act 1969, s 1(1)
Durham v BAI (Run Off) Ltd, CA [2011] 1 All ER 605; [2011] 1 All ER (Comm) 811
SC(E) [2012] 1 WLR 867; [2012] ICR 574

"*Contracting authority*"—Public Contracts Regulations 2006, reg 3(1)
Alstom Transport v Eurostar International Ltd, Roth J [2013] PTSR 454

"*Contributory infringement*"—Patents Act 1977, s 60(2)
Grimme Landmaschinenfabrik GmbH & Co KG v Scott (trading as Scotts Potato Machinery), CA [2011] Bus LR D129

"*Controlled waste*"—Environmental Protection Act 1990, s 75(2)(4) (as amended) **R v W,** CA [2012] PTSR 617

"*Controller*"—Parliament and Council Directive 95/46/EC, art 2(d)
Google Spain SL v Agencia Española de Protección de Datos (AEPD) (Case C-131/12), ECJ [2014] QB 1022; [2014] 3 WLR 659

"*Conversion or enlargement of a building*"—Defective Premises Act 1972, s 1 **Jenson v Faux,** CA [2011] 1 WLR 3038

"*Copies*"—Police and Criminal Evidence Act 1984, s 15(7)
R (Bhatti) v Croydon Magistrates' Court, DC [2011] 1 WLR 948

"*Correction of a mistake*"—Land Registration Act 2002, Sch 4, paras 1, 5(a) **Baxter v Mannion,** Henderson J [2010] 1 WLR 1965
CA [2011] 1 WLR 1594

"*Costs . . . incurred*"—Landlord and Tenant Act 1985, s 20B (as inserted)
Burr v OM Property Management Ltd, CA [2013] 1 WLR 3071

"*Court*"—Solicitors Act 1974, s 87 **Tel-Ka Talk Ltd v Revenue and Customs Comrs (Law Society intervening),** Senior Costs Judge Hurst [2011] STC 497

"*Court*"—Human Rights Act 1998, Sch 1, Pt I, art 5.4 **R (Morales) v Parole Board,** Silber J [2011] 1 WLR 1095

"*Court having jurisdiction in particular in criminal matters*"—Council Framework Decision 2005/214/JHA, art 1(a)(iii) **Proceedings concerning Baláž (Case C-60/12),** ECJ [2014] RTR 61

"*Creating*"—Race Relations Act 1976 (c 74), s 3A(1) (as inserted) **Conteh v Parking Partners Ltd,** EAT [2011] ICR 341

"*Credit*"—Consumer Credit Act 2006 (Commencement No 4 and Transitional Provisions) Order 2008, art 4(1) **Santander UK plc v Harrison,** Males J [2013] Bus LR 501

"*Creditor*"—Consumer Credit Act 1974, s 141 **Link Financial Ltd v Jones,** Hamblen J [2013] 1 WLR 693

1994 found by the Lexis Library, and the Witnesses Act 1806. The Criminal Justice Act 2003 and the Counter-Terrorism Act 2008 are not indexed by Westlaw UK under "Right to Silence".

Searches using standard index terms can be combined with additional keywords in both the Lexis Library and Westlaw UK, if you wish to make a more specific search. If the subject index terms available from the databases are not helpful for the subject you wish to search, the advice given in para.7.10 on using keywords for subject searching for case law applies here also. It makes sense to turn to textbooks and other secondary sources first, in order to have a good grasp of possible key terms before making your search. Highly specific searches, using terms known to appear in legislation, are more likely to be successful than searches using wider, general, subject words. A useful list of relevant legislation can be found, for example, if you have determined in advance that you wish to search for sections of Acts relating to "registration of marriage" and "foreign marriage" having determined that "foreign marriage" (rather than, e.g. marriage abroad) is a term used in UK legislation.

If you do not have access to the Lexis Library or Westlaw UK, the legislation.gov.uk website (para.4.15) provides an alternative approach to searching the full text of legislation using keywords. The "Advanced Search" allows words in legislation titles to be combined with "Keywords in content", but there is no added subject indexing. The BAILII database (para.4.8) can also be used in much the same way. In both cases, sections of Acts containing your search words are highlighted.

TIPS • *Place phrases in quotation marks when searching Westlaw UK, otherwise your search will find sections of Acts in which the search words appear, but not necessarily next to each other. The Lexis Library treats consecutive words as phrases.*

Other online sources for tracing legislation by subject

Catalogues of official publications offer an alternative to full text databases of legislation for tracing legislation by subject. The tso shop website (para.6.15) enables statutes to be searched by title keyword and searches to be restricted to Acts. Using the UKOP database (para.6.16) "Flexible Search" widens the range of subject searching, as the UKOP thesaurus enables results to be found using both the search words you have entered and alternative, closely related, terms. 7.22

Halsbury's Statutes of England

Halsbury's Statutes provides the amended text of legislation which is still in force, along with annotations detailing, for example, statutory instruments made under the Act, case law, judicial interpretation of words and phrases and references to relevant sections of *Halsbury's Laws*. 7.23

The various volumes of the main work are arranged alphabetically by broad subject areas. Acts dealing with agriculture, for example, are found in Vol.1, whereas statutes on the subject of wills are found in the final volume.

The annual *Table of Statutes and General Index* provides a comprehensive subject index to the volumes to enable you to find statutes on a particular topic. The index will refer you to the appropriate volume and page number. In the *Table of Statutes and General Index* volume there is a separate subject index to the *Current Statutes Service*, which contains those Acts that were passed after the main volumes were issued. If you are looking for the latest Acts on a particular subject, look also in the subject index at the front of the looseleaf Vol.1 of the *Current Statutes Service*. This indexes the material that has been added to the Service since the annual *Table of Statutes and General Index* was published.

Once you have identified those Acts which are of relevance to you, it is essential to consult both the *Cumulative Supplement* and the *Noter-Up* to see if there have been any changes in the law. An explanation of how to do this, along with further details of *Halsbury's Statutes*, can be found at para.4.17.

Other print sources for tracing legislation on a subject

7.24 *Halsbury's Laws* (para.7.3) contains references to relevant statutes, although the text of the Acts is not printed. The *Current Law Monthly Digests* and *Year Books* (para.7.12 and para.7.13) are arranged by subject and include entries for new statutes and statutory instruments as well as for cases on a subject. A brief summary appears under the appropriate subject heading.

HOW TO TRACE STATUTORY INSTRUMENTS ON A SUBJECT

7.25 Statutory instruments on a particular subject can be traced by consulting:

- Online sources (para.7.26); and
- *Halsbury's Statutory Instruments* (para.7.27).

For an explanation of the nature and purpose of statutory instruments, see para.4.26.

Online sources for tracing statutory instruments

7.26 The full-text databases of legislation noted in para.7.21 all provide access to statutory instruments. The considerations relevant to searching for statutory instruments are consequently much the same. The Lexis Library "Legislation" search is a particularly useful starting point for keyword searching, as the database source can be limited so that only statutory instruments are searched. In Westlaw UK, the legislation search includes both statutes and statutory instruments. A subject index approach to searching for statutory instruments is the most effective approach for these databases as also noted in para.7.21. Both the Lexis Library and Westlaw UK contain statutory instruments in force. The Justis UK Statutory Instruments database contains the full text of all statutory instruments from 1987 onwards, and a further archive database contains statutory instruments published between 1671 and 1986. However, only a few libraries are likely to subscribe to the archive.

The "Advanced Search" of the legislation.gov.uk website provides an alternative approach to searching for statutory instruments and key search considerations are as noted in para.7.21. Complete coverage begins in 1987. Selected statutory instruments are available for the period 1948 to 1986.

Halsbury's Statutory Instruments

7.27 *Halsbury's Statutory Instruments* is a series which covers every statutory instrument of general application in force in England and Wales. It reproduces the text of a selected number and provides summaries of others. The series is arranged alphabetically by subject and is kept up to date by a *Service* binder containing notes of changes in the law and the text of selected new instruments. A full description of the work can be found in para.4.29.

If you are looking for statutory instruments dealing with a particular subject, you should start by looking up your subject in the *Consolidated Index*. This paperback volume is issued annually and indexes the contents of all the main volumes. The entries give you the volume number (in bold type) and page number in the main work and the number of the statutory instrument (in brackets).

Occasionally you will find that the volume to which you are referred has been reissued since the latest *Consolidated Index* was published. The references from the *Consolidated Index* will no longer be correct and in this case you will need to refer to the subject index at the back of the new volume.

Once you have traced the relevant statutory instruments on your subject in the main volumes, it is important to turn to the *Service* binder to find out if the information you have traced is still up to date. To do this, turn to the "Monthly Survey" section of the *Service* binder and look up the relevant subject title. This shows new statutory instruments which have appeared since the main volume was compiled. It tells you which statutory instruments printed in the main volumes are no longer law and provides you with a page-by-page guide to changes made since the main volume was published.

SUMMARY: HOW TO USE HALSBURY'S STATUTORY INSTRUMENTS TO FIND INFORMATION ON A SUBJECT

1. Consult the *Consolidated Index*. This tells you the volume, page number and statutory instrument numbers you require.
2. To check if there have been any changes in the law, look in the "Monthly Survey" pages of the *Service* binder.

Tracing recent statutory instruments

The legislation.gov.uk website (at *http://www.legislation.gov.uk*) lists statutory instruments in number order on its "Browse Legislation" page, making it possible to check for the most recent statutory instruments added to the site. The website also features a "New Legislation" page. If you suspect that a statutory instrument is very recent, it might also be convenient to check entries in the TSO *Daily List* (para.6.15). The print *Current Law Monthly Digest* has the advantage of listing relatively recent statutory instruments under subject headings. 7.28

All draft statutory instruments awaiting approval are also published in full text on the legislation.gov.uk website and they remain on the site until they are superseded by a statutory instrument, or, in some cases, until they are withdrawn. Draft statutory instruments can be found on the "Browse Legislation" page.

FINDING BOOKS ON A SUBJECT

Your first task is to find out what suitable books are available in your own library. Start with your library catalogue. All catalogues allow you to search for keywords in the titles of books. This means you can search for title words that match your subject. A keyword search on "negligence", 7.29

for example, picks up the titles "Introduction to negligence", "The law of negligence" and so on. If you do not find books on your subject, try some alternative headings or look under a more general, or a more specific subject. Negligence, for instance, is part of the law of torts and there will be a chapter on negligence in all general textbooks on the law of torts.

Library catalogue records usually also add subject keywords to the details given for a particular book. As a result a search on "negligence" is likely to find a number of books that do not contain the word "negligence" in the book title. If you wish to limit a search to title words only, look for an "Advanced Search" option, enabling title-only searches.

The subject classification number (or classmark) given to a particular book provides an alternative approach to subject searching. To use subject classifications, search for any book that matches your subject interest, even if it is hopelessly out of date. The classification assigned to that book can then be used to find other books that have been given the same classification. These books may have completely different title words. In most catalogues, the classification for a book in the catalogue record can be used as a link to retrieve a list of books sharing the same classification. If this is not the case, use the classification code as a keyword, e.g. "KN10". Subject classifications are often added to the classification used to determine the place of a book on the library shelves, so a wider range of books can be found using a classification search than would be found browsing the library shelves (even if none to the library's books were on loan).

Remember too that footnotes and bibliographies (lists of books) in textbooks and journal articles refer you to other books, journals and cases on a subject. Check in the library catalogue to find out if these are available in your library. Government reports on a subject may not be entered, and you need to make use of other catalogues and indexes to trace these publications (see para.6.15 and para.6.18).

You are not restricted to your own catalogue if you wish to trace books on a subject. The online catalogues of all of the UK universities, along with the British Library, can be searched. COPAC (at *http://www.copac.jisc.ac.uk*) provides a particularly useful starting point for UK academic research libraries as it provides access to the merged catalogues of the largest research libraries in the UK and Ireland. This means that a single catalogue search can find details of a book held by, among others, the Cambridge University Library, the Bodleian Library, Trinity College Dublin and the Institute of Advanced Legal Studies. The Institute of Advanced Legal Studies collections can also be searched via the Institute's own library pages (at *http://www.ials.sas.ac.uk*). The British Library Integrated catalogue (at *catalogue.bl.uk*) includes both the main reference and document supply collections.

If you are interested in tracing US publications, the WorldCat catalogue (at *http://www.worldcat.org*) is the largest online catalogue available. It has records which are based largely, though not exclusively, on US university holdings. The Library of Congress catalogue (at *https://catalog.loc.gov*) provides another starting point for US publications.

Google Books

7.30 Google Books (at *https://books.google.co.uk*) should not be overlooked as a means of finding books on a subject. The inclusion of the full text of books in the indexes used by Google Books means that a subject approach is possible which usefully complements the more traditional use of library catalogues (para.7.29). To use Google Books, search using keywords you would like to see in chapter headings, key paragraphs etc. trying to be as specific as possible. Where book previews are available, these words can be seen in "Snippet" views of the relevant pages of the books. Searches using wide subject terms such as "negligence" or "medical negligence" will tend to place books with these terms to the top of the results list, but details of many books will be returned and it can be difficult to assess the value of the books found. Search results can be improved using the "Search Tools" option, which allows results to be sorted by date to show recent books first. Date ranges can also be specified and results limited to books only ("Magazines" are also included in the search).

Google Books indexes the extensive range of books scanned by Google from university libraries, adding content where publishers have allowed Google Book indexing. However, key titles will be missing from Google Books where publishers have not allowed indexing by the site. Where publisher content is indexed, Google Books—unlike an academic library—does not select books of academic value only. As a result, it would be unwise to rely exclusively on Google Books to find books on a subject.

Legal bibliographies

Bibliographies list books that have been published on a subject, both in the UK and elsewhere. A number of possible sources are given below. The *Current Law Monthly Digest* and *Current Law* (para.7.31) provide the only current print listings of UK law books by subject. **7.31**

Current Law

At the back of each *Current Law Monthly Digest* is a list of new books published during that month (mainly British, with a few foreign works in English). When the *Monthly Digests* are replaced by the *Current Law Year Book*, a list of books published during the year is printed at the back of the Year Book. **7.32**

Bibliographies of older material

Print bibliographies are no longer a guide to current UK legal publishing, but this does not entirely exhaust their usefulness, especially if your field of interest is legal history or jurisprudence. Szladit's, C., *Bibliography on Foreign and Comparative Law* (2001) is a detailed bibliography covering books and articles on foreign and comparative law published in English. Raistrick, D., *Lawyer's Law Books* (1995), a single-volume bibliography, listing textbooks by subject. Sweet & Maxwell's *Legal Bibliography of the British Commonwealth* (1955–1964) is the oldest general UK legal bibliography that may still be available. **7.33**

Many other specialist legal bibliographies have also been published, e.g. P. O'Higgins and M. Partington, *Social Security Law in Britain and Ireland: a Bibliography* (1986); E. Beyerly, *Public International Law: a Guide to Information Sources* (1991); and R.W.M. Dias, *Bibliography of Jurisprudence* (1979).

Law Books and Serials in Print

The US published *Law Books and Serials in Print, 40th edn,* (2015) is a three volume work still published in print. It includes listings of books by subject heading in Vol.1. *Current Publications in Legal and Related Fields*, another US bibliography, was published in 59 volumes between 1952 and 2011 and is now available online from HeinOnline. **7.34**

The British National Bibliography

7.35 The most comprehensive source of information for British books which have been published since 1950 is the *British National Bibliography* (BNB). Your library may not have retained the annual print volumes of the BNB, but all BNB records can be searched from the BNB page of the British Library website (at *http://bnb.bl.uk*).

An initial keyword search can be used to find a book of interest and subject heading and Dewey classifications for the book then used to provide a systematic search for similar material. A search for "EU copyright law", for example, finds book records using the subject keyword combination "Copyright—European Union countries" and the Dewey classification "346.240482" which can be used as links to retrieve lists of books as described in para.7.29.

The BNB home page also provides a link to weekly lists of books recently added to the BNB online, arranged in Dewey classification order. Entries for law books are at the numbers 340–349.

Sources for books in print

7.36 A number of sources enable you to search for the titles of books in print. Publishers' websites list current and forthcoming publications and most organise their titles by subject. Commercial books in print databases also allow subject searching using keywords. Library staff may be able to help you make use of books in print databases such as Nielson BookData Online, the major commercial source for information on UK books in print, or book supplier databases such as those of Coutts or Dawsons. These can be useful as a guide to the current availability of books.

The Amazon website (at *http://www.amazon.co.uk*) remains a convenient site for keyword searches for books in print, as most publishers supply the site with title information. The American site (at *http://www.amazon.com*) is also worth searching, as are other European Amazon websites (e.g. *http://www.amazon.de* and *http://www.amazon.fr*).

The ability to find out-of-print titles through Amazon sellers can also be supplemented by the use of AbeBooks website (at *http://www.abebooks.co.uk*).

THESES

7.37 If you are undertaking a comprehensive piece of research, you may need to find out if any theses have already been written on that subject. Theses are increasingly being made available online in full text, but a comprehensive search still requires the use of indexes and catalogues to trace those only held in print.

The EThOS website from the British Library (at *http://ethos.bl.uk*) provides details of PhD theses from the majority of UK universities. It also provides the access route to UK theses online. Many recent theses are available from the site in open access versions and can be downloaded in full. Most UK universities also participate in a thesis request service provided by EThOS. If a university is participating in the service, the print version of the thesis requested is digitised and then made available from the website. The earliest theses available for digitisation requests date from the early 20th Century. Many universities cover the cost of the digitisation, others require the requester to pay. You will need to register with the EThOS site in order to make a request. You will find, though, that some theses are blocked for access by embargo conditions set by the thesis author. Be prepared, in addition, to wait a few weeks for a thesis to be digitised from print and become available for download. When a thesis is digitised, it is available for subsequent users of the site. The "Advanced Search" on the website allows search terms to be limited to abstracts, titles etc. Both simple and advanced searches also allow search results to be limited to theses available for immediate download.

However, the EThOS database does not contain a record of all research theses from all UK universities. The *Index to Theses*, more fully, the *Index to Theses Accepted for Higher Degrees by the Universities of Great Britain and Ireland*, is, as the title suggests, the major source for a comprehensive search for British and Irish theses. Coverage is extensive, but it does rely on universities to submit theses information. The *Index* is available online from ProQuest as ProQuest Dissertations & Theses: UK & Ireland. This is a subscription database, so you will need to check if your library can provide access. An additional print source of information for UK law theses, *Legal Research in the United Kingdom, 1905–1984*, was published by the Institute of Advanced Legal Studies, and updated until 1988 by the *List of Current Legal Research Topics*.

Details of the vast majority of North American theses can be found in *Dissertation Abstracts International*, which also includes some non-North American theses. Abstracts are available from 1980. The publishers, UMI, have made the *Dissertation Abstracts International* database available to a number of online database providers. The WorldCat catalogue (at *http://www.worldcat.org*) provides an alternative if *Dissertation Abstracts International* is not available, as search results can be limited to display theses only.

Open access US theses can be found using the PQDT Open website (at *http://pqdtopen.proquest.com*). European theses available in full text open access versions can be found using the DART-Europe E-theses Portal (at *http://www.dart-europe.eu*).

8 European Union law

INTRODUCTION

8.1 European Union law is as much part of the law of the UK as the laws passed by the UK Parliament. For this reason, UK legal sources should, and often will, include references to relevant EU law. However, because this is not always so, and because EU law is organised in a different way from English law, students also need to become familiar with the sources of EU law.

The sources of EU law are made available by the EU from the Europa website (para.8.2), the main source for official EU information. Treaties, legislation and case law are available from the EUR-Lex web pages (para.8.3) and case law is also available from the EU Court of Justice (paras 8.17–18).

Your library may also have retained print sources of legislation and case law, especially if it is a designated European Documentation Centre (EDC). Further information on EU information sources in the UK can be found using European Commission Representation in the UK website (at *http://ec.europa.eu/unitedkingdom*) and the Europe in the UK website (at *http://www.europe.org.uk*).

THE EUROPA WEBSITE

8.2 The Europa website (at *http://www.europa.eu*) provides a wealth of information from EU institutions. The "About the EU", "EU by Topic" and "Documents and publications" sections of the website all provide useful approaches to finding legal information. The European Commission Press Release Database (at *http://europa.eu/rapid*) also carries recent news items from the EU.

A subject approach to legal information is possible using the "EU by Topic" section of the website. A number of major subject areas are listed, e.g. "Employment and Social Affairs", "Competition", and "Environment". Within each heading, a "Legislation" section lists summaries of policy and legislation in the relevant area. Further links are provided to the relevant full text. The "EU institutions and bodies" section for each subject area also provides links to important bodies within the major institutions. If the "Environment" heading is selected, for example, the Committee on the Environment, Public Health and Food Safety of the European Parliament is listed with a link to the relevant page of the European Parliament website. The "Publications, newsletters and statistics" section for each subject area provides links to key publications.

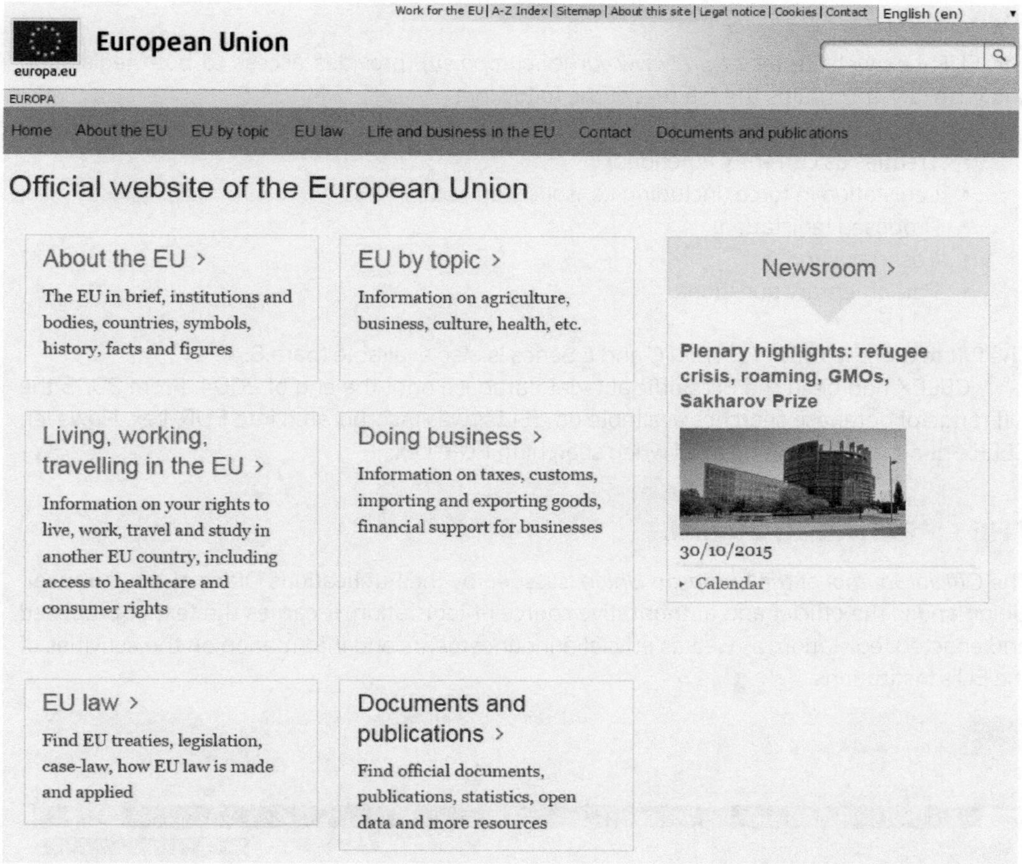

Fig 8.1 Europa website home page

The "About the EU" section of the website is useful if you wish to find further information on the activities of any of the major institutions: the European Parliament, the Council of the European Union, the European Commission and the Court of Justice of the European Communities. Brief summaries can be found under "EU institutions and other bodies".

The "Documents and publications" section of the Europa website provides, in turn, a listing of key sources for official documents published by EU institutions. These include green papers and white papers (proposals for legislation) from the European Commission, and presidency conclusions from the European Council.

Also on the Europa website, the Eurostat pages (at *http://ec.europa.eu/eurostat*), bring together statistics from the EU's statistical information service. The European Commission Library and e-Resources Centre pages (at *http://ec.europa.eu/libraries*) provide, in addition, access to ECLAS, the European Commission's Central Library catalogue, a useful source of information for books and journal articles relevant to the EU (para.8.25).

Search results from the Europa website's search can be filtered by document format and date, which can be helpful if you are looking for particular documents using keywords.

EUR-LEX

8.3 The EUR-Lex website (at *http://www.eur-lex.europa.eu*), provides access to both legislation and case law. It contains the full text of the following:

- Treaties as currently amended;
- Legislation in force (including consolidated texts);
- Proposed legislation;
- Case-law; and
- Parliamentary questions.

The full text of the *Official Journal C* and *L* Series is also available (para.8.4).

CELEX had been the EU's official legal database until the end of 2004. From 2005 the full range of database searches available on CELEX was incorporated into EUR-Lex. However, CELEX numbers can still be used when searching EUR-Lex.

THE OFFICIAL JOURNAL

8.4 The *Official Journal of the European Union* is issued by the Publications Office of the European Union and is the official and authoritative source of legislation. It carries the text of proposed and enacted legislation, as well as official announcements and information on the activities of the EU's institutions.

Fig 8.2 EUR-Lex website home page

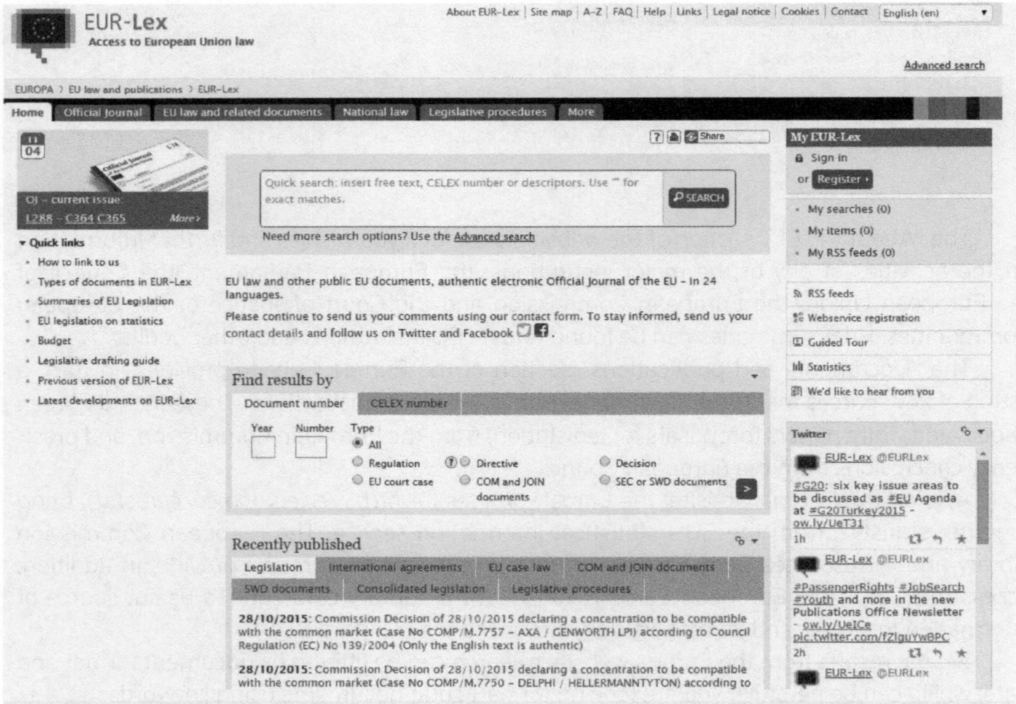

Your library is unlikely to hold print versions of current or recent issues of the *Official Journal*, however the publication format of PDF versions of the journal is identical. These can be found in the "Official Journal" section of the EUR-Lex site (at *http://www.eur-lex.europa.eu*). The Journal is published in two sequences:

1. *L series* (*Legislation*): this consists of the texts of enacted legislation, divided into a further two sequences.
   (a) acts whose publication is obligatory (primarily regulations, directives addressed to all Member States);
   (b) acts whose publication is not obligatory (all other legislation).
2. *C series* (*Information and Notices*): this is arranged in five parts, as follows:
   - Part I, Resolutions, recommendations and opinions, including, e.g. Council resolutions and recommendations; recommendations from the European Central Bank;
   - Part II, Information, including:
   Information from European Institutions and Bodies, e.g. Commission decisions on competition cases or state aid, opinions from the Court of Auditors;
   - Part III, Preparatory Acts: proposed legislation;
   - Part IV, Notices, including:
   Notices from European Institutions and Bodies, e.g. Euro exchange rates, opinions and reports from the Commission; European Parliament minutes of proceedings and texts adopted;
   - Part V, Announcements, including:
   Administrative procedures, e.g. Commission calls for research, Procedures relating to the implementation of competition policy, Court proceedings: notes of new cases.

Usually only two or three parts of the C series are present in any one issue.

Public procurement notices are also published as a supplement to the *Official Journal*. The notices are presented online as the Tenders Electronic Daily (TED) database (at *http://www.ted.europa.eu*), which provides details of current business tender opportunities.

Standard citations to the *Official Journal* use the form:

[2015] O.J. L115/11

The issue number is given for the "L" or "C" series, followed by the page number. The *Official Journal* may also be cited, e.g. O.J. no.L115 6 May 2015, p.11; or O.J. 2015, L115/11.

TREATIES

The treaties page of the EUR-Lex website (para.8.3) displays links to the original founding treaties of the European Communities. These were: 8.5

- The Treaty establishing the European Economic Community, 1957;
- The Treaty establishing the European Atomic Energy Community, 1957; and

Fig 8.3
Example contents page of the *Official Journal L Series*

Official Journal of the European Union — L 239

English edition — **Legislation** — **Volume 58** — **15 September 2015**

Contents

- The Treaty establishing the European Coal and Steel Community, 1951 (expired 2002).

The Treaty on European Union, 1992, (the Maastricht Treaty), later revised not just the content, but also the name of the original EEC Treaty, so that it became the Treaty establishing the European Community (EC Treaty). Further revisions to the EC Treaty and the Treaty on European Union were subsequently made by:

- The Treaty of Amsterdam, 1997;
- The Treaty of Nice, 2001; and
- The Treaty of Lisbon, 2007.

The Treaty of Lisbon introduced a further significant change of treaty name, renaming the EC Treaty, the Treaty on the Functioning of the EU. It also substantially renumbered the articles of the treaty.

Fortunately consolidated versions of both the Treaty on European Union and the Treaty on the Functioning of the European Union have been published in the *Official Journal* following the adoption of the Treaty of Lisbon in December 2009. The consolidated versions can be found on the "Treaties" page of the EUR-Lex website (at *http://www.eur-lex.europa.eu*). The treaties page also notes some amendments to both treaties made since the last consolidated versions were published in 2012. The two treaties taken together are now founding treaties of the European Union. Ratified by national governments, they constitute EU primary legislation. EU directives and regulations are, for this reason, secondary legislation (see para.8.6 below).

If you wish to examine the original texts of the various EU treaties, as published in the *Official Journal*, these can also be found on the EUR-Lex "Treaties" page. The Treaty of Lisbon, for example, was published in the *Official Journal* C Series, in issue 306 (17 December 2007). The Treaty was also published as a UK Command Paper, Cm.7294, on the same day.

In addition to these official sources, many of the important texts of primary materials are published in student textbooks. *Blackstone's Statutes on EU Treaties and Legislation*, for example, edited by Nigel Foster, and currently revised annually (26th edn 2015–2016).

SECONDARY LEGISLATION

Secondary legislation is that which is created by the institutions of the European Union in implementing the powers granted to them in the relevant treaties. There are a number of different types of legislative acts: 8.6

- Regulations;
- Directives;
- Decisions;
- Recommendations; and
- Opinions.

The nature of each type of act is explained in art.288 of the Treaty on the Functioning of the European Union.

The legislative process of the EU is very different from that of the UK. Draft legislation or proposals are put forward by the Commission and the final versions are published as *Commission Documents* (known as *COM Docs*). They are also published in the *Official Journal C Series*. Proposals are then considered by the European Parliament and the European Economic and Social Committee (EESC) or the Committee of the Regions (CoR), which publish *Reports* or *Opinions*. The European Parliament may also initiate proposals for legislation.

Consultative documents from the relevant bodies are available online from EU sources, though the websites involved are not always easy to navigate. *COM Docs* are included in EUR-Lex under "Preparatory Acts" in the "EU law and related documents" section of EUR-Lex. EESC and CoR Opinions are published in the *Official Journal C Series*. Recent EESC

Opinions are available on their website (at *http://www.eesc.europa.eu*). Committee of the Regions Opinions are available from the Committee website (at *http://www.cor.europa.eu*). Resolutions of the European Parliament (but not the full report) are published in the *Official Journal C Series*. Full reports of debates can be found in the "Plenary" section of the European Parliament website (at *http://www.europarl.europa.eu*). Minutes of European Parliament committees, along with other relevant documents, can be found in the "Committees" section of the site.

Once the various suggestions from these bodies have been considered, and the original proposals amended if necessary, the Council of the European Union will adopt a directive or regulation and the text is published in the *Official Journal L Series*. Directives must then be implemented in the law of the Member States.

Citation of legislative acts

8.7 For legislation published from 2015 onwards, the citation of a legislative act is made up of the following elements:

1. Form of legislation and institutional origin, e.g. Council Directive, Commission Regulation;
2. Treaty basis placed in brackets–usually (EU);
3. The year and number of the act;
4. Date and title;
5. Official Journal reference, e.g. [2015] O.J. L27/1.

A 2015 example would be:

> European Parliament and Council Directive (EU) 2015/720 of 29 April 2015 amending Directive 94/62/EC as regards reducing the consumption of lightweight plastic carrier bags [2015] O.J. L115/11

Citation for a pre-2015 directive adds the treaty basis to the year and number, as follows:

> Council Directive 2010/18/EU of 8 March 2010 implementing the revised framework on parental leave [2010] O.J. L68/13

Pre-2015 regulations are cited with the number first and the year following. The treaty basis is also given in brackets. An example would be:

> Commission Regulation (EU) No.1266/2010 of 22 December 2010 amending Directive 2007/68/EC as regards labelling requirements for wines.

Prior to the adoption of the Lisbon Treaty the institutional treaty basis was given as "EC" for the EC Treaty, or "EEC" for the EEC Treaty. Both can be seen in the title of the following directive:

> Commission Directive 95/12/EC of 23 May 1995 implementing Council Directive 92/75/EEC with regard to energy labelling of household washing machines.

Fig 8.4 First page of Directive 2003/88/EC

18.11.2003 EN Official Journal of the European Union L 299/9

DIRECTIVE 2003/88/EC OF THE EUROPEAN PARLIAMENT AND OF THE COUNCIL
of 4 November 2003
concerning certain aspects of the organisation of working time

THE EUROPEAN PARLIAMENT AND THE COUNCIL OF THE EUROPEAN UNION,

Having regard to the Treaty establishing the European Community, and in particular Article 137(2) thereof,

Having regard to the proposal from the Commission,

Having regard to the opinion of the European Economic and Social Committee [1],

Having consulted the Committee of the Regions,

Acting in accordance with the procedure referred to in Article 251 of the Treaty [2],

Whereas:

(1) Council Directive 93/104/EC of 23 November 1993, concerning certain aspects of the organisation of working time [3], which lays down minimum safety and health requirements for the organisation of working time, in respect of periods of daily rest, breaks, weekly rest, maximum weekly working time, annual leave and aspects of night work, shift work and patterns of work, has been significantly amended. In order to clarify matters, a codification of the provisions in question should be drawn up.

(2) Article 137 of the Treaty provides that the Community is to support and complement the activities of the Member States with a view to improving the working environment to protect workers' health and safety. Directives adopted on the basis of that Article are to avoid imposing administrative, financial and legal constraints in a way which would hold back the creation and development of small and medium-sized undertakings.

(3) The provisions of Council Directive 89/391/EEC of 12 June 1989 on the introduction of measures to encourage improvements in the safety and health of workers at work [4] remain fully applicable to the areas covered by this Directive without prejudice to more stringent and/or specific provisions contained herein.

(4) The improvement of workers' safety, hygiene and health at work is an objective which should not be subordinated to purely economic considerations.

[1] OJ C 61, 14.3.2003, p. 123.
[2] Opinion of the European Parliament of 17 December 2002 (not yet published in the Official Journal) and Council Decision of 22 September 2003.
[3] OJ L 307, 13.12.1993, p. 18. Directive as amended by Directive 2000/34/EC of the European Parliament and of the Council (OJ L 195, 1.8.2000, p. 41).
[4] OJ L 183, 29.6.1989, p. 1.

(5) All workers should have adequate rest periods. The concept of 'rest' must be expressed in units of time, i.e. in days, hours and/or fractions thereof. Community workers must be granted minimum daily, weekly and annual periods of rest and adequate breaks. It is also necessary in this context to place a maximum limit on weekly working hours.

(6) Account should be taken of the principles of the International Labour Organisation with regard to the organisation of working time, including those relating to night work.

(7) Research has shown that the human body is more sensitive at night to environmental disturbances and also to certain burdensome forms of work organisation and that long periods of night work can be detrimental to the health of workers and can endanger safety at the workplace.

(8) There is a need to limit the duration of periods of night work, including overtime, and to provide for employers who regularly use night workers to bring this information to the attention of the competent authorities if they so request.

(9) It is important that night workers should be entitled to a free health assessment prior to their assignment and thereafter at regular intervals and that whenever possible they should be transferred to day work for which they are suited if they suffer from health problems.

(10) The situation of night and shift workers requires that the level of safety and health protection should be adapted to the nature of their work and that the organisation and functioning of protection and prevention services and resources should be efficient.

(11) Specific working conditions may have detrimental effects on the safety and health of workers. The organisation of work according to a certain pattern must take account of the general principle of adapting work to the worker.

(12) A European Agreement in respect of the working time of seafarers has been put into effect by means of Council Directive 1999/63/EC of 21 June 1999 concerning the Agreement on the organisation of working time of seafarers concluded by the European Community Shipowners' Association (ECSA) and the Federation of Transport Workers' Unions in the European Union (FST) [5] based on Article 139(2) of the Treaty. Accordingly, the provisions of this Directive should not apply to seafarers.

[5] OJ L 167, 2.7.1999, p. 33.

A legislative act is given a date of enactment, but this does not indicate the date when the act is published in the *Official Journal*. This can be up to several months later.

How to find the text of a regulation or directive

8.8 Suppose you wish to look for the current text of the following directive:

> European Parliament and Council Directive 2003/88/EC of 4 November 2003 concerning certain aspects of the organisation of working time

How should you set about finding it? The best approach is to use the EUR-Lex website (at *http://www.eur-lex.europa.eu*). A search can be made directly from the EUR-Lex homepage using the year and number of the directive. The search form can also be used to specify that you wish to search for a directive rather than a regulation or decision.

The relevant year is entered as a four digit number, 2003 in the example given. The document number is 88. Both are given in full in the directive citation. Citations for pre-2000 directives require the initial numbers in the citation to be translated into a four digit year, so that Directive 93/104/EC is entered as year 1993 and document number 104.

Once these details have been entered, your search will display a results screen with the full title and *Official Journal* reference for the directive. Select "Text" to see the full text of the directive. A summary of the legislation may also be available.

The "Linked documents" entry for a directive lists any amendments or repeals and provides links to the full text of any related legislation. For Directive 2003/88/EC, which repeals an earlier working time directive (93/104/EC), the "Linked documents" entry provides a link to the directive repealed. If a directive has been amended a number of times, the "Linked documents" entry includes a link to a consolidated version of the text, incorporating all the amendments made. The full text displayed in your initial search result is the original text of the directive.

The bibliographic information associated with the text of directives, showing related documents, can also be found using the "EU" search in Westlaw UK (para.2.4). To find a directive, use the standard abbreviation for a directive in the "Case or Document No." search box, e.g. "2003/88/EC". A search by publication reference is also possible. The "Related information" section displays links to documents related to a particular directive.

TIPS • *Always check "Linked documents" when tracing the text of a directive on the EUR-Lex site. Links are provided to amending legislation, consolidated texts and important cases.*

How to trace legislation on a subject without a reference

8.9 If you have been told, for example, that there is a directive on part-time working or bathing water quality, but you do not have a number or a date, you will need to use a subject approach. In most cases, choosing the correct terminology is the first problem you will encounter. Directives are commonly given colloquial titles which in many cases contain the keywords needed to search an online database. A search for directives containing the words "parental leave" or "bathing water quality" using EUR-Lex, or Westlaw UK, for example, finds the relevant directive. Be prepared, though, to try alternative terms. A directive on the energy labelling of household electric refrigerators is not found, for example, if you use the word "fridges" rather than "refrigerators".

Because of the advantages provided by the linked legislation entries for legislation noted in para.8.8, the EUR-Lex website provides a good starting point for searching for a directive using keywords. Use the "Advanced Search" and limit the collection to be searched to "Legislation". This means that your keyword searches will only find legislation and not all categories of material found on EUR-Lex. "Directives" can also be specified as the legislation type.

A search on "bathing water quality" then finds Directive 2006/7/EC on the management of bathing water quality, which repeals an earlier directive, 76/160/EEC. The "Linked documents" entry confirms the repeal of the earlier directive and also notes amendments made by a 2009 regulation on regulatory procedure. A consolidated text for the directive is also provided, incorporating the changes made.

More complex searches can be carried out using search terms such as "or" and "not". These are explained on the "Search using search terms" screen. Searches can also be limited using standard subject themes.

The "EU" search page of Westlaw UK provides an alternative for finding legislation by keyword. To use Westlaw UK, enter "bathing water quality" in the "Parties or title" search box. It is not, unfortunately, possible to restrict the search to legislation, which means that the results for the search include a significant number of European Court of Justice cases, though these, may, of course, be of interest. There is no consolidated version of Directive 2006/7/EC, incorporating later amendments. This is only available in the EUR-Lex website.

If you are not sure of the keywords to use in searching for a directive, another approach is to use the "Directory code" headings available from the EUR-Lex "Advanced Search". A standard EU analytical table of headings is displayed, enabling the bathing water quality directive to be found, for example, under the following string of headings: "Environment, consumers and health protection"; "Pollution and nuisances"; and "Water protection and management". The headings used are not always particularly helpful. In this case, there are many entries under "Water protection and management", but it is possible to further refine the search by type of legislation to find a useful list of directives on water protection and management.

How to check if legislation is in force

If you have used EUR-Lex to find a directive or regulation as described in para.8.8, the "Linked Documents" section will confirm whether it is still in force. If you used Westlaw UK, any directive no longer in force is accompanied by a "no entry" icon indicating that the directive has been suspended or repealed. 8.10

If you are searching EUR-Lex using the "Advanced Search" (see para.8.9), a tick box can be used once the "Legislation" collection has been specified, restricting the search to legislation in force. This can save possible confusion. If you search for directives using the keywords "working time" and tick the "Limit to legislation in force" box, only current in-force directives are retrieved. You do not see Directive 93/104/EC and its various amending directives. Both the older Directive 93/104/EC and the current Directive 2003/88/EC are directives "concerning certain aspects of the organisation of working time".

An analytical overview of all legislation in force can also be found if you select the "Directory of European Union legislation" from the EUR-Lex home page (at *http://eur-lex.*

europa.eu). The directory uses the standard EU classification scheme noted in para.8.9 and links are provided to the full text of legislation listed under each heading.

How to trace proposals for legislation

8.11 In the UK, draft legislation is introduced into Parliament and becomes law during the same parliamentary session. This is not the case with EU legislation, which may take years to either become law or ultimately fail to become law. How would you know if legislation has been proposed on a particular subject?

The ability to discover EU policies and activities by subject area noted in para.8.2 can help identify key legislative initiatives. Once areas of proposed legislation have been identified, the European Commission's PreLex database then provides a useful means of identifying particular legislative proposals and confirming their current status. Links to relevant COM documents and *Official Journal* entries are included. The database can be found from the "Legislation" page of the European Commission pages on the Europa website (at *http://ec.europa.eu/legislation*). To find the search link, select "PreLex–decisions and laws in the pipeline".

If initiatives on the regulation of organic production, for example, have been identified as an area of interest, use the "Search In legislative procedures" link on the Pre-Lex "Legislative procedures" page to open an "Advanced Search" in EUR-Lex with the "Legislative procedures" collection specified. A search for "organic production" finds a proposal for a regulation of the European Parliament and of the Council "on organic production and labelling of organic products", COM (2014) 180.

The COM document itself can be found and dates are given for the proposal's transmission to the European Parliament, the opinion of the European Economic and Social Committee and so on. A link is also provided for the relevant entry for the proposal in the European Parliament's "Legislative Observatory" database. The Legislative Observatory (OEIL) database (at *http://www.europarl.europa.eu/oeil*) contains the details of all procedures or proposals before the Parliament, along with those concluded since July 1994. Legislative Opinions of the European Parliament can be found, along with the text of relevant committee reports.

How to trace whether a directive has been implemented in the United Kingdom

8.12 Directives, once adopted by the Council of the European Union, must be implemented by Member States by the most appropriate method for each country. In the UK, this is generally done by passing an Act of Parliament or issuing a statutory instrument. Member States are given a set period of time in which to do this. Tracing UK legislation implementing a directive can be problematic.

The European Commission has developed a web gateway, N-Lex (at *http://eur-lex.europa.eu/n-lex*), to help solve the problem of tracing implementing legislation. It provides a common search page which can be used to search national databases of legislation for Member States. Unfortunately the search link to the UK legislation.gov.uk web pages does not work well. UK legislation is best searched directly using the various sources described earlier in this book. The legislation searches of Westlaw UK or the Lexis Library provide an effective approach, as does a direct search of the legislation.gov.uk website: to use these databases, follow the approach outlined for searching for legislation by subject in para.7.21.

To search for legislation implementing the bathing water quality directive, for example, use a keyword search to find references to "2006/7/EC". The search finds the Bathing Water Regulations 2008/1097, along with an explanatory memorandum which includes the statement that Bathing Water Regulations 2008/1097 "transpose the requirements of EC Directive 2006/7/EC".

A convenient print alternative for tracing implementing legislation is provided by the *EU Legislation Implementator* volume of *Halsbury's Statutory Instruments* (para.7.28). If you have already discovered the reference for a directive, a chronological listing of directives enables you to look up the implementing UK legislation. All three statutory instruments noted above for Directive 96/34/EC can be traced from the entry for the directive. The *EU Legislation Implementator* is revised annually.

TIPS • *The EU Legislation Implementator volume of Halsbury's Statutory Instruments provides a convenient quick reference source for UK implementing legislation. The full text can then be found online using UK legislation databases.*

CASE LAW

There are two courts which interpret and enforce law of the European Union. The first, the European Court of Justice (ECJ), has been in existence since the European Communities were founded. The second, the Court of the First Instance (CFI), gave its first judgments in 1990. The ECJ hears all types of cases, including appeals from the CFI, but the CFI only hears competition, anti-dumping and staff cases. The case law of both courts has assumed a position of great importance. 8.13

The *Official Journal C Series* carries notices of cases pending before the courts. Brief details only of the nature of the proceedings and the judgment are provided.

European Court Reports

The official source of European Court judgments is the *Reports of Cases before the Court*. These are more commonly known as the *European Court Reports* (abbreviated to E.C.R.). In this series, the opinion of the Advocate General is given alongside the judgment. This is an important stage in the proceedings before the ECJ. The Advocate General's opinion is not binding on the court, but it is of great use to students of EU law in that it will include a thorough analysis of the facts and legal arguments in the case. Usually three or five judges hear the case. In contrast to the UK, they then present a single agreed judgment text. 8.14

There is an English language set of the *Reports* covering the judgments of the courts since 1954. Since 1990, the *Reports* have been split into two parts in each issue. Part I contains ECJ cases and Part II contains CFI cases. Since 1994 staff cases have been published in a separate series known as *Reports of European Community Staff Cases* (ECS-SC). These are not all translated into other languages.

Although the E.C.R. is the official series, it suffers from major delays in publication. Precise and accurate translation into the various EU languages results in delays of up to two years which makes it impossible to use it for recent cases. However, both opinions of the Advocate General and judgments of the European Court of Justice are available online from the Court website (at *http://www.curia.europa.eu*). They can also be found on the EUR-Lex website (at *http://www.eur-lex.europa.eu*). These sites provide the official online source of all opinions and judgments from the ECJ. As with all EU websites, there is no subscription charge for access. (See paras 8.18–8.22 for more on searching using these sites.)

Citation of European Court of Justice and Court of First Instance cases

8.15 The case citation is made up as follows:

1. Case Number and year of registration;
2. Names of the parties;
3. *European Court Reports* citation

An example would be:

Case C-59/89 *Commission v Germany* [1991] E.C.R. I-2607

After 1990, each case is preceded by the letter C (ECJ) or the letter T (CFI). Also note that a case with a reference . . . /07, for example, means that the application or reference to the court was made in 2007. The judgment was not given in that year. This means that you cannot automatically go to the E.C.R. for the year 2007 to find the judgment.

A European Case-Law Identifier (ECLI) was introduced in 2015, using four elements separated by colons. In the following example:

Case C-403/03 *Schempp v Finanzamt Munchen*, EU:C:2005:446

- EU indicates that it is a decision delivered by an EU Court or Tribunal;
- C indicates that this decision was delivered by the Court of Justice;
- 2005 indicates that the decision was delivered during 2005;
- 446 indicates that it is the 446th ECLI attributed in that year;

Paragraphs in judgments are cited as, e.g 'EU:C:2005:446, para.22'.

The ECLI is treated as a neutral citation in standard citation, preceding the report citation, e.g.

Case C-403/03 *Schempp v Finanzamt Munchen* EU:C:2005:446, [2005] E.C.R. I-6421

Other sources of case law

8.16 A number of UK published law reports publish reports of ECJ cases. The *Common Market Law Reports* (C.M.L.R) provides the main alternative to the *European Court Reports*. It is published by Sweet & Maxwell and also covers the cases with an EU dimension in national courts. C.M.L.R. appears sooner than the *European Court Reports* with a full, if not official, report. Both the Advocate General's opinion and the judgment made in a case are included in the reports. Whilst it does not report all cases, it does report all cases of significance. The reports are available online from Westlaw UK (para.2.4).

The *All England Reporter (European Cases)*—All E.R. (EC)—has published decisions from the ECJ and the CFI since 1995. The reports are available online from the Lexis Library

Fig 8.5 Example page from the *Common Market Law Reports* (from Westlaw UK)

Status: Positive or Neutral Judicial Treatment

*1356 Dano v Jobcenter Leipzig (European Commission and others, intervening)

(Case C-333/13)

Before the Court of Justice (Grand Chamber)

11 November 2014

[2015] 1 C.M.L.R. 48

Presiding, Skouris P ; Lenaerts VP ; Tizzano , Bay Larsen , von Danwitz , Vajda , Rodin PC ; Juhász , Borg Barthet , Malenovský , Levits , Berger (Rapporteur) and da Cruz Vilaça JJ ; A.G. Wathelet :

11 November 2014

Discrimination; EU law; EU nationals; Entitlement; Free movement of persons; Jobseeking; Rights of entry and residence; Social security benefits

H1 *Free movement of persons—non-discrimination—access to basic jobseekers provision—art.18 TFEU—Regulation 883/2004—Directive 2004/38—application for jobseekers provision in Germany—refusal—challenge—"special non-contributory cash benefits"—non-exportability of special non-contributory cash benefits—within scope of art.4 of Regulation 883/2004—derogation from non-discrimination—social assistance—equal treatment with Member State nationals—conditions of Directive 2004/38—preventing unreasonable burden on social assistance—sufficient resources—specific examination of financial situation—no right to benefit.*

H2 D and her son, who were both Romanian nationals, applied for basic jobseekers provision in Germany. D could not write, and had difficulty reading, the German language. She had not been trained in a profession and had not worked in either Germany or Romania. There was no evidence that D had sought a job in Germany. JL refused the application for the provision, and that refusal was confirmed on appeal. D and her son issued proceedings before the *Sozialgericht Leipzig* (Social Court, Leipzig), which sought a preliminary ruling from the Court of Justice. The Court held that Regulation 883/2004 , as amended by Regulation 1244/2010 , had to be interpreted as meaning that "special non-contributory cash benefits", as referred to in arts 3(3) and 70 of the regulation, fell within the scope of art.4 of the regulation. However, art.24(1) of Directive 2004/38 , read in conjunction with art.7(1)(b) thereof, and art.4 of Regulation 883/2004 , as amended by Regulation 1244/2010 , precluded legislation of a Member State under which nationals of other Member States were excluded from entitlement to certain "special non-contributory cash benefits" within the meaning of art.70(2) of Regulation 883/2004 , although those benefits were granted to nationals of the host Member State who were in the **1357* same situation, insofar as those nationals of other Member States did not have a right of residence under Directive 2004/38 in the host Member State.

H3 Request for a preliminary ruling from the *Sozialgericht Leipzig* (Germany) under art.267 TFEU .

Held:

Application to "special non-contributory cash benefits"

H4 (a) Article 3 of Regulation 883/2004 defined the matters covered by the regulation, expressly stating in art.3(3) that the regulation "shall also apply to the special non-contributory cash benefits covered by Article 70 [of the regulation]." It was clear from the wording of art.3 of Regulation 883/2004 that the regulation applied to special non-contributory cash benefits. [48]–[49]

H5 (b) Article 70(3) of Regulation 883/2004 provided that art.7 of the regulation, which governed the waiving of residence rules, and the other chapters of Title III thereof, which was devoted to the various categories of benefits, were not to apply to special non-contributory cash benefits.

(para.2.3). *European Community Cases* (C.E.C) is another source of case law. Only very important cases are covered. Specialist law report series such as *Fleet Street Reports or Industrial Relations Law Reports* also include relevant EU case law.

Both Westlaw UK and the Lexis Library can also be used to search for judgments online as noted in the following sections.

How to find a Court of Justice judgment or opinion if you have the reference

8.17 Suppose you are given the following case reference:

Case C-310/08 *Harrow LBC v Ibrahim.*

How do you find it? Both the Court of Justice website (at *http://www.curia.europa.eu*) and the EUR-Lex website (at *http://www.eur-lex-europa.eu*) provide free public access to the full text of judgments and opinions. Whichever route you choose, the final text of the opinion or judgment is the same.

Judgments can be found on the ECJ Curia website (at *http://www.curia.europa.eu)* using the site's search form. The *Harrow LBC v Ibrahim* case can then be found using either the case number or the "Names of parties" search. The Advocate General's opinion and the judgment are found as separate entries in the database along with links to the *Official Journal* notices for the application and judgment for the case under "List of documents".

Numerical access to case law is also possible from the EUR-Lex home page (at *http://www.eur-lex.europa.eu*). Search using the case number and a four digit year, so that 310/08 is searched as year 2008 and number 310. Links for the judgment and opinion are provided in the search results, but these can be more difficult to interpret than results from the Curia search.

An alternative route to ECJ cases is provided by Westlaw UK (para.2.4) and the Lexis Library (para.2.3). There are some advantages to using Westlaw UK in particular.

All ECJ cases can be found in Westlaw UK using the EU search page. A search using "C-310/08" in the "Case or Document No." search box finds both the opinion and judgment for the case. The "Books" section at the end of the judgment text in Westlaw UK includes, in addition, brief notes of articles on the case in European journals.

The *Common Market Law Reports* are also included in Westlaw UK. As noted in para.8.16, these report all significant ECJ cases. To check for a reported version of the *Harrow LBC v Ibrahim* case, use the "Cases" search page in Westlaw UK. The "Citation" search on the page only recognises the *European Court Reports* citation for the case, [2010] I–1065, not the case number, so you may need to search by party name. However a search finds the case reported in the *Common Market Law Reports*, [2010] 2 C.M.L.R. 51. The importance of the case for UK law also meant that it was reported in the *Human Rights Reports* and the *Public and Third Sector Law Reports*. Citations and links to full text are available to these reports from the Westlaw UK results page. The "Case Analysis" entry for the case in Westlaw UK also provides references for a significant number of journal articles commenting on the case.

EU cases can also be found using the Lexis Library "Cases" search. Searches can be limited to "Court of Justice of the EU".

TIPS • *Use "Free text" or party name searches to find ECJ cases in UK law reports. Case numbers are not recognised in the "Cases" citation search of either Westlaw UK or the Lexis Library.*

How to find a judgment of the Court of Justice on a subject

What can you do if you want to find cases on, for instance, the Common Customs Tariff? 8.18

Both the Court of Justice website and the EUR-Lex websites allow the full text of judgments and opinions to be searched. Keywords can be entered using the full Court of Justice search form (at *http://curia.europa.eu/juris*) and general themes selected using a "Subject-matter" search. For the customs tariff, these are "Free movement of goods" and "Customs Union".

Using EUR-Lex, select the "Advanced Search" from the home page (at *http://eur-lex.europa.eu*) and choose the "EU case law" collection. Then use either keywords or the "Directory of Case Law". The subject category "Common Customs Tariff" can be found in the directory under "Free Movement of Goods" and "Customs Union".

Searches can also be made using the "EU" search page in Westlaw UK or in the "Cases" search in the Lexis Library. The advice given in para.7.10 on searching full-text databases of UK case law holds equally well for searches of EU case law. Unless you are only interested in very recent cases, for example, your first concern, if searching for cases on the Common Customs Tariff, will be to find a way of further restricting your search so that a manageable list of results can be found. Are you for instance interested in cases where issues of nomenclature are important? Or is it another aspect of cases discussing the Commons Customs Tariff that interests you?

How to trace further information on a case

If a case has been reported in a UK published law report, the Westlaw UK "Cases" search (para.3.15), is a useful source of case summaries and further information. As noted in para.8.17, the "Case Analysis" entry for *Harrow LBC v Ibrahim,* for example, displays references to journal articles discussing the case. Later cases citing the case are also noted. 8.19

The Westlaw UK "Cases" search can be particularly useful for tracing information on key cases that have had a significant impact on EU law. A search for "Factortame", for example, under "Cases Cited" in the "Advanced Search" finds a number of UK cases for which the *Factortame* case has been significant. The results page lists cases which have applied, followed, or considered *Factortame*, both in the ECJ and in UK domestic courts. Citations for case comment in journal articles are also given in the relevant "Case Analysis" entries.

How to trace cases which have interpreted EU legislation

Commonly in research, there is a need to trace cases which are concerned with the interpretation of the provisions of EU law. For example, how do you find ECJ cases which have interpreted Directive 93/104/EC on the organisation of working time? 8.20

The best approach is to search for the directive using EUR-Lex as described in para.8.8. Once the directive has been found, the "Linked documents" entry provides links to any EU cases providing interpretation. A number of cases are listed for Directive 93/104/EC, including C–84/94 *United Kingdom v Council of the European Union*, which declared the directive void.

An alternative approach is to use the Westlaw UK "Cases" search (para.3.15) to search for UK reported cases which have interpreted the directive. Results will include ECJ cases reported in reports such as the *Common Market Law Reports* along with UK domestic reported cases. Search using "93/104" as a search term.

How to trace recent judgments

8.21 If you wish to go directly to the full text of a judgment (or opinion) which you know to be very recent, the Curia website (at *http://www.curia.europa.eu*) provides a convenient list of recent judgments under the "Case-law" section of the website.

Updates on recent judicial proceedings are also available from the "Press and Media" section of the Curia website. Brief notes of recent judgments are available along with notes of opinions and new cases brought before the court. A link is provided to the full text of each press release.

LEGAL ENCYCLOPEDIAS

8.22 The print loose-leaf *Encyclopedia of European Union Laws (Sweet & Maxwell)* provides coverage of all EU constitutional texts. *Halsbury's Laws of England* (para.7.3) is also a potential source of information on EU Law. If you are using the online version from the Lexis Library, a search on Directive 2003/88 on working time, for example, finds a section summarising EU requirements and noting UK implementation. Relevant ECJ cases are also noted.

BOOKS

8.23 The European Commission publishes a wide range of material providing introductions, overviews and summaries of topics. All these will be available to you if your library is a European Documentation Centre (see para.8.1). The library catalogue will help you locate them.

The library catalogue can also help you find relevant textbooks. These may include books on political and economic aspects of European integration found outside the law section of your library. Remember that books in almost any area of law can provide discussion of EU law. Though there will be a specific section on EU law within your library, the textbooks found there are not the only ones that can help you understand EU law.

ECLAS, the European Commission's own library catalogue can provide an effective means of tracing details of books of all kinds of EU law and wider EU related issues. The Central Library page of the European Commission site provides a link to the catalogue search page (at *http://ec.europa.eu/eclas/F*). Limit the language choice to "English" and the format choice to "Books" to find books in English on a subject, e.g. competition law.

JOURNALS

8.24 Many legal journals cover EU topics in a selective manner. Major English language journals that specialise in the subject include the *Common Market Law Review*, the *European Law Review*, the *European Business Law Review*, the *European Competition Law Review*, *International and Comparative Law Quarterly* and the *Yearbook of European Law*. Your library may be able to provide access to recent issues both online and in print (see para.5.2).

How to find articles on EU law

If you are looking for recent articles on EU law the best source for coverage in UK law journals is the *Legal Journals Index*. See para.5.8 for further information on searching the index using keywords. Citations for ECJ cases and EC legislation can also be used to trace articles. 8.25

The European Commission's ECLAS catalogue (at *http://ec.europa.eu/eclas/F*) can also help trace journal articles on EC law. Limit the format choice to "Articles" and the language to "English" to find details of English language journal articles on a subject, e.g. "Common Customs Tariff".

The General Report on the Activities of the European Union

The *General Report on the Activities of the European Union* can be accessed from the "Documents and publications" page of the Europa website (at *http://www.europa.eu*). The *General Review* is an annual review, summarising key developments in particular areas. EU actions can be reviewed under standard subject headings, e.g. "Environment", for the previous year. If you turn to previous issues of the *General Review* a picture can be built up of the development of EU policy in an area. 8.26

CURRENT INFORMATION

Recent EU developments can be traced using European Commission Press Release Database (at *http://www.europa.eu/rapid*). Searches can be limited by policy area or by institution. The database includes press releases, news updates and announcements. 8.27

If your library has a subscription to the Nexis news service (see para.5.24), you can also access the full-text news coverage of many European newspapers.

Appendix I Sources of Law for Scotland, Northern Ireland and Wales

SCOTS LAW

Case Law

A1.1 Westlaw UK (para.2.4) provides access to the two major series of Scottish law reports: *Session Cases* cited, e.g.:

Clark v TripAdvisor LLC [2014] *CSIH 110; 2015 S.C. 368*

Scots Law Times cited, e.g.:

W v Advocate General for Scotland [2015] *CSOH 111; 2015 S.L.T. 537*

Neutral citations have been used for Scottish cases since 2005. The examples above show neutral citations for the Court of Session, Inner House (CSIH) and the Court of Session, Outer House (CSOH).

Standard citation adds an abbreviation for the relevant court for cases pre-dating the use of neutral citations, e.g.

Burnett's Trustee v Grainger 2002 S.C. 580 (IH)

The Lexis Library (para.2.3) provides access to the *Session Cases, Scottish Criminal Case Reports* and *Scottish Civil Law Reports*, along with *Scottish Case Digests*.

Judgments are available from the Scottish Court Service (at *http://www.scotcourts.gov.uk*); also from the BAILII website (at *http://www.bailii.org).*

Acts of the Scottish Parliament

A1.2 Acts of the Scottish Parliament are cited, e.g.:

Mental Health (Scotland) Act 2015 (asp 9)

The official printed version is provided by Queen's Printer for Scotland (at *http://www.gov.scot/Topics/Government/queensprinterforscotland*). Legislation links on the website are to legislation held on the legislation.gov.uk website (para.2.13). Links are provided to amending legislation. BAILII (at *http://www.bailii.org*) provides non-subscription access to the original versions of Scottish Acts. Justis UK Statutes (para.2.6) and Lawtel (para.2.5) also provide access to the original unamended text, along with links to amending legislation.

The Lexis Library (para.2.3) and Westlaw UK (para.2.4) provide access to the amended text of Acts in force.

Scottish Statutory Instruments

Scottish Statutory Instruments are cited, e.g.: A1.3

Scottish Parliament (Disqualification) Order 2015, SSI 2015/350

The legislation.gov.uk website (para.2.13) and BAILII (para.2.15) provide non-subscription access.

The Lexis Library (para.2.3) and Westlaw UK (para.2.4) provide subscription access.

The Scottish Parliament

The *Official Report* of the Scottish Parliament can be found on the Parliament website (*http://www.scottish.parliament.uk*). The "Parliamentary Business" section of the website provides links to the full text of Bills, Committee web pages, research briefings and the Official Report of Proceedings. A1.4

The Scottish Executive

Papers from the Scottish Executive can be found on its website (at *http://www. gov.scot*). A1.5

Official Publications

Official Publications can be traced using the databases described in para.6.16. A1.6

Encyclopedias

The *Laws of Scotland: Stair Memorial Encyclopedia* is available from the Lexis Library (para.2.3). *Laws of Scotland* provides a comprehensive statement of the law of Scotland, comparable to that provided for England and Wales by *Halsbury's Laws of England* (para.7.3). A1.7

Westlaw UK (para.2.4) provides access to the full text of *Renton and Brown Criminal Procedure* and *Renton and Brown Criminal Procedure Legislation*.

NORTHERN IRELAND LAW

Case Law

The Lexis Library (para.2.3) provides full text access to the *Northern Ireland Law Reports*, cited, e.g.: A1.8

R. v McGreechan [2014] *NICA 5*, [2015] N.I. 44

The *Northern Ireland Judgments Bulletin* is only available in print. It is cited, e.g.:

Re Wilson's Application [2012] NIQB 102, [2014] N.I.J.B. 101

Neutral citations have been used for Northern Ireland cases since 2001. The examples above show neutral citations for the Northern Ireland Court of Appeal (NICA) and the Northern Ireland Queen's Bench Division (NIQB).

Judgments reported in the N.I.J.B. (along with other "unreported" judgments) can be found for the mid-1980s onwards using the Lexis Library "Cases" search. Judgments from 2000 onwards are available from the Northern Ireland Court Service (at *http://www.courtsni.gov.uk*); also the BAILII website (para.2.15).

Northern Ireland Statutes

A1.9 Northern Ireland Statutes from 1922 onwards can be found using the legislation.gov.uk website (para.2.13).

Acts of the Northern Ireland Assembly are cited, e.g.:

Justice Act (Northern Ireland) 2015

Orders in Council (used for primary legislation 1972–2009) cited e.g.:

Criminal Justice (Northern Ireland) Order 2008

Acts of the Northern Ireland Parliament (1921–1972) cited e.g.:

Wild Birds Protection Act (NI) 1931

Westlaw UK (para.2.4) provides updated versions of Northern Ireland Orders in Council for 1991 onwards, along with updated Acts of the Northern Ireland Assembly.

Statutory Rules of Northern Ireland

A1.10 The unamended text of all secondary legislation for Northern Ireland from 1996 onwards can be found on the legislation.gov.uk website (para.2.13). A selection of Statutory Rules is available for 1991–1995.

Northern Ireland Assembly

A1.11 The *Official Report* of debates for the Assembly is available from the Northern Ireland Assembly website (at *http://www.niassembly.gov.uk*). Assembly and Committee Reports (published as Northern Ireland Assembly Papers) are also available.

Northern Ireland Executive and Government Departments

A1.12 Links for Northern Ireland government departments and the Office of the First Minister and Deputy First Minister can be found using the nidirect website (at *http://www.nidirect.gov.uk*). The Northern Ireland Executive website (at *http://www.northernireland.gov.uk*) provides information on the background and work of the Northern Ireland Executive.

Official Publications

A1.13 Official Publications can be traced using the databases described in para.6.16.

Updates on Cases and Legislation

A1.14 The *Current Law Monthly Digest* (para.7.12) provides updates on Northern Ireland legislation by subject. Northern Ireland cases are also noted where they appear in selected UK law reports (cases reported in the *Northern Ireland Law Reports* are not included).

The *Bulletin of Northern Ireland Law* provides a comprehensive digest of legal developments in Northern Ireland for the period 1981–2012. Publication has been discontinued and online access is no longer available.

Encyclopedias

Valentine: All the Law of Northern Ireland is available as an additional subscription from the Lexis Library (para.2.3). It provides a subject approach to legislation in force in Northern Ireland along with summaries of key cases. A1.15

WALES LEGISLATION

Acts and Measures of the National Assembly for Wales

Acts of the National Assembly for Wales can be found on the legislation.gov.uk website and are cited, e.g.: A1.16

Higher Education (Wales) Act 2015 (anaw 1)

Measures of the National Assembly for Wales (primary legislation for the period 2008–2011) are cited, e.g.:

Learner Travel (Wales) Measure 2008 (nawm 2)

The Lexis Library (para.2.3) and Westlaw UK (para.2.4) provide updated versions of primary legislation.

Wales Statutory Instruments

Statutory instruments made by the National Assembly for Wales can be found on the legislation.gov.uk website and are cited, e.g.: A1.17

The Care Leavers (Wales) Regulations SI 2015/1820 (W 262)

National Assembly for Wales

The "Assembly Business" section of the National Assembly for Wales website (at *http://www.assembly.wales*) provides links to the Record of Proceedings, and the progress of Assembly Bills. A guide to the legislative process is also available. A1.18

Welsh Government

The Welsh Government website (at *http://gov.wales*) provides information on Welsh Government in devolved areas. A1.19

Appendix II Sources of International Law

CASE LAW

A2.1 Case law from a number of international courts and tribunals is available online. These include (among others):

- African Court of Human and Peoples Rights (at *http://www.african-court.org*);
- Central American Court of Justice (at *http://portal.ccj.org.ni*);
- COMESA Court of Justice (at *http://www.comesa.int*);
- East African Court of Justice (at *http://eacj.org*);
- Inter-American Court of Human Rights (at *http://www.corteidh.or.cr*);
- International Centre for the Settlement of Investment Disputes (at *http://www.worldbank.org/icsid*);
- International Court of Justice (ICJ) (at *http://www.icj-cij.org*);
- International Criminal Court (ICC) (at *http://www.icc-cpi.int*);
- International Criminal Tribunal for Yugoslavia (at *http://www.icty.org*);
- International Tribunal for the Law of the Sea (at *http://www.itlos.org*);
- Permanent Court of Arbitration (at *http://www.pca-cpa.org*);
- Special Court for Sierra Leone (at *http://www.rscsl.org*).

Case law from a wide range of international courts can be searched from the following websites:

- World Courts (at *http://www.worldcourts.com*);
- Worldlii International Courts & Tribunals Collection (at *http://www.worldlii.org/int/cases*).

Your library may also have a subscription to Oxford Reports on International Law—an online subscription service which brings together decisions on public international law from international law courts, domestic courts, and ad hoc tribunals.

SPECIALIST WEBSITES

A2.2 There are a number of specialist websites that can help identify international organisations, conventions and treaties. These include:

- American Society of International Law—Electronic Resource Guide (at *http://www.asil.org/erg*);

- Eagle-I Internet Portal for Law (Institute of Advanced Legal Studies) (at *http://ials.sas.ac.uk/eaglei/project/eiproject.htm*);
- Electronic Information System for International Law (at *http://www.eisil.org*);
- Flare Index to Treaties (at *http://ials.sas.ac.uk/library/flag/introtreaties.htm*); and
- United Nations Treaty Collection (at *http://treaties.un.org*).

BOOKS

A number of "cases and materials" collections are available for international law: A2.3

- M. Evans, *Blackstone's International Law Documents*, 12th edn (OUP, 2015);
- D. Harris and S. Sivakumaran, *Cases and Materials on International Law*, 8th edn (Sweet & Maxwell, 2015).

A listing of useful international law websites can be found in:

- M. Shaw, *International Law*, 7th edn (OUP, 2014)

Appendix III Abbreviations of Reports, Series and Journals

A3.1 This alphabetical list contains a selection of the more commonly used abbreviations in the UK, the EU and the Commonwealth. It is not exhaustive and further information can be found in D. Raistrick, *Index to Legal Citations and Abbreviations* and in the I.A.L.S. *Manual of Legal Citations*, Vols. I and II, the *Index to Legal Periodicals*, the *Legal Journals Index*. *The Digest* (Cumulative Supplement) and the *Current Law Citators* also contain lists of abbreviations, at the front.

A.C.—Law Reports Appeal Cases 1891—present
A.J.—Acts Juridica
A.J.I.L.—American Journal of International Law
A.L.J.—Australian Law Journal
A.L.R.—American Law Reports Annotated
A.L.R.—Australian Law Reports, formerly Argus Law Reports
All E.R.—All England Law Reports 1936—present
All E.R. Rep.—All England Law Reports Reprint 1558–1935
Am. J. Comp. L.—American Journal of Comparative Law
Anglo-Am. L.R.—Anglo-American Law Review
Ann. Dig.—Annual Digest of Public International Law Cases (1919–1949). (From 1950 this series has been published as the International Law Reports—I.L.R.)
App. Cas.—Law Reports Appeal Cases 1875–1890
B.C.L.C.—Butterworths Company Law Cases
B.D.I.L.—British Digest of International Law
B.F.S.P.—British and Foreign State Papers
B.I.L.C.—British International Law Cases
B.J.A.L.—British Journal of Administrative Law
B.J. Crim.—British Journal of Criminology
B.J.L.S.—British Journal of Law and Society
B.L.R.—Building Law Reports
B.L.R.—Business Law Review
B.N.I.L.—Bulletin of Northern Ireland Law
B.T.R.—British Tax Review
B.Y.I.L.—British Yearbook of International Law
Bull. E.C.—Bulletin of the European Communities
Business L.R.—Business Law Review
C.A.R.—Criminal Appeal Reports
C.A.T.—Court of Appeal Transcript (unpublished)
C.B.R.—Canadian Bar Review
C.D.E.—Cahiers de Droit Européen
C.J.Q.—Civil Justice Quarterly

C.L.—Current Law
C.L.J.—Cambridge Law Journal
C.L.P.—Current Legal Problems
C.L.R.—Commonwealth Law Reports (Australia)
C.M.L.R.—Common Market Law Reports
C.M.L. Rev.—Common Market Law Review
C.P.D.—Law Reports Common Pleas Division 1875–1880
C.T.S.—Consolidated Treaty Series
Calif. L. Rev.—California Law Review
Camb. L.J.—Cambridge Law Journal
Can. B.R.—Canadian Bar Review
Ch.—Law Reports Chancery Division 1891–present
Ch.D.—Law Reports Chancery Division 1875–1890
Co. Law.—Company Lawyer
Colum. L. Rev.—Columbia Law Review
Com. Cas.—Commercial Cases 1895–1941
Constr. L.J.—Construction Law Journal
Conv.; Conv.—N.S.—Conveyancer and Property Lawyer
Cox C.C.—Cox's Criminal Law Cases
Cr. App. R.; Cr. App. Rep.—Criminal Appeal Reports
Cr. App. R.(S)—Criminal Appeal Reports (Sentencing)
Crim. L.R.—Criminal Law Review
D.L.R.—Dominion Law Reports (Canada)
D.U.L.J.—Dublin University Law Journal
E.C.R.—European Court Reports
E.G.—Estates Gazette
E.G.L.R.—Estates Gazette Law Reports
E.H.R.R.—European Human Rights Reports
E.I.P.R.—European Intellectual Property Review
E.L. Rev.—European Law Review
E.R.—*English Reports*
Eng. Rep.—*English Reports*
Eur. Comm. H.R. D.R.—European Commission for Human Rights Decisions and Reports
Eur. Court H.R. Series A/Series B—European Court of Human Rights Series A & B
Euro C.L.—European Current Law
Ex.D.—Law Reports Exchequer Division 1875–1880
F.L.R.—Family Law Reports
F.L.R.—Federal Law Reports
F.S.R.—Fleet Street Reports
F.T.—Financial Times
Fam.—Law Reports Family Division 1972–present
Fam. Law—Family Law
Grotius Trans.—Transactions of the Grotius Society

H.L.R.—Housing Law Reports
Harv. L. Rev.—Harvard Law Review
I.C.J. Rep.—International Court of Justice Reports
I.C.J.Y.B.—International Court of Justice Yearbook
I.C.L.Q.—International and Comparative Law Quarterly
I.C.R.—Industrial Cases Reports 1975–present
I.C.R.—Industrial Court Reports 1972–1974
I.J.; Ir. Jur.—Irish Jurist
I.L.J.—Industrial Law Journal
I.L.M.—International Legal Materials
I.L.Q.—International Law Quarterly
I.L.R.—International Law Reports
I.L.R.M.—Irish Law Reports Monthly
I.L.T.; Ir.L.T.—Irish Law Times
I.R.—Irish Reports
I.R.L.R.—Industrial Relations Law Reports
I.R.R.R.—Industrial Relations Review & Reports
Imm.A.R.—Immigration Appeal Reports
Ir. Jur.—Irish Jurist
I.T.R.—Industrial Tribunal Reports
J.B.L.—Journal of Business Law
J.C.—Session Cases: Justiciary Cases (Scotland)
J.C.L.—Journal of Criminal Law
J.C.M.S.—Journal of Common Market Studies
J.I.S.E.L.—Journal of the Irish Society for European Law
J.I.S.L.L.—Journal of the Irish Society for Labour Law
J.L.S.—Journal of Law and Society
J.L.S.—Journal of the Law Society of Scotland
J. Legal Ed.—Journal of Legal Education
J.O.—Journal Officiel des Communautés Européennes
J.P.—Justice of the Peace Reports (also Justice of the Peace (journal))
J.P.I.L.—Journal of Personal Injury Litigation
J.P.L.—Journal of Planning and Environment Law
J.R.—Juridical Review
J.S.P.T.L.—Journal of the Society of Public Teachers of Law
J.S.W.L.—Journal of Social Welfare Law
K.B.—Law Reports: King's Bench Division 1901–1952
K.I.R.—Knight's Industrial Reports
L.A.G. Bul.—Legal Action Group Bulletin
L.G.C.—Local Government Chronicle
L.G.R.—Knight's Local Government Reports
L.J.—Law Journal 1866–1965 (newspaper)
L.J. Adm.—Law Journal: Admiralty N.S. 1865–1875
L.J. Bcy.—Law Journal: Bankruptcy N.S. 1832–1880

L.J.C.C.R.—Law Journal: County Courts Reports 1912–1933
L.J.C.P.—Law Journal: Common Pleas N.S. 1831–1875
L.J. Ch.—Law Journal: Chancery N.S. 1831–1946
L.J. Eccl.—Law Journal: Ecclesiastical Cases N.S. 1866–1875
L.J. Eq.—Law Journal: Equity N.S. 1831–1946
L.J. Ex.—Law Journal: Exchequer N.S. 1831–1875
L.J. Ex. Eq.—Law Journal: Exchequer in Equity 1835–1841
L.J.K.B. (or Q.B.)—Law Journal: King's (or Queen's) Bench N.S. 1831–1946
L.J.M.C.—Law Journal: Magistrates' Cases N.S. 1831–1896
L.J.N.C.—Law Journal: Notes of Cases 1866–1892
L.J.N.C.C.R.—Law Journal Newspaper: County Court Reports 1934–1947
L.J.O.S.—Law Journal (Old Series) 1822–1831
L.J.P.—Law Journal: Probate, Divorce and Admiralty N.S. 1875–1946
L.J.P.D. & A.—Law Journal: Probate, Divorce and Admiralty N.S. 1875–1946
L.J.P. & M.—Law Journal: Probate and Matrimonial Cases N.S. 1858–1859, 1866–1875
L.J.P.C.—Law Journal: Privy Council N.S. 1865–1946
L.J.P.M. & A.—Law Journal: Probate, Matrimonial and Admiralty N.S. 1860–1865
L.J.R.—Law Journal Reports 1947–1949
L. Lib.J.—Law Library Journal
L.M.C.L.Q.—Lloyd's Maritime and Commercial Law Quarterly
L.N.T.S.—League of Nations Treaty Series
L.Q.R.—Law Quarterly Review
L.R.A. & E.—Law Reports: Admiralty and Ecclesiastical Cases 1865–1875
L.R.C.C.R.—Law Reports: Crown Cases Reserved 1865–1875
L.R. C.P.—Law Reports: Common Pleas Cases 1865–1875
L.R. Ch. App.—Law Reports: Chancery Appeal Cases 1865–1875
L.R. Eq.—Law Reports: Equity Cases 1866–1875
L.R. Ex.—Law Reports: Exchequer Cases 1865–1875
L.R.H.L.—Law Reports: English and Irish Appeals 1866–1875
L.R. P. & D.—Law Reports: Probate and Divorce Cases 1865–1875
L.R.P.C.—Law Reports: Privy Council Appeals 1865–1875
L.R.Q.B.—Law Reports: Queen's Bench 1865–1875
L.R.R.P.; L.R. R.P.C.—Law Reports: Restrictive Practices Cases 1957–1973
L.S.—Legal Studies
L.S. Gaz.—Law Society Gazette
L.T.—Law Times
L.T.R.; L.T. Rep.—Law Times Reports (New Series) 1859–1947
L.T.Jo.—Law Times (newspaper) 1843–1965
L.T.O.S.—Law Times Reports (Old Series) 1843–1860
L. Teach.—Law Teacher
Law & Contemp. Prob.—Law and Contemporary Problems
Lit.—Litigation
Liverpool L.R.—Liverpool Law Review

Ll. L.L.R.; Ll.L.R.; LL.L. Rep.—Lloyd's List Law Reports later Lloyd's Law Reports
Lloyd's L.R.; Lloyd's Rep.—Lloyd's List Law Reports later Lloyd's Law Reports
M.L.J.—Malayan Law Journal
M.L.R.—Modern Law Review
Man. Law—Managerial Law
Med. Sci. & Law—Medicine, Science & the Law
Mich. L. Rev.—Michigan Law Review
N.I.—Northern Ireland Law Reports
N.I.J.B.—Northern Ireland Law Reports Bulletin of Judgments
N.I.L.Q.—Northern Ireland Legal Quarterly
N.I.L.R.—Northern Ireland Law Reports
N.L.J.—New Law Journal
N.Y.U.L. Rev.—New York University Law Review
N.Z.L.R.—New Zealand Law Reports
New L.J.—New Law Journal
O.J.—Official Journal of the European Communities
O.J.C.—Official Journal of the European Communities: Information and Notices
O.J.L.—Official Journal of the European Communities: Legislation, e.g. 1972, L139/28
O.J.L.S.—Oxford Journal of Legal Studies
P.—Law Reports: Probate, Divorce and Admiralty 1891–1971
P. & C.R.—Planning (Property from 1968) and Compensation Reports
P.C.I.J.—Permanent Court of International Justice Reports of Judgments
P.D.—Law Reports: Probate Division 1875–1890
P.L.—Public Law
P.N.—Professional Negligence
Q.B.—Law Reports: Queen's Bench Division 1891–1901, 1952–present
Q.B.D.—Law Reports: Queen's Bench Division 1875–1890
R.D.E.—Rivista di Diritto Europeo
R.G.D.I.P.—Revue Générale de Droit International Public
R.M.C.—Revue du Marché Commun
R.P.C.—Reports of Patent, Design & Trade Mark Cases
R.R.—*Revised Reports*
R.R.C.—Ryde's Rating Cases
R.T.R.—Road Traffic Reports
R.V.R.—Rating & Valuation Reporter
Rec.—Recueil des Cours
Rec.—Recueil de la Jurisprudence de la Cour (Court of Justice of the European Communities)
S.A.—South African Law Reports
S.C.—Session Cases (Scotland)
S.C. (H.L.)—Session Cases: House of Lords (Scotland)
S.C.(J.)—Session Cases: Justiciary Cases (Scotland)
S.C.C.R.—Scottish Criminal Case Reports
S.I.—Statutory Instruments

S.J.—Solicitors Journal
S.L.R.—Law Reporter/Scottish Law Review
S.L.T.—Scots Law Times
S.R.—Statutory Rules (Northern Ireland)
S.R. & O.—Statutory Rules and Orders
S.T.C.—Simon's Tax Cases
Scolag.—Bulletin of the Scottish Legal Action Group
Sol. Jo.—Solicitors Journal
St. Tr.; State Tr.—State Trials 1163–1820
Stat.L.R.—Statute Law Review
State Tr. N.S.—State Trials (New Series) 1820–1858
T.C.—Reports of Tax Cases
T.L.R.—Times Law Reports
TSO—The Stationery Office, 1996–present
Tax Cas.—Reports of Tax Cases
Tul. L. Rev.—Tulane Law Review
U. Chi. L. Rev.—University of Chicago Law Review
U.K.T.S.—United Kingdom Treaty Series
U.N.T.S.—United Nations Treaty Series
U.N.J.Y.—United Nations Juridical Yearbook
U.N.Y.B.—Yearbook of the United Nations
U. Pa. L. Rev.—University of Pennsylvania Law Review
U.S. —United States Supreme Court Reports
U.S.T.S.—United States Treaty Series
V.A.T.T.R.—Value Added Tax Tribunal Reports
V.L.R.—Victorian Law Reports (Australia)
W.I.R.—West Indian Reports
W.L.R.—Weekly Law Reports
W.N.—Weekly Notes
W.W.R.—Western Weekly Reporter
Y.B.—Yearbook (old law report), e.g. (1466) Y.B.Mich. (the term) 6 Edw. 4, pl.18, fol.7 (plea, folio)
Y.B.W.A.—Yearbook of World Affairs
Yale L.J.—Yale Law Journal
Yearbook E.C.H.R.—Yearbook of the European Convention on Human Rights

Appendix IV How Do I Find? A Summary of Sources for English Law

ABBREVIATIONS

A4.1 Cardiff Index to Legal Abbreviations (para.3.5)
D. Raistrick, *Index to Legal Citations and Abbreviations*.
The front pages of: *Current Law Case Citator* (para.3.5)

BOOKS

Tracing books on a subject

A4.2 Use the library catalogue (para.7.29).
Use Google Books (para.7.30).
Use Google Scholar (para.5.7).
Consult catalogues and bibliographies (see below).
Non-legal databases also include book references (para.5.13).

Tracing books by author or title

A4.3 Use the library catalogue (para.7.29).
Consult catalogues and bibliographies (see below).

CATALOGUES AND BIBLIOGRAPHIES

A4.4 COPAC catalogue of UK research libraries (para.7.29).
Other catalogues of specialist and national libraries (para.7.29).
Legal bibliographies (para.7.31).
British National Bibliography (para.7.35).
Sources for books in print (para.7.36).

FINDING CASES

If you know the name of the case

A4.5 (Summary: after para.3.20)
Westlaw UK "Cases" search (para.3.15).
Current Law Case Citators (para.3.16).
Online databases of case law (para.2.2, para.3.8).
The Digest (para.3.15).
English Reports (for English cases before 1865) (para.3.10).

For recent Law Reports

Westlaw UK "Cases" search (para.3.15). ▶ A4.6
Current Law (para.3.16).
Cases reported in *The Times* (para.5.24).

For recent judgments

The BAILII website (para.3.20) ▶ A4.7
Online updates on recent cases (para.3.22).
"Case law" search from the ICLR website (para.3.22).
Other databases of judgments (para.3.19 and para.3.20).

Tracing cases on a subject

Westlaw UK "Cases" search (para.7.9). ▶ A4.8
Current Law (para.7.12 and para.7.13).
The Digest (para.7.14).
Full-text case law databases (para.7.10).
Halsbury's Laws of England (para.7.4).
Databases providing updates to recent cases (para.3.22).

Tracing the subsequent judicial history of a case

Westlaw UK "Case Analysis" (para.7.9). ▶ A4.9
Current Law (para.7.12 and para.7.13).
The Digest (para.7.14).
Full-text case law databases (para.7.10).
Law Reports Index (table of cases judicially considered) (para.7.16).

Are there any journal articles on this case?

Westlaw UK "Case Analysis" (para.7.9). ▶ A4.10
Latest issue of *Current Law Monthly* (entries in the Cumulative Table of Cases).
Lawtel "Articles Index" (para.5.11).
Legal Journals Index (para.5.8).

GENERAL STATEMENTS OF THE LAW

Textbooks (para.7.29). ▶ A4.11
Halsbury's Laws of England (para.7.3).
Specialised legal encyclopedias (para.7.6).

OFFICIAL PUBLICATIONS

Tracing official publications

UKOP database (para.6.16). ▶ A4.12
Other databases for tracing official publications (para.6.16).
tsoshop website (para.6.15)

HMSO catalogues (pre-1996 publications) (para.6.15).
ProQuest House of Commons Papers (para.6.16).
General Index to Accounts and Papers (para.6.16).
Printed indexes to the House of Commons Parliamentary Papers (para.6.16).

JOURNAL ARTICLES

Articles on a subject

A4.13 *Legal Journals Index* (para.5.8).
HeinOnline (para.5.9)
Lawtel "Articles Index" (para.5.11).
Index to Legal Periodicals (para.5.10).
Index to Foreign Legal Periodicals (para.5.12).
Current Law Monthly Digests (under appropriate subject heading) (para.7.12) and *Current Law Year Books* (at the back of the volumes) (para.7.13).
Library keyword searches (para.5.6)
Google Scholar (para.5.7)
Other non-legal journal indexes (para.5.13 et seq.)

Articles on a case

A4.14 *Legal Journals Index* (para.5.8).
Lawtel "Articles Index" (para.5.11).
Latest issue of *Current Law Monthly* (entries in the Cumulative Table of Cases).

Articles on an Act

A4.15 *Legal Journals Index* (para.5.8).
Westlaw UK "Legislation Analysis" (para.4.18).
Current Law Legislation Citators (para.4.19).
Indexes to journals (under the appropriate subject heading).

Tracing journals

A4.16 Consult the library's catalogue or journal finder (para.1.9).
If the journal is not available in your library, use other catalogues, as for books (para.7.29)—ask the library staff for advice.

STATUTES

Collections of the Statutes

Older statutes

A4.17 *Statutes of the Realm* (para.4.22).
Statutes at Large (various editions) (para.4.23).
Acts and Ordinances of the Interregnum (para.4.24).

Modern statutes

BAILII United Kingdom Statutes (para.4.8). **A4.18**
Justis UK Statutes (para.4.9).
Current Law Statutes (para.4.11).
Lexis Library "Legislation" search (para.4.13).
Westlaw UK "Legislation" search (para.4.14).
Legislation.gov.uk (para.4.15).
Halsbury's Statutes (para.4.16).

Collections of Acts by subject

Halsbury's Statutes (para.4.16, para.7.23). **A4.19**

Annotated editions of statutes

Current Law Statutes (para.4.11).
Halsbury's Statutes (para.4.16, para.7.23).

Statutes in force

Halsbury's Statutes (para.4.16, para.7.23). **A4.20**
Westlaw UK "Legislation Analysis" (para.4.18).
Lexis Library "Legislation" search (para.4.13).
Westlaw UK "Legislation" search (para.4.14).
Chronological Table of the Statutes (para.4.20).
Current Law Legislation Citators (para.4.19).
Is It In Force? (para.4.17).

Tracing statutes on a subject

Halsbury's Statutes (para.4.17, para.7.23). **A4.21**
Full-text databases of legislation (para.7.21) (other online sources para.7.22).
Halsbury's Laws (para.7.3).

Print indexes to statutes

Chronological Table of the Statutes (shows whether Acts of any date are still in force) (para.4.20). **A4.22**
Is It In Force? (para.4.17).
Halsbury's Statutes (alphabetically arranged by subject. Consult alphabetical list of statutes, then look in the *Cumulative Supplement* and *Noter-Up* service to check if an Act is still in force) (para.7.23).
Public General Acts: Tables and Index (annual—brings the information in the Chronological Table of Statutes up to date) (para.4.6).

Local and personal Acts—Indexes

Legislation.gov.uk—Acts available 2001 onwards (para.2.13) **A4.23**
Index to Local and Personal Acts 1801–1947 (para.4.25).

Supplementary Index to the Local and Personal Acts 1948–1966 (para.4.25).
Local and Personal Acts; Tables and Index (para.4.25).

Is this Act still in force? Has it been amended?

A4.24 *Is It In Force?* (shows whether Acts passed since 1961 are still in force) (para.4.17).
Chronological Table of the Statutes (indicates if an Act of any date is in force) (para.4.20).
Westlaw UK "Legislation Analysis" (para.4.18).
Current Law Legislation Citators (para.4.19).
Full-text databases of legislation in force (para.4.12).
Halsbury's Statutes (consult the main volumes, the *Cumulative Supplement* and the looseleaf *Service* volume) (para.4.16).

What cases have there been on the interpretation of this Act?

A4.25 Westlaw UK "Legislation Analysis" (para.4.18).
Current Law Legislation Citators (para.4.19).
Halsbury's Statutes (para.7.23).

What Statutory Instruments have been made under this Act?

A4.26 Westlaw UK "Legislation Analysis" (para.4.18).
Current Law Legislation Citators (para.4.19).
Halsbury's Statutes (para.4.16).

Have any journal articles been written about this Act?

A4.27 Westlaw UK "Legislation Analysis" (para.4.18).
Current Law Legislation Citators (para.4.19).
Legal Journals Index (para.5.8).
Other indexes to journal articles (see heading "Journal Articles", above).

Has this Act been brought into force by a Statutory Instrument?

A4.28 *Halsbury's Statutes* (para.4.16).
Westlaw UK "Legislation Analysis" (para.4.18).
Current Law Legislation Citators (para.4.19).

STATUTORY INSTRUMENTS

Collections of Statutory Instruments

A4.29 *Statutory Rules and Orders and Statutory Instruments Revised* (all statutory instruments in force in 1948) (para.4.26).
Statutory Instruments (annual volumes—subject index in last volume of each year) (para.4.26).
Halsbury's Statutory Instruments (selective—arranged by subject) (para.4.29).
Justis UK Statutory Instruments database (para.4.26).
Full-text databases of legislation (para.4.12).

Is this Statutory Instrument in force? Has it been amended?

Halsbury's Statutory Instruments (para.4.29). A4.30
Full-text databases of legislation in force (para.4.12).

What Statutory Instruments have been made under this Act?

Westlaw UK "Legislation Analysis" (para.4.18). A4.31
Current Law Legislation Citator (para.4.19).
Halsbury's Statutes (para.4.16).

Has an Act been brought into force by a Statutory Instrument?

Is It in Force? (para.4.17). A4.32
Westlaw UK "Legislation Analysis" (para.4.18).
Current Law Legislation Citators (para.4.19).

Indexes to Statutory Instruments

Halsbury's Statutory Instruments (chronological, alphabetical and by subject) (para.4.29, para.7.27). A4.33
TSO Daily Lists (includes all new Instruments as they are published) (para.6.15).

THESES

EThOS website (para.7.37). A4.34
Index to Theses (para.7.37).
Dissertation Abstracts (para.7.37).

WORDS AND PHRASES

For the meaning of words and phrases, use legal dictionaries (para.1.10). A4.35
For Latin phrases, use legal dictionaries and *Broom's Legal Maxims* (para.1.11).

Judicial and statutory definitions of words and phrases

Words and Phrases Legally Defined (para.7.19). A4.36
Stroud's Judicial Dictionary.
The entry "Words and Phrases" in: *Law Reports: Consolidated Index*; *Current Law Monthly Digests* and *Current Law Year Books*; and indexes to the *All England Law Reports*, *Halsbury's Laws*, and *The Digest*.

Index

LEGAL TAXONOMY
FROM SWEET & MAXWELL

This index has been prepared using Sweet and Maxwell's Legal Taxonomy. Main index entries conform to keywords provided by the Legal Taxonomy except where references to specific or non-standard terms (denoted by quotation marks) have been included. These keywords provide a means of identifying similar concepts in other Sweet & Maxwell publications and online services to which keywords from the Legal Taxonomy have been applied. Readers may find some minor differences between terms used in the text and those which appear in the index. Suggestions to **sweetandmaxwell.taxonomy@thomson.com.**

(all references are to paragraph number)